The Ideal Life

The Ideal Life

Henry Drummond

WHITAKER
HOUSE

Publisher's note: This new edition from Whitaker House has been updated for the modern reader. Some words, expressions, sentence structure, and punctuation have been revised for clarity, readability, and accuracy. Some of the material in the endnotes appeared in parentheses in the text of the original edition. Other endnotes have been added by the Whitaker House editorial department. In addition, a number of biblical references have been added to indicate exact quotation of Scripture or allusions to Scripture.

All Scripture quotations are taken from the King James Version of the Holy Bible. Boldface type in Scripture quotations indicates the author's emphasis.

THE IDEAL LIFE:
Listening for God's Voice, Discerning His Leading

ISBN: 978-1-62911-152-0
eBook ISBN: 978-1-62911-129-2
Printed in the United States of America
© 2014 by Whitaker House

Whitaker House
1030 Hunt Valley Circle
New Kensington, PA 15068
www.whitakerhouse.com

Library of Congress Cataloging-in-Publication Data (Pending)

1 2 3 4 5 6 7 8 9 10 11 12 ⅎ 22 21 20 19 18 17 16 15 14

CONTENTS

NOTE FROM THE ORIGINAL PUBLISHERS

The addresses that make up this volume were written by Professor Drummond between the years 1876 and 1881, and are now published to meet the wishes of those who heard some of them delivered, and in the hope that they may continue his work.

They were never prepared for publication and have been printed from his manuscripts with a few obvious verbal corrections. A few paragraphs used in later publications have been retained.

Of the memorial sketches, the first was originally published in the *Contemporary Review*, the second in the *North American Review*.

December 1897

ILL TEMPER

The Elder Brother

"And he was angry, and would not go in."
—Luke 15:28

Those who have studied the paintings of Sir Noel Paton must have observed that part of their particular beauty lies, by a trick of art, in their partial ugliness. There are flowers and birds, knights and ladies, gossamer-winged fairies and children of seraphic beauty. But in the corner of the canvas, or just at their feet, there is some uncouth and loathsome form—a toad, a lizard, a slimy snail—to lend, by contrast with its repulsiveness, a lovelier beauty to the rest. Likewise, in ancient sculpture, the griffin and the dragon grin among the angel faces on the cathedral front, heightening the surrounding beauty by their deformity.

Many of the literary situations of the New Testament powerfully exhibit this species of contrast. The twelve disciples—one of them is a devil. Jesus upon the cross, pure and regal—on either side a thief. And, as conspicuously, here in this fifteenth chapter of Luke, the most exquisite painting in the Bible is touched off at the foot with the black thundercloud of the elder brother—perfect, as a mere dramatic situation. But this conjunction, of course, is more than artistic. Apart from its reference to the Pharisees, the association of the two characters side by side—the prodigal and his brother—has a deep moral significance.

When we look into sin—not in its theological aspects, but in its everyday clothes—we find that it divides itself into two kinds. We find that there are sins of the body and sins of the disposition. Or, more narrowly, sins of the passions, including all forms of lust and selfishness, and sins of the temper. In the New Testament, the prodigal is the example of sins of passion; the elder brother, of sins of temper.

Sins of Temper

At a first glance, one would say that it was the younger brother in this picture who was the thundercloud. It was he who had dimmed all the virtues, and covered himself and his home with shame. And people have always pointed to the runaway son, in contrast with his domestic brother, as the example of all that is worst in human character. Possibly, the estimate is wrong. Possibly, the elder brother is worse. We judge sins, as we judge most things, by their outward form. We arrange the vices of our neighbors according to a scale that society has tacitly adopted, placing the more gross and public at the foot, the slightly less gross higher up; and then, by some strange process, the scale becomes obliterated. Finally, it vanishes into space, leaving lengths of itself unexplored, its sins unnamed, unheeded, and unshunned. But we have no balance to weigh sins. *Coarser* and *finer* are merely words of our own. The chances are, if anything, that the finer are the lower. The very fact that the world sees the coarser sins so well is against the belief that they are the worst. The subtle and unseen sin, that sin in the part of the nature most near to the spiritual, ought to be more degrading than any other. Yet, for many of the finer forms of sin, society has yet no brand. This sin of the elder brother is a mere trifle, only a little bit of temper, and scarcely worthy the recording.

Now, what was this little bit of temper? For Christ saw fit to record it. The elder brother, who was hardworking, patient, dutiful—let him get full credit for his virtues—comes in from his long day's work in the fields. Every night, for years, he has plodded home like this, heavy-limbed but light-hearted, for he has done his duty, and honest sweat is on his brow. But, too often, a person's sense of responsibility for his character ends with the day's work. And we always meet the temptation that is to expose us when we least expect it. Tonight, as he nears the old homestead, he hears the noise of mirth and music. He makes out the strain of a dancing measure—a novel sound, surely, for the dull farm.

"Your brother has come," the servant says, "and they have killed the fatted calf." His brother! Happy hour! How long they mourned for him! How glad the old man would be! How the family prayer had found him out at last and brought the erring boy to his parents' roof! But no—there is no joy on that face; it is the thundercloud.

"Brother, indeed," he mutters; "the scapegrace! Killed the fatted calf, have they? More than they ever did for me. I can teach them what I think of their merrymaking. And talk of the reward of virtue! Here I have been unhonored and ignored all these years, and this young roué from the swine troughs assembles the whole countryside to do him homage." *"And he was angry, and would not go in."*

"Oh, he is acting like a spoiled child!" one is inclined to say at first; but it is more than this. It is the thundercloud, a thundercloud that has been brewing under all his virtues, all his life. The subtle fluids from a dozen sins have come together for once, and now they are scorching his soul. Jealousy, anger, pride, lack of love, cruelty, self-righteousness, sulkiness, touchiness, doggedness, all mixed up together into one ill temper. This is a fair analysis. The above are the staple ingredients of ill temper. And yet, men laugh over it. "Only temper," they call it—a little hotheadedness, a momentary ruffling of the surface, a mere passing cloud. But the passing cloud is composed of drops, and the drops here betoken an ocean, foul and rancorous, seething somewhere within the life—an ocean made up of jealousy, anger, pride, lack of love, cruelty, self-righteousness, sulkiness, touchiness, and doggedness, lashed into a raging storm.

This is why temper is significant. Its significance lies not in what it is but in what it reveals. Except for this, it would not be worth notice. It is the intermittent fever that tells of un-intermittent disease; the occasional bubble escaping to the surface, betraying the rottenness underneath; a hastily prepared specimen of the hidden products of the soul, dropped involuntarily when you are off guard. In short, it is the lightning-form of a dozen hideous and unchristian sins.

One of the first things to startle us—leaving now mere definition—about sins of temper, is their strange compatibility with high moral character. The elder brother, without doubt, was a man of high principle. Years ago, when his father divided his living between the brothers, he had the chance to sow his wild oats, if he liked. As he was the elder brother, the larger portion fell to him. Now was his time to see the world, enjoy life, and break with the monotony of home. Like a dutiful son, he chose his career. The old home would be his world, the old people his society. He would be his father's right hand, and cheer and comfort his declining years. So, to the servants he became a pattern of industry; to the neighbors an example of thrift and faithfulness; a model young man to all the country, and even more so in contrast to his vagabond brother. For association with lofty character is a painful circumstance of this deformity. And it suggests strange doubts as to the real virtue of much that is reckoned virtue and gets credit for the name. In reality, we have no criterion for estimating at their true worth those who figure as models of all the virtues. Everything depends on motive. The virtues may be real or only apparent, even as the vices may be real though not apparent.

For instance, some people are kept from going astray by mere cowardice. They do not have character enough to lose their character. For it often requires a strong character to go wrong. It demands a certain originality and courage, and a pocketing of pride, of which not all are capable, before a person can make up his mind to fall out of step with society and scatter his reputation to the winds. So, it comes to pass that many very mean men retain their outward virtue. Conversely, among the prodigal sons of the world are often found characters of singular beauty. The prodigal, no doubt, was a better man to meet and spend an hour with than his immaculate brother. A wealth of tenderness and generosity, truly sweet and noble dispositions, constantly surprise us in characters hopelessly under the ban of men. But it is an instance of misconception as to the nature of sin that with most people this counts for nothing; although in those whose defalcation is in the lower region it counts, and counts almost for everything.

Many of those who sow to the flesh regard their form of sin as trifling compared with the inconsistent and unchristian graces of those who profess to sow to the spirit. For example, many people who think nothing of getting drunk would scorn to do an ungenerous deed or speak a withering word. And, as has already been said, it is really a question whether they are not right. One person sins high up in his nature, the other low down; and the vinous spendthrift, on the whole, may be a better person than the acid Christian. "*Verily I say unto you,*" said Jesus to the chief priests and elders, "*that the publicans and the harlots go into the kingdom of God before you*" (Matthew 21:31).

The fact, then, that there are these two distinct sets of sins, and that few of us indulge both, but most of us indulge one or the other, explains compatibility of virtuous conduct with much unloveliness of disposition. And, it is this very association that makes sins of temper appear so harmless. There cannot be much wrong, we fancy, where there is so much general good. How often it is urged as an apology for garrulous people that they are the soul of kindness if we only knew them better. And how often it is maintained as a setoff against crossness and pitiable explosions of small distempers that those who exhibit them are, in their normal mood, above the average in demonstrative tenderness. And this is what makes it so hard to cure. We excuse the partial failure of our characters on the ground of their general success. We who are so good can afford to be a little bad. A true logic would say we can only afford to be a little better. If the fly in the ointment is a very small fly, why have a very small fly? Temper is the vice of the virtuous. Christ's sermon on the elder brother is evidently a sermon pointedly to the virtuous—not to make bad people good but to make good people perfect.

The Effects of Sins of Temper

Passing now from the nature and relations of sins of this particular class, we come briefly to look at their effects. And these are of two kinds: the influence of temper on the intellect, and the influence of temper on the moral and religious nature.

With reference to the first, it has sometimes been taken for granted that a bad temper is a positive acquisition to the intellect. Its fieriness is supposed to communicate combustion to surrounding faculties and to kindle the system into intense and vigorous life. Darwin quoted a physician, who told him, "A man when excessively jaded will sometimes invent imaginary offenses and put himself into a passion, unconsciously for the sake of reinvigorating himself."[1] Now, of course, passion has its legitimate place in human nature, and, when really controlled, instead of controlling, becomes the most powerful stimulus to the intellectual faculties. Luther referred to this when he said, "I never work better than when I am inspired by anger; when I am angry, I can write, pray, and preach well, for then my whole temperament is quickened, my understanding sharpened, and all mundane vexations and temptations depart."[2]

The point, however, at which temper interferes with the intellect is in all matters of judgment. A quick temper really incapacitates sound judgment. Decisions are struck off at a white heat, without time to collect grounds or hear explanations. Once they are made, it takes a humbler spirit than most of us possess to reverse them. We ourselves are prejudiced in their favor simply because we have made them, and subsequent courses must generally do homage to our first precipitancy. No doubt, the elder brother secretly confessed himself a fool the moment his back was turned on the door. But he had taken his stand; he had said, "I will not go in." And neither his father's entreaties nor his own sense of the growing absurdity of the situation—think of the man standing outside his own door—were able to shake him. Temptation betraying a man into an immature judgment, quickly followed by an irrelevant action, and the whole having to be defended by subsequent conduct, after making such a fuss about it—such is the natural history on the side of intellect of a sin of temper.

Among the scum left behind by such an action, apart from the consequences to the individual, are results always disastrous to others. For this is another trait of sins of temper—their worst influence is upon others. It is generally, too, the weak who are the sufferers; for temper is the prerogative of superiors. And inferiors, down to the bottom of the scale, have not only to bear the brunt of the storm but also to sink their own judgment and spend their lives in ministering to what they know to be caprice. So, their whole training is systematically false, and their own mental habits become disorganized and ruined. When the young, again, are disciplined by the iron instead of the golden rule, the consequences are still more fatal. They feel that they do not get a fair hearing. Their case is summarily dismissed untried; and that sort of nursery lynch law to which they are constantly subjected carries with it no explanation of moral principles, muzzles legitimate feelings, and really inflicts a punishment infinitely more serious than is intended, in crushing out all sense of justice.

But it is in their moral and social effects that the chief evil lies. It is astonishing how large a part of Christ's precepts is devoted solely to the inculcation of happiness. How much of His life, too, was spent simply in making people happy! There was no word more often on His lips than "blessed"; and it is recognized by Him as a distinct end in life—*the* end for this life—to secure the happiness of others. This simple grace, too, needs little equipment. Christ had little. One need scarcely even be happy oneself. Holiness, of course, is a greater word, but we cannot produce that in others. That is reserved for God Himself. But what is put in our power is happiness; and, for that, each person is his brother's keeper. Now, society is an arrangement for producing and sustaining human happiness, and temper is an agent for thwarting and destroying it. Look at the parable for a moment, and see how the elder brother's wretched pettishness, explosion of temper, and churlishness spoiled the happiness of a whole circle.

First, it certainly spoiled his own. One can well guess how ashamed of himself he must have been when the fit was over. Yet these things are never over as quickly as they seem. Self-disgust and humiliation may come at once, but a good deal else within has to wait until the spirit is tuned again. For instance, prayer must wait. An individual cannot pray until the sourness is out of his soul. He must first forgive his brother who trespassed against him before he can go to God to have his own trespasses forgiven. (See Matthew 5:23–24.)

Then, look at the effect on the father, or on the guests, or even on the servants: That scene outside had cast its miserable gloom on the entire company. But there was one other who felt it with a tenfold keenness—the prodigal son. We can imagine the effect on him. This was home, was it? Well, it was a pity he ever returned. If this was to be the sort of thing he could expect, he had better go. Happier a thousand times among the swine than to endure the boorishness of his self-contained, self-righteous brother. Yes, many times we drive men from Christ's door by our sorry entertainment. The church is not spiritualized enough yet to entertain the world. We have no spiritual courtesies. We cultivate our faith and proclaim our hope but forget that a greater than these is charity. (See 1 Corinthians 13:13.) Until men can say about us, "They suffer long and are kind, are not easily provoked, do not behave themselves unseemly, bear all things, think no evil," we have no chance against the world. (See 1 Corinthians 13:4–5.) One repulsive Christian will drive away a score of prodigals. God's love for poor sinners is very wonderful, but God's patience with ill-natured saints is a deeper mystery.

The worst of the misery caused by ill temper is that it does no good. Some misery is beneficial, but this is gratuitous woe. Nothing in the world causes such rankling, abiding, unnecessary, and unblessed pain. And Christ's words, therefore, when He refers to the breach of the law of love are most severe. *"But whoso shall offend one of these little ones which believe in me,"* He says, *"it were better for him that a millstone were hanged about his neck, and that he were drowned in the depth of the sea"* (Matthew 18:6). That is to say, it is Christ's deliberate verdict that it is better not to live than not to love.

In its ultimate nature, distemper is a sin against love. And, however impossible it may be to realize that now, however we may condone it as a pardonable weakness or a small infirmity, there is no greater sin. A sin against love is a sin against God, for God is love. (See 1 John 4:8, 16.) He who sins against love, sins against God.

The Cure for Sins of Temper

This tracing of the sin to its root now suggests this further topic—its cure. Christianity professes to cure anything. The process may be slow, the discipline may be severe, but it can be done. But is not temper a constitutional thing? Is it not hereditary, a family failing, a matter of temperament? And can that be cured? Yes, if there is anything in Christianity. If there is no provision for that, then Christianity stands convicted of being unequal to human need. In the case before us, what course, then, did the father take to pacify the angry passions of his ill-natured son? Note that he made no attempt in the first instance to reason with him. To do so is a common mistake, and utterly useless both to ourselves and others. We are perfectly convinced of the puerility of it all, but that does not help us in the least to mend it. The malady has its seat in the affections, and therefore the father went there at once. Reason came in its place, and the son was supplied with valid arguments against his conduct—stated in the last verse of the chapter—but he was first plied with love.

"Son," said the father, "*thou art ever with me, and all that I have is thine*" (Luke 15:31). Analyze these words, and underneath them you will find the rallying cries of all great communities. There lie liberty, equality, and fraternity—the happy symbols with which men have sought to maintain governments and establish kingdoms. "*Son*"—there is liberty. "*Thou art ever with me*"—there is unity, fraternity. "*All that I have is thine*"—there is equality. If any appeal could rouse a person to give up himself, to abandon selfish ends, under the strong throb of a common sympathy, it is this formula of the Christian republic. Take the last characteristic, equality—"*All that I have is thine*." It is absurd to talk of your rights here and your rights there. You have all rights. "*All that I have is thine*." There is no room for selfishness if there is nothing more that one can possess. And God has made the equality. God has given us all. And, once the memory of His great kindness to us, His particular kindness, is moved within, the heart must melt to Him, and flow out to all mankind as brothers.

It is quite idle, by force of will, to seek to empty the angry passions out of our life. Who has not made a thousand resolutions in this direction, only—and with unutterable mortification—to behold them dashed to pieces with the first temptation? The soul is to be made sweet not by taking out the acidulous fluids but by putting something else in—a great love, God's great love. This works a chemical change upon these "fluids," renovates and regenerates them, dissolves them in its own rich, fragrant substance. If a person lets this into his life, his cure is complete; if not, it is hopeless.

In the New Testament, the character who is hardest to comprehend is the unmerciful servant. (See Matthew 18:23–35.) For his base extravagance, his wife and children were to be sold, and he was to be imprisoned. He cries for mercy on his knees, and the 10,000 talents—a hopeless and enormous debt—is freely cancelled. He goes straight from the kind presence of his lord, and, meeting some poor wretch who owes him a hundred pence, seizes him by the throat and hauls him to the prison cell from which he himself has just escaped. How a man can rise from his knees, where, forgiven much already, he has just been forgiven more, and go straight from the audience chamber of his God to speak hard words and to do hard things, is all but incredible. In wasting his master's money, this servant truly must have wasted away his own soul. But grant a man any soul at all, love must follow forgiveness.

Being forgiven much, he must love much—not as a duty but as a necessary consequence. He must become a humbler, tenderer man, generous and brotherly. Rooted and grounded in love, his love will grow until it embraces the earth. Only then he dimly begins to understand his father's gift—*"All that I have is thine."* The world is his; he cannot injure his own. The ground of benevolence is proprietorship. And all who love God are the proprietors of the world. The meek inherit the earth (see Matthew 5:5)—all that He has is theirs. All that God has—what is that? Mountain and field, tree and sky, castle and cottage, white man, black man, genius and dullard, prisoner and pauper, sick and aged—all these are mine. If they be noble and happy, I must enjoy them; if they be great and beautiful, I must delight in them; if they be poor and hungry, I must clothe them; if they be sick and in prison, I must visit them. (See Matthew 25:31–46.) For they are all mine, all these, and all that God has beside, and I must love all and give myself for all.

Here the theme widens. From Plato to Herbert Spencer, reformers have toiled to frame new schemes of sociology. There is none as grand as the sociology of Jesus. But we have not found out the New Testament sociology yet; we have spent the centuries over its theology. Surely, man's relation to God may be held as settled now. It is time to take up the other problem: man's relation to man. With a former theology, man as man, as a human being, was of no account. He was a mere theological unit, the x of doctrine, an unknown quantity. He was therefore taught to believe, not to love. Now we are learning slowly that to believe *is* to love; that the first commandment is to love God, and the second, *"like unto it"*—another version of it—is to love man. (See Matthew 22:36–39.) Not only the happiness of, but also the efficiency of, the passive virtues, love is coming to be recognized as a power, as a practical success in the world. The fact that Christ led no army, wrote no book, built no church, spent no money, but that He loved, and so conquered—this is beginning to strike men. And Paul's argument is gaining adherents—that when all prophecies are fulfilled, and all our knowledge becomes obsolete, and all tongues grow unintelligible, this thing, love, will abide and see them all out one by one into the oblivious past. (See 1 Corinthians 13.) The hope for the world is that we will learn to love; and, in learning that, unlearn all anger and wrath and evil-speaking and malice and bitterness.

And this will indeed be the world's future. This is heaven. The curtain drops on the story of the prodigal, leaving him in but the elder brother out. And why is obvious. It is impossible for such a man to be in heaven. He would spoil heaven for all who were there. Except such a man be born again, he cannot enter the kingdom of God. To get to heaven, we must take it in with us.

There are many heavens in the world even now from which we all shut ourselves out by our own exclusiveness—heavens of friendship, of family life, of Christian work, of benevolent ministrations to the poor and ignorant and distressed. Because of some personal pique, some disapproval of methods; because the lines of work of some of the workers are not exactly to our taste, we play the elder brother. We are angry and will not go in. This is the naked truth of it: We are simply angry and will not go in. And, if we could only see it, this bears its own worst penalty. For there is no severer punishment than just to be left outside, perhaps, to grow old alone, unripe, loveless, and unloved. We are angry and will not go in. All sins mar God's image, but sins of temper mar God's image, God's work, and man's happiness.

WHY CHRIST MUST DEPART
A Sermon Before Communion

"It is expedient for you that I go away."
—John 16:7

It was on a Communion night like this that the words were spoken. They fell upon the disciples like a thunderbolt startling a summer sky. He had lived among them for three years. They had lately learned to love Him. Day after day, they had shared together the sunshine and the storm, and their hearts clung to Him with a strange tenderness. And just when everything was at its height, when their friendship was now pledged indissolubly in the first most solemn sacrament, the unexpected words come: "I must say good-bye; *'it is expedient for you that I go away.'"* It was a crushing blow to the little band. They had staked their all upon that love. They had given up homes, businesses, and friends, and had promised to follow Him. And now He says, "I must go"!

Let us see what He means by it. The words may help us to understand more fully our own relationship with Him now that He is gone.

The Way Jesus Broke the News

The first thing that strikes one is the way Jesus took to break the news. It was characteristic. His sayings and doings always came about in the most natural way. Even His profoundest statements of doctrine were invariably apropos of some often trivial circumstance happening in the day's events. In the same way, He did not now suddenly deliver the doctrine of the ascension. It leaked out as if it were in the ordinary course of things.

The supper was over, but the friends had much to say to one another that night, and they lingered around the table. They did not know it was the last supper, never dreamed of it; but there had been an unusual sweetness in their conversation, and they talked on and on. The hour grew late, but John still leaned on his Master's breast; and the others, grouped around in the twilight, drank in the solemn gladness of the Communion evening. Suddenly, a shadow falls over this scene. A sinister figure rises stealthily, takes the bag, and makes for the door unobserved. Jesus calls him, hands him the piece of bread. The spell is broken. A terrible revulsion of feeling comes over Him— as if a stab in the dark had struck into His heart. He cannot go on now. It is useless to try. He cannot keep up the perhaps forced spirits. (See John 13:21–30.)

"*Little children,*" He says very solemnly, His voice choking, "*yet a little while I am with you*" (John 13:33). He also says, "*Whither I go, ye cannot come*" (John 13:33).

The hour is late. They think He is getting tired. He means to retire to rest. But Peter asks straight out, "*Lord, whither goest thou?*" (John 13:36). Into the garden? Back to Galilee? It never occurred to one of them that He meant the Unknown Land.

"*Whither I go,*" He replies a second time, "*thou canst not follow me now; but thou shalt follow me afterwards*" (John 13:36). "Afterwards"! The blow slowly falls. In a dim, bewildering way, it begins to dawn upon them. It is separation.

We can judge the effect from the next sentence. He says, *"Let not your heart be troubled"* (John 14:1). He sees their panic and consternation; and doctrine has to stand aside until experiential religion has ministered. And then it is only at intervals that He gets back to it; almost every sentence is interrupted. Questionings and misgivings are started, explanations are insisted on, but the terrible truth will not hide. He always comes back to that—He will not temper its meaning; He still insists that it is absolute, literal. And finally He states it in its most bare and naked form: *"It is expedient for you that I go away."*

Jesus' Reasons for Going Away

Why did Jesus go away? We all remember a time when we could not answer that question. We wished He had stayed, and were here now. This children's hymn expresses a real human feeling, and our hearts still burn as we read it:

> I think, when I read that sweet story of old,
> When Jesus was here among men,
> How He called little children as lambs to His fold,
> I should like to have been with them then.
> I wish that His hands had been placed on my head,
> That His arms had been thrown around me,
> And that I might have seen His kind look when He said,
> "Let the little ones come unto Me."[3]

Jesus must have had reasons for disappointing a human feeling so deep, so universal, and so sacred. We may be sure, too, that these reasons intimately concern us. He did not go away because He was tired. It is quite true that He was *"despised and rejected of men"* (Isaiah 53:3); it is quite true that the pitiless world hated and spurned and trod on Him. But that did not drive Him away. It is quite true that He longed for His Father's house and pined and yearned for His love. But that did not draw Him away. No. He never thought of Himself. He says, *"It is expedient for you"*—not *"for Me"*—*"that I go."*

Note His reasons for going away.

1. To Prepare a Place for Us

The first reason is one of His own stating: *"I go to prepare a place for you"* (John 14:2). And the very mention of this is a proof of Christ's considerateness. The burning question with every person who thought about his life in those days was, "Where is this life leading?" The present—alas!—was dim and inscrutable enough, but the future was a fearful and unsolved mystery. So, Christ put that right before He went away. He gave this unknown future form and color. He told us—and it is only because we are so accustomed to it that we do not wonder more at the magnificence of the concept—that when our place in this world knows us no more, there will be another place ready for us. We do not know much about that place, but the best thing we do know is that He prepares it. *"Eye hath not seen, nor ear heard, neither have entered into the heart of man, the things which God hath prepared for them that love him"* (1 Corinthians 2:9). It is better to think of this, to let our thoughts rest on the fact that He prepares it, than to fancy details of our own.

But that does not exhaust the matter. Consider the alternative. If Christ had not gone away, what then? We would not, either. The circumstances of our future life depended upon Christ's going away to prepare them; but the fact of our going away at all depended on His going away. We could not follow Him hereafter, as He said we should, unless He led first. He had to be the Resurrection and the Life.

And preparing a way for us was part of preparing a place for us. He prepared a place for us by the way He took to prepare a place. It was a very wonderful way.

Once, in a lonely valley in Switzerland, a small band of patriots marched against an invading force ten times their strength. One day, they found themselves at the head of a narrow pass, confronted by a solid wall of spears. They made assault after assault, but that bristling line remained unbroken. Time after time, they were driven back, decimated with hopeless slaughter. The forlorn hope rallied for the last time. As they charged, their leader suddenly advanced before them with outstretched arms, and every spear for three or four yards of the line was buried in his body. He fell dead. But he prepared a place for his followers. Through the open breach, over his dead body, they rushed to victory and won freedom for their country.

In the same way, the Lord Jesus went before His people, the Captain of our salvation, sheathing the weapons of death and judgment in Himself, and preparing a place for us with His dead body. It is well for us not only that He went away, but also that He went by way of the cross.

2. To Be Very Near to Us

Another reason why He went away was to be very near. It seems a paradox, but He went away really in order to be near. Suppose, again, He had not gone away; suppose He were here now. Suppose He were still in the Holy Land, in Jerusalem. Every ship that started for the East would be crowded with Christian pilgrims. Every train flying through Europe would be thronged with people going to see Jesus. Every mailbag would be full of letters from those in difficulty and trial, and gifts of homage to manifest men's gratitude and love.

Let us say that you are in one of those ships. When you arrive after the long voyage, the port is blocked with vessels of every flag. With much difficulty, you land and join one of the long trains starting for Jerusalem. As far as the eye can reach, the caravans move across the desert in an endless stream. You do not mind the scorching sun, the choking dust, the elbowing crowds, the burning sands. You are in the Holy Land, and you will see Jesus! Yonder, at last, in the far distance, are the glittering spires of the Holy Hill—above all, the shining temple dome beneath which He sits. But what is that dark, seething mass stretching for leagues and leagues between you and the Holy City? They have come from the north and from the south and from the east and from the west, as you have, to look upon their Lord. They wish…

That His hands might be placed on their head;
That His arms might be thrown around them.

But it cannot be. You have come to see Jesus, but you will not see Him. They have been there weeks, months, years, and have not seen Him. They are a yard or two nearer, and that is all. The thing is impossible. It is an anticlimax, an absurdity. It would be a physical impossibility; it would be a social outrage.

Now Christ foresaw all this when He said it was expedient that He should go away. Observe that He did not say it was necessary; it was *expedient*.

The objection to the opposite plan was simply that it would not have worked. So He says to you, "It is very kind and earnest of you to come so far, but you mistake. Go away back from the walls of the Holy City, over the sea, and you will find Me in your own home. You will find Me where the shepherds found Me, doing their ordinary work; where the woman of Samaria found Me, drawing the water for the forenoon meal; where the disciples found Me, mending nets in their working clothes; where Mary found Me, among the commonplace household duties of a country village."

Indeed, what would religion be if the soul-sick had to take their turn like the outpatients waiting outside the infirmary at the poor-hour? How would it be with the old who were too frail to travel to Him, or the poor who could not afford it? How would it be with the blind, who could not see Him; or the deaf, who could not hear Him? It would be physically impossible for millions to obey the Lord's command *"Come unto me,...and I will give you rest"* (Matthew 11:28).

For their sakes, it was expedient that He should go away. It was a great blessing for the world that He went. Access to Him is universally complete from every corner of every home in every part of the world. For the poor can have Him with them always. The soul-sick cannot be out of reach of the Physician. The blind can see His beauty now that He has gone away. The deaf can hear His voice when all others are silent, and the dumb can pray when they cannot speak.

Yes, the visible incarnation must, of necessity, be brief; only a small circle could enjoy His actual presence. But a kingdom like Christianity needed a risen Lord. It was expedient for the whole body of its subjects that He went away. He would be nearer man by being apparently further. The limitations of sense subjected Him while He stayed. He was subject to geography, locality, space, and time. But by going away, He was in a spaceless land, in a timeless eternity, able to be with all men always, *"even unto the end of the world"* (Matthew 28:20).

3. So That We Might See Him Better

Another reason why Jesus went away—although this, also, is a paradox—was that we might see Him better. When a friend is with us, we do not really see him as well as when he is away. We see only points, details. It is like looking at a great mountain: You see it best a little way off. Clamber up the flanks of Mont Blanc, and you see very little—a few rocks, a pine or two, a blinding waste of snow; but come down into the valley of Chamonix, and there the monarch dawns upon you in all his majesty.

Christ is the most gigantic figure of history. To take in His full proportions, one must be both near and away. The same is true of all greatness. It is said of all great poets, philosophers, politicians, and men of science that their generation never knew them. They dawn upon us as time rolls past. Then, their life comes out in its true perspective, and the symmetry of their work is revealed. Likewise, we never know our friends until we lose them. We often never know the beauty of a life that is lived very near our own until the hand of death has taken it away. It was expedient for us, therefore, that Jesus should go—that we might see the colossal greatness of His stature, appreciate the loftiness and massiveness of His whole character, and feel the perfect beauty and oneness of His life and work.

4. So That We Might Walk by Faith

Still another reason Jesus went away was that we might walk by faith. After all, if He had stayed, we would have been walking by sight, with all its inconveniences. And this is the very thing religion is continually trying to undo. The strongest temptation for every person is to guide himself by what he can see and feel and handle. This is the core of ritualism, the essence of idolatry. Men want to see God; therefore, they make images of Him. We do not laugh at ritualism; it is intensely human. It is not so much a sin of presumption as a sin of mistake. It is a trying to undo the going away of Christ. It is a trying to make believe that He is still here. And the fatal fallacy of it is that it defeats its own end. He who seeks God in tangible form misses the very thing he is seeking, for God is a Spirit. (See John 4:24.) The desire burns within him to see God; the desire is given to him to make him spiritual, by giving him a spiritual exercise to do; and he cheats himself by exercising the flesh instead of the spirit. Hunger and thirst for God are an endowment to raise us out of the seen and the temporal. But instead of letting the spiritual appetite elevate us into the spirit, we are apt to degrade the very instrument of our spiritualization and make it minister to the flesh.

It was expedient that Jesus would become a Spirit in order that the disciples would be spiritualized. To all men, life in the body is short. The mortal dies and puts on immortality. (See 1 Corinthians 15:53.) So, Christ's great aim is to strengthen the afterlife. For this reason, Jesus gave exercises in faith to be the education for immortality. Therefore, He went away to strengthen the spirit for eternity.

It is not because there is any deep, mysterious value in faith itself that it plays so great a part in religion. It is not because God arbitrarily chooses that we should walk by faith rather than by sight. It is because it is essential to our future; it is because this is the faculty that, of all others, is absolutely necessary to life in the spirit.

For our true life will be lived in the spirit. In the hereafter, there will be nothing carnal. Christ is therefore solicitous to educate our faith, for sight will be useless. In the hereafter, there will be no eye, no pupil, no retina, no optic nerve; so, faith is the spiritual substitute for them that Christ would develop in us by going away.

5. So That the Comforter Might Come

But the great reason has yet to be mentioned. Jesus went away so that the Comforter might come. We have seen how His going away was a provision for the future life. The absent Lord prepares a place there; the absent object of faith educates the souls of the faithful to possess and enjoy it. But He also provides for the life that now is. And His going away has to do with the present as much as with the life to come.

One day, when Jesus was in the region of Perea, a message came to Him that a very dear friend was sick. This friend lived in a distant village with his two sisters. The sisters were greatly concerned about their brother's illness, and had sent in haste for Jesus. Now, Jesus loved Mary and Martha and their brother Lazarus (see John 11:5); but He was so situated at the time that He could not go. Perhaps He was too busy; perhaps He had other similar cases on hand. At any event, He could not go. When He ultimately went, it was too late.

Hour after hour, the sisters waited for Him. They could not believe He would not come; but the slow hours dragged themselves along by the dying man's couch, and he was dead and laid in the grave before Jesus arrived. We can imagine one of Jesus' thoughts, at least, as He stands and weeps by that grave with the inconsolable sisters: "It is expedient that I go away. I would have been present at his deathbed scene if I had been away. I will depart and send the Comforter. There will be no summons of sorrow that He will not be able to answer. He will abide with men forever. He will come and go everywhere. He will be like the noiseless, invisible wind, blowing all over the world, wherever He wishes." (See John 3:8.)

The doctrine of the Holy Spirit is very simple. Men stumble over it because they imagine it to be something very mysterious and unintelligible. But the whole matter lies here. Our text is the key to it. The Holy Spirit is just what Christ would have been had He been here. He ministers comfort just as Christ would have done, only without the inconveniences of circumstance, without the restrictions of space, and without the limitations of time. In addition, we need a personal Christ, but we cannot have that; at least, we cannot *each* have that. So, the only alternative is a spiritual Christ; that is, a Holy Spirit, and then we can all have Him.

"He will reprove the world of sin, and of righteousness, and of judgment" (John 16:8). Christ had to go away to make room for a person of the Trinity who could deal with the world. He Himself could reprove only the individual of sin, of righteousness, and of judgment. But work on a larger scale is done now that He is gone. This is what Jesus referred to when He said, *"Greater works than these shall* [you] *do"* (John 14:12).

And yet, Christ did not go away so that the Spirit might take His place. Christ is with us Himself. He is with us, and yet He is not with us; that is, He is with us by His Spirit. The Spirit does not reveal the Spirit. He does not speak of Himself; He reveals Christ. (See John 15:26; 16:13–15.) He is the nexus, the connection, between the absent Christ and the world—a spiritual Presence that can penetrate where the physical Christ could not go. It was expedient for the present Christ to go away so that the universal Christ might come to all.

Practical Effects of Jesus' Going Away

Finally, if all this was expedient for us, this strange relation of Jesus to His people ought to have a startling influence upon our life. Expediency is a practical thing. Going away was a terrible risk. Has the expedience that Christ adopted been worthwhile to you and me? The following three great practical effects, at least, are obvious.

1. We Experience a Personal Christ

Christ ought to be as near to us as if He were still here. Nothing so simplifies the whole religious life as this thought. A present, personal Christ solves every difficulty and meets every requirement of Christian experience. There is a historical Christ, a national Christ, a theological Christ—we each want Christ. So we have Him. For purposes of expediency, for a little while, He has become invisible. It is our part to have Him.

> More present to Faith's vision keen
> Than any other vision seen;
> More near, more intimately nigh,
> Than any other earthly tie.[4]

2. We Have an Incentive to Honest Faithfulness

Next, consider what an incentive to honest faithfulness this is. The kingdom of heaven is like a man traveling to a far country. Before he went, he called his servants and gave to each his work. (See Matthew 25:14–30.)

Are we doing our work faithfully? Are we doing it at all? The visible eye of the Master is off us. No one inspects our work. Wood, hay, stubble—no man knows. It is the test of the absent Christ. He is training us to a kind of faithfulness whose high quality is unattained by any other earthly means. It was after the Lord had gone that the disciples worked. They grew fast after that—in vigor, in usefulness, in reliance, in strength of character. Hitherto, they had rested in His love. Did you ever think what a risk it was for Him to go away? It was a terrible risk—to leave us here all by ourselves. And yet this was one of His ways of elevating us. Nothing exalts a person like having confidence placed in him. So Jesus went away and let them try themselves.

We cannot always sit at the Communion table. We partake of the feast not so much as a luxury, though it is that, but to give us strength to work. We think our Sabbath services, our prayers, and our Bible reading are our religion. It is not so. We do these things to help us to be religious in other things. These are the mere meals, and a workman gets no wages for his meals. The wages are for the work he does. The value of today's Communion is not estimated yet. It will take the coming week to put the value upon it. In itself, it counts little; we will see what it is by what we will be.

Every communicant is left by Christ with a solemn responsibility. Christ's confidence in us is unspeakably touching. Christ was sure of us; He felt the world would be safe in our hands. He was away, but we would be Christs to it. The Light of the World was gone, but He would light a thousand lights, and leave each one of us to illuminate one corner of its gloom.

3. We Can Await His Soon Return

Last, He is gone only for a little while: *"Behold, I come quickly"* (Revelation 3:11; 22:7, 12). The probation will soon be past. "Be good children until I come back," He has said, like a mother leaving her little ones, "and *'I will come again, and receive you unto myself; that where I am, there ye may be also.'"* (See John 14:3.) So, we wait until He comes again—we wait until it is expedient for Him to come back.

So I am [waiting] quietly
Every day.
Whenever the sun shines brightly
I rise and say,
"Surely it is the shining of His face...."

*****

And when a shadow falls across the window
Of my room,
Where I am working my appointed task,
I lift my head to watch the door, and ask
If He is come....[5]

3

GOING TO THE FATHER
Written After the Death of a Friend

"…I go unto my Father."
—John 14:12

You can unlock a person's whole life if you watch what words he uses most. We each have a small set of words, which, though we are scarcely aware of it, we always work with, and which really express all that we mean by life or have found out of it. For such words preserve the past for us. They have become ours by a natural selection, throughout our career, of all that is richest and deepest in our experience. So, our vocabulary is our history, and our favorite words are ourselves.

Have you ever noticed Christ's favorite words? If you have, you must have been struck by two things: their simplicity and their fewness. Some half dozen words preserve His entire theology—words that are, without exception, humble, elementary, simple monosyllables. They are words such as these: *world, life, trust, love.*

The Greatest Word of Christ

But none of these was the greatest word of Christ. His great word was new to religion. When He came, there was no word rich enough to carry the new truth He was bringing to men. So, He imported into religion one of the grandest words of human language, transfigured it, and gave it back to the world illuminated and transformed, as the watchword of the new religion. That word was *Father*.

The world's obligation to the Lord Jesus is that He gave us that word. We never would have thought of it; if we had, we never would have dared to say it. It is a pure revelation. Surely, it is the most touching sight of the world's past to see God's only begotten Son coming down from heaven to try to teach the stammering, mute inhabitants of this poor planet to say, *"Our Father"* (Matthew 6:9; Luke 11:2).

That word has gathered the great family of God together; and when we come face-to-face with the real, the solid, and the moving in our religion, it is to find all its complexity resolvable into this simplicity—that God, whom others call King Eternal and Infinite Jehovah, is our Father, and we are His children.

This, after all, is religion. And to live daily in this simplicity is to live like Christ.

It takes a great deal to succeed as a Christian—such a great deal that many do not succeed. And the great reason for this lack of success is the lack of a central word. People will copy anything rather than a principle. A relationship is always harder to follow than a fact. We study the details of Christ's actions, the point of this miracle and of that, the circumferential truth of this parable and of that; but to copy details is not to copy Christ. To live greatly like Christ is not to agonize daily over details, to make anxious comparisons with what we do and what He did, but a much simpler thing. It is to reecho Christ's word. It is to have that calm, patient, assured spirit that reduces life simply to this: a going to the Father.

Probably, not one person in a hundred has a central word in his Christian life; and the consequence is that there is probably nothing in the world as disorderly and slipshod as personal spiritual experience. With most of us, it is a thing without stability or permanence; it is changed by every trifle we meet, by each new mood or thought. It is a series of disconnected approaches to God, a disorderly succession of religious impulses, an irregulation of conduct—now on this principle, now on that; one day because we read something in a book, the next because it was contradicted in another. And when circumstances lead us to really examine ourselves, everything is indefinite, hazy, and unsatisfactory; and perhaps all that we have for the Christian life are the shreds of the last few Sabbaths' sermons and a few borrowed patches from other people's experience. So we live in perpetual spiritual oscillation and confusion, and we are almost glad to let any friend or any book upset the most cherished thought we have.

The thing that steadied Christ's life was the thought that He was going to His Father. This one thing gave it unity, harmony, and success. During His whole life, He never forgot His word for a moment. There is no sermon of His where it does not occur; there is no prayer, however brief, where it is missed. In that first memorable sentence of His, which breaks the solemn spell of history and makes one word resound through thirty silent years, the one word is this; and all through the after years of toil and travail, the "Great Name" was always hovering on His lips or bursting out of His heart. In its beginning, and in its end, from the early time when He spoke of His Father's business until He finished the work that was given Him to do, Jesus' life, disrobed of all circumstance, was simply this: *"I go unto my Father."*

If we take this principle into our own lives, we will find that it influences us in three ways:

1. It explains life.

2. It sustains life.

3. It completes life.

1. The Principle of "Going to the Father" Explains Life

Few people, I suppose, do not feel that life needs explaining. We think we see through some things in it—partially. Yet, most of it, even to the wisest mind, is enigmatic. Those who know it best are the most bewildered by it, and those who stand upon the very rim of the vortex confess that, even for them, it is overspread with cloud and shadow. "What is my life?" "Where am I going?" "From where do I come?" These are the questions that are not worn down yet, although the whole world has handled them.

To these questions, there are but three answers—one by the poet, one by the atheist, and one by the Christian.

The Poet's Answer

The poet tells us, and philosophy says the same—only less intelligibly—that life is a sleep, a dream, a shadow. It is a vapor that appears for a little while and then vanishes away; it is a meteor hovering for a moment between two unknown eternities; it is like bubbles that form and burst upon the river of time. This philosophy explains nothing. It is a taking refuge in mystery. "Where am I going?" The poet virtually answers, "I am going to the Unknown."

The Atheist's Answer

The atheist's answer is just the opposite. He knows no unknown. He understands all, for there is nothing more than what we can see or feel. Life is what matter is; the soul is phosphorus. "Where am I going?" "I go to dust," he says; "death ends all." And this explains nothing. It is worse than mystery. It is contradiction. It is utter darkness.

The Christian's Answer

But the Christian's answer explains something. Where is he going? *"I go unto my Father."* This is not a definition of his death—there is no death in Christianity. Rather, it is a definition of the Christian life. It is always a going to the Father. Some travel swiftly, some are long upon the road, some meet many pleasant adventures by the way, others pass through fire and peril; but, though the path be short or winding, and though the pace be quick or slow, it is a going to the Father.

Now, this explains life. It clarifies the two most inexplicable things in life. For one thing, it explains why there is more pain in the world than pleasure.

God knows, although we scarcely do, that there is something better than plea-sure—progress. Pleasure, mere pleasure, is animal. God gives that to the but-terfly. But progress is the law of life to the immortal. So God has arranged our life as progress, and its working principle is evolution. Not that there is no pleasure in it. The Father is too good to His children for that. But the shadows are all shot through it, for He fears lest we forget there is anything more. Yes, God is too good to leave His children without indulgences, without far more than we deserve; but He is too good to let them spoil us. Our pleasures are therefore mere entertainments. We are entertained like passing guests at the inns on the roadside. Yet, even after the choicest meals, we dare not linger. We must take the pilgrim's staff again and go on our way to the Father.

Sooner or later, we find out that life is not a holiday but a discipline. Earlier or later, we all discover that the world is not a playground. It is quite clear that God intends it for a school. The moment we forget that, the puzzle of life begins. We try to play in school; the Master does not mind that so much for its own sake, for He likes to see His children happy. But in our playing, we neglect our lessons. We do not see how much there is to learn, and we do not care. But our Master cares. He has a perfectly overpowering and inexplicable solicitude for our education; and because He loves us, He sometimes comes into the school and speaks to us. He may speak very softly and gently, or very loudly. Sometimes, a look is enough, and we understand it, like Peter, and go out at once and weep bitterly. (See Luke 22:61–62.) Sometimes, the voice is like a thunderclap, startling a summer night. But one thing we may be sure of: The task He sets us to is never measured by our delinquency. The discipline may seem far less than what we deserve, or even to our eye ten times more. But it is not measured by these—it is measured by God's concern for our progress, measured solely by His love, measured solely that the student may be better educated when he arrives at his Father. The discipline of life is a preparation for meeting the Father. When we arrive there to behold His beauty, we must have the educated eye, and that must be trained here. We must become so pure in heart; and it requires much practice so that we will see God. That explains life—why God puts man in the cru-cible and makes him pure by fire.

When we see Him, we must speak to Him. We have that language to learn. And that is perhaps why God makes us pray so much. Then, we are to walk with Him in white. Our sanctification is a putting on of this white. But there has to be much disrobing first, much putting off of filthy rags. This is why God causes man's beauty to consume away like the moth. He takes away the moth's wings and gives the angel's, and man goes the quicker and the lovelier to the Father.

Besides all this, it is quite true, indeed, that sometimes shadow falls more directly from definite sin. But, even then, its explanation is the same. We lose our way, perhaps, on the way to the Father. The road is rough, and we choose the way with the flowers beside it, instead of the path of thorns. Thus, purposely or carelessly, we often lose the way. So, the Lord Jesus has to come and look for us. And He may have to lead us through desert and danger before we regain the road—before we are as we were—and the voice says to us sadly once more, "This is the way to the Father."

The other thing that this truth explains is why there is so much that is unexplained. After we have explained all, there is much left. It is said that all our knowledge is but different degrees of darkness. But we know *why* we do not know why. It is because we are going to our Father. We are only going— we are not there yet. Therefore, patience. *"What I do thou knowest not now; but thou shalt know hereafter"* (John 13:7). Hereafter, because the chief joy of life is to have something to look forward to. But hereafter for a deeper reason. Knowledge is given only for action; knowing exists only for doing. And, already, nearly all men know to do more than they do. So, until we do all that we know, God retains the balance for that time when we can use it. In the larger life of the hereafter, more will be given, proportionate to the vaster sphere and the more ardent energies.

Therefore, necessarily, much of life is still twilight. But our perfect refuge is to anticipate a little, and to go in thought to our Father; and, like children tired out with efforts to put together the disconnected pieces of a puzzle, wait to take the fragments to our Father.

And yet, even that sometimes fails. He seems to hide from us, and the way is lost, indeed. The footsteps that went before us up until then cease, and we are left alone in the chill, dark night. If we could only see the road, we would know it went to the Father. But we cannot say we are going to the Father; we can say only that we would like to go. "Lord," we cry, "we do not know where You are going, so how can we know the way?" "Where I go," is the inexplicable answer, "you don't know now." Well is it for those who at such times are near enough to catch the rest: "But you will know hereafter." (See John 13:36–14:21.)

2. The Principle of "Going to the Father" Sustains Life

A year or two ago, in the pages of one of our magazines, some of the greatest and choicest minds of this country labored to answer the question "Is life worth living?" It was a triumph for religion, some thought, that the keenest intellects of the nineteenth century would be stirred with themes like this. It was not so; it was the surest proof of the utter heathenism of our age. Is life worth living? We might as well ask, "Is air worth breathing?" Taking the definition of life here suggested, the real question is this: "Is going to the Father worthwhile?"

Yet, we can understand the question. On any other definition, we can understand it. On any other definition, life is very far from being worth living. Without that, life is worse than an enigma; it is an inquisition. Life is either a discipline or a most horrid cruelty. Man's best aims here are persistently thwarted, his purest aspirations degraded, his intellect systematically insulted, his spirit of inquiry crushed, his love mocked, and his hope stultified. There is no solution whatever to life without this; there is nothing to sustain either mind or soul amid its terrible mystery but this; there is nothing even to account for mind and soul. And it will always be a standing miracle that men of powerful intellect who survey life, who feel its pathos and bitterness, and are shut up all the time to impenetrable darkness by their beliefs—I say, it will always be a standing miracle how such men, with the terrible unsolved problems all around them, can keep reason from reeling and tottering from its throne. If life is not a going to the Father, it is not only not worth living, but it is also an insult to the living. And it is one of the strangest mysteries how men who are large enough in one direction to ask that question, and too limited in another to answer it, would voluntarily continue to live at all.

There is nothing to sustain life but this thought. And it does sustain life. Take even an extreme case, and you will see how. Take the darkest, saddest, most pathetic life of the world's history. That was Jesus Christ's. See what this truth was to Him in practical terms. It gave Him a life of absolute composure in a career of most tragic trials.

You have often noticed, and it is inexpressibly touching, how, as His life narrows, and troubles thicken around Him, He leans more and more upon this. And when the last days draw near—as the memorable chapters in John reveal them to us—with what clinging tenderness He alludes in almost every second sentence to "My Father." There is a wistful eagerness in these closing words that is strangely tender—like one ending a letter at sea when land is coming into sight.

This is the Christian's only stay in life. It provides rest for his soul, work for his character, and an object—an inconceivably sublime object—for his ambition. It does not stagger him to be a stranger here, to feel the world passing away. The Christian is like the pearl diver who is out of the sunshine for a little while, spending his short day amid rocks and weeds and dangers at the bottom of the ocean. Does he desire to spend his life there? No, but his Master desires that he do so. Is his life there? No, his life is up above. A communication is open to the surface, and the fresh, pure life comes down to him from God. Is he not wasting time there? He is gathering pearls for his Master's crown. Will he always stay there? When the last pearl is gathered, the "Come up higher" will beckon him away, and the weights that kept him down will become an *"exceeding…weight of glory"* (2 Corinthians 4:17), and he will go, he and these he brings with him, to his Father.

To change the metaphor, he feels like a man in training for a race. It is still months away, but it is nearer to him than tomorrow, nearer than anything else. Great things are always near things. So, he lives in his future. Ask him why he practices this deliberate abstinence from luxury in eating and drinking. "I am keeping my life," he says. Why this self-denial, this separation from worldliness, this change to a quiet life from revelries far into the night? He is keeping his life. He cannot have both the future and the present; and he knows that every regulated hour, and every temptation scorned and set aside, is adding a nobler tissue to his frame and keeping his life for the prize that is to come.

Trial to the Christian is training for eternity, and he is perfectly content, for he knows that *"he that loveth his life shall lose it; and he that hateth his life in this world shall keep it unto life eternal"* (John 12:25). He is keeping his life until he gets to the Father.

3. The Principle of "Going to the Father" Completes Life

Life has been defined as "a going to the Father." It is quite clear that there must come a time in the history of all those who live this life when they reach the Father. This is the most glorious moment of life. Angels attend at it. Those on the other side must hail the completing of another soul with ineffable rapture. When they are yet a great way off, the Father runs and falls on their neck and kisses them. (See Luke 15:20.)

On this side, we call that experience death. It means reaching the Father. It is not departure; it is arrival. Not sleep, but waking. To those who live like Christ, life is not a funeral procession. It is a triumphal march to the Father— and an entry at the end in God's own chariot in the last hour of all. No, as we watch a life that is going to the Father, we cannot think of night, of gloom, of dusk and sunset. It is life that is the night, and death that is the sunrise.

"Pray moderately," says an old saint, "for the lives of Christ's people."[6] Pray moderately. He means that we may want these lives to remain on our side of eternity, but Christ may need them on His. He has seen them a great way off and has set His heart upon them, and has asked the Father to make them come quickly. He says, *"I will that they also, whom thou hast given me, be with me where I am"* (John 17:24). So, it is better that they should go to the Father.

The Words "I Go to the Father" Speak to Us All

Jesus' words have different emphases to different people. There are three types of people to whom they come home with a particular emphasis:

1. Those Who Are Straying from God

These words speak to those who are staying from God. "I do not wonder at what men Suffer," says John Ruskin, "but I wonder often at what they

Lose."[7] My fellow pilgrim, you do not know what you are losing by not going to the Father. You live in an appalling mystery. You have nothing to explain your life, nor to sustain it; no boundary line on the dim horizon to complete it. When life is done, you are going to leap into the dark. You will cross the dark river and land on the further shore alone. No one will greet you. You and the Inhabitant of Eternity will be strangers. Will you not arise and go to your Father today?

2. God's People

Next, they speak to all God's people. Let us remember that we are going to the Father. Even now, we are the sons of God. Oh, let us live like it—simpler, uncomplaining, useful, separate; joyful as those who march with music, yet sober as those who are to company with Christ. The road is heavy—high road and low road—but we will soon be home. God grant us a sure arrival at our Father's house.

3. Those Who Mourn the Death of a Loved One

And this voice whispers yet one more message—to those who mourn. Did death end all? Is it well with the child? It is well. The last inn by the roadside has been passed—that is all. And a voice called to us, "Good-bye! I go to my Father."

THE ECCENTRICITY
OF RELIGION

"They said, He is beside himself."
—Mark 3:21

The most sorrowful life in the history of the world is the life of the Lord Jesus. Those who study it find a fresh sorrow every day. Before He came, it was already foretold that He would be acquainted with grief. (See Isaiah 53:3.) But no imagination had ever conceived the darkness of the reality.

It began with one of the bitterest kinds of sorrow—the sorrow of an enforced silence. For thirty years, He saw, but dared not act. The wrongs He came to redress were there. The hollowest religion ever known—a mere piece of acting—was being palmed off around Him on every side as the religion of the living God. He saw the poor trodden upon, the sick untended, the widow unavenged, His Father's people scattered, His truth misrepresented, and the whole earth filled with hypocrisy and violence. He saw this, grew up among it, knew how to cure it. Yet, He was silent; He did not open His mouth. (See Isaiah 53:7.) It is impossible to comprehend how He held in His breaking spirit until the slow years dragged themselves out.

Then came the public life, the necessity to breathe its atmosphere—the temptation, the contradiction of sinners, the insults of the Pharisees, the attempts on His life, the dullness of His disciples, the Jews' rejection of Him, the apparent failure of His cause, Gethsemane, Calvary. Yet, these were but the more marked shades in the darkness that blackened the whole path of the Man of Sorrows.

But, in the Scripture passage that contains our text, we are confronted with an episode in His life that is not included in any of these, an episode that had a bitterness all its own; and such as has fallen to the lot of few to know. It was not the way the world treated Him; it was not the Pharisees. It was not something that came from His enemies; it was something His friends did. When He left the carpenter's shop and went out into the wider life, His friends were watching Him. For some time, they had noticed a certain strangeness in His manner. He had always been strange among His brothers, but now it was growing upon Him. He has said much stranger things of late, made many strange plans, gone away on curious errands to strange places. What did it mean? Where was it to end? Was the family to be responsible for all this eccentricity? One sad day, it culminated. It was quite clear to them now. He was not responsible for what He was doing. It was His mind that had become affected. He was "*beside himself.*" In plain English, *He was mad!*

That is an awful thing to say when it is true, and a more awful thing when it is not; but it is a still more awful thing when the accusation comes from those whom we love, from those who know us best. It was not the voice of an enemy; it came from His own home. It was His own mother, perhaps, and His brothers, who pointed that terrible finger at Him, apologized for Him, entreated the people not to mind Him, for He was beside Himself—He was mad.

Surely, there should have been one spot upon God's earth for the Son of Man to lay His head (see Matthew 8:20; Luke 9:58)—one roof in Nazareth, at least, with Mother's ministering hand and Sister's love for the weary Worker. But His very home is closed to Him. He has to endure these things: the furtive glances of eyes that once loved Him, the members of the household watching Him and whispering one to another; the cruel suspicion; the laying of hands upon Him, hands that once had been kind to Him; and finally, the overwhelming announcement of the verdict of His family: *"He is beside himself."* Truly, *"he came unto his own, and his own received him not"* (John 1:11).

What makes it seemly today to dig up this harrowing memory and to emphasize a thought that we cannot but feel lies on the borderland of blasphemy? Because the significance of that scene is still intense. It has a particular lesson for us who are to profess ourselves followers of Christ—a lesson in counting the cost. From first to last, Christ's life was a dramatized parable; it was too short and too significant to allow even a scene that might well rest in solemn shadow to pass by unused.

From the World's Standpoint, Jesus Was "Beside Himself"

Observe that, from the world's standpoint, the charge was true. It is useless to denounce this as a libel; a bitter, blasphemous slander. That was not so—it was true. There was no alternative. Either He was the Christ, the Son of the Living God, or He was beside Himself. A holy life is always a phenomenon. The world does not know it. It is either supernatural or morbid.

For what is "being beside oneself"? What is madness? It is eccentricity— "ec-centr-icity," having a different center from other people. For instance, suppose a person devotes his life to collecting objects of antiquarian interest—old coins perhaps, or old editions of books. His center is odd; his life revolves in an orbit of his own. Therefore, his friends say that he is eccentric.

Or, imagine an engine with many moving wheels, large and small, cogged and plain, but each revolving upon a central axis and describing a perfect circle. But, at one side, there is one small wheel that does not turn in a circle. Its motion is different from all the rest, and the changing curve it describes is unlike any ordinary line of the mathematician. The engineer tells you that this is the *eccentric*, because it has a different center.

Now, when Jesus Christ came among men, He found nearly all of them revolving in one circle. There was but one center to human life—self. Man's chief end was to glorify himself and enjoy himself forever. Then, as now, by the all-but-unanimous consensus of the people, this present world was sanctioned as the legitimate object of all human interest and enterprise. By the whole gravitation of society, Jesus—as a Man—must have been drawn to the very verge of this vast vortex of self-indulgence, personal ease, and pleasure that had sucked in the populations of the world since time began. But He stepped back. He absolutely refused to be attracted. He put everything out of His life that had even a temptation in it to the world's center.

He humbled Himself—there is no place in the world's vortex for humbleness. He became of no reputation—nor is there a place for namelessness. He emptied Himself—gravitation cannot act on emptiness. So, the prince of this world came but found nothing in Him. (See John 14:30.) He found nothing, because the true center of that life was not to be seen. It was with God. The unseen and the eternal moved Him. He did not seek His own happiness but that of others. He went about doing good. His object in going about was not gain but to do good.

All this was very eccentric. It was living on altogether new lines. Christ did God's will. He did not please Himself. His center was to one side of self—He was "beside" Himself. From the world's viewpoint, it was simply madness.

Think about this idea of His, for instance, of starting out into life with so quixotic an idea as that of doing good; the simplicity of the expectation that the world ever would become good. Think of this irrational talk about meat to eat that they did not know about; about living water; these extraordinary Beatitudes, declaring sources of happiness that had never been heard of; these paradoxical utterances of which He was so fond, such as that the way to find life was to lose it, and to lose life in this world was to keep it to life eternal. What could these be but mere hallucinations and dreams! It was inevitable that men would laugh and sneer at Him. He was unusual. He would not go with the multitude. And men were expected to go with the multitude. What the multitude thought, said, and did were the right things to have thought, said, and done. And if anyone thought, said, or did differently, his folly be on his own head. He was beside Himself. He was mad.

Christ's Followers Will Likewise Be Considered "Besides Themselves"

Everyone who lives like Christ produces the same reaction upon the world. This is an inevitable consequence. If we are true to Christ, what men said of Him, they will say of you and me. The servant is not above his master. (See John 13:16; 15:20.) Jesus said, *"If they have persecuted me, they will also persecute you"* (John 15:20). A Christian must be different from other people. Time has not changed the essential difference between the spirit of the world and the spirit of Christ. They are radically and eternally different. And still, from the world's standpoint, Christianity is eccentricity. For what, again, is Christianity? It is the projection into the world of those lines along which Christ lived. It is a duplicating in modern life of the spirit, the method, and the aims of Jesus; a following through the world of the very footprints He left behind. And if these footprints were at right angles to the broad, beaten track that the world went along in His day, they will be so still. It is useless to say the distinction has broken down. These two roads are still at right angles.

The day may come when the path of righteousness will be the glorious highway for all the earth. But it is not now. Christ did not expect it would be so. He made provision for the very opposite. He prepared His church beforehand for the reception it would get in the world. He gave no hope that it would be an agreeable one. Light must conflict with darkness, truth with error. There is no sanctioned place in the world as yet for a life with God as its goal, and self-denial as its principle. Meekness must be victimized; spirituality must be misunderstood; true religion must be mocked. Holiness must make a strong ferment and reaction, in family or community, office or workshop, wherever it is introduced. Jesus said,

> *Think not that I am come to send peace on earth: I came not to send peace, but a sword. For I am come to set a man at variance against his father, and the daughter against her mother, and the daughter in law against her mother in law. And a man's foes [He might well say it] shall be they of his own household.* (Matthew 10:34–36)

True religion is no milk-and-water experience. It is a fire. It is a sword. It is a burning, consuming heat that must radiate upon everything around.

The change to the Christlike life is so remarkable that when one really undergoes it, he cannot find words in common use by which he can describe its revolutionary character. He has to recall the very striking phrases of the Bible, which once seemed such exaggerations: *"new man"* (Ephesians 4:24; Colossians 3:10), *"new creature"* (2 Corinthians 5:17; Galatians 6:15), *"new heart"* (see, for example, Ezekiel 11:19), and *"new birth"* (see, for example, John 3:3). His very life has been taken down and recrystallized around the new center. He has been born again.

The impression his friends receive from him now is the impression of eccentricity. The change is bound to strike them, for it is radical, central. They will call in unworthy motives to account for the difference; they will say it is a mere temporary fit and will pass away. They will say he has shown a weakness that they did not expect from him, and try to banter him out of his novel views and stricter life. This, in its mildest form, is the modern equivalent of *"He is beside himself."* And it cannot be helped. It is the legitimate reproach of the cross. The words are hard but not new. Has it not come down that long line of those of whom the world was not worthy? Its history—alas!—is well-known. It fell on the first Christians in a painful and even vulgar form.

The little church had just begun to live. The disciples stood after the great day of Pentecost contemplating that first triumph of Christ's cause with unbounded joy. At last, an impression had been made upon the world. The enterprise was going to succeed, and the whole earth would fill with God's glory. They little calculated that the impression they made on the world was the impression of their own ridiculousness. The people asked, *"What meaneth this?"* (Acts 2:12). "It means," the disciples would have said, "that the Holy Spirit, who was to come in Christ's name, was here, that God's grace was stirring the hearts of men and moving them to repent." The people had a different answer. *"These men,"* was the coarse reply, *"are full of new wine"* (Acts 2:13). This time, they are not insane—they are intoxicated!

Time passes, and Paul tells us the charge was laid at his door. He had made that great speech in the hall of the Caesarian palace before Agrippa and Festus. He told them of the grace of God in his conversion, and he closed with an eloquent confession of his Lord. What impression had he made upon his audience? The impression of a madman. *"As he thus spake for himself, Festus said with a loud voice, Paul, thou art beside thyself; much learning doth make thee mad"* (Acts 26:24).

Poor Paul! How you feel for him when the cruel blow is struck. But there was no answer to it. From their viewpoint, it was perfectly true. And so it has been with all saints to the present hour. It does not matter if they speak words of soberness, like Paul. It does not matter if they are men of burning zeal, like Francis Xavier and George Whitefield; men of calm spirit like Gerhard Tersteegen and Thomas à Kempis; men of learning like Augustine, or of ordinary gifts like John Wesley—the effect of all saintly lives upon the world is the same. They are to the Jews a stumbling block and to the Greeks foolishness. (See 1 Corinthians 1:23.)

It is not simply working Christianity that is an offense. To the natural man, the whole spiritual life is an eccentric thing. For instance, take such a manifestation as personal prayer. The scientific men of the day have examined it and pronounced it "hallucination." Or take public prayer: a congregation of people with heads bowed, eyes shut, and voices hushed, invoking, confessing, pleading, and entreating One who, though not seen, is said to see; who, speaking not, is said to answer. From the world's standpoint, there is no other name for this incantation but eccentricity, delusion, madness. We are not ashamed of the terms. They are the guarantee of quality. And all high quality in the world is subject to the same reproach. For we are discussing a universal principle. It applies to inventors, to discoverers, to philosophers, to poets, to all men who have been better or higher than their time. These men are never understood by their contemporaries. And if there are martyrs of science—the centers of science being seen, demonstrated, and known in this world—how much more must there be martyrs for religion, whose center is beyond the reach of earthly eye?

The More Active Religion Is, the More Unpopular It Is

It follows that the more active religion is, the more unpopular it must be. At first, Christ's religion did not trouble His friends. For thirty years, in any case, they were content to put up with it. But as it grew in intensity, they lost patience. When He called the twelve disciples, they gave Him up. His work went on, and the world said nothing for some time. But, as His career became more and more aberrant, the family feeling spread and gained universal ground. Even the most beautiful and tender words He uttered were quoted in evidence of His state. For John tells us that, after Jesus' exquisite discourse about the Good Shepherd, there was *"a division…among the Jews for these sayings. And many of them said, He hath a devil, and is mad; why hear ye him?"* (John 10:19–20). It seemed utter raving.

Have you ever noticed—and there is nothing more touching in history—how Christ's path narrowed?

Some books call the first great, active period of His ministry "the year of public favor." On the whole, it was a year of triumph. The world received Him for a time. Vast crowds followed Him. John the Baptist's audience left him and gathered around the new voice. Palestine rang with the name of Jesus. Noblemen, rulers, and rabbis vied with one another in entertaining Him. But the excitement died down suddenly and soon.

The next year is called "the year of opposition." The applause was over. The crowds thinned. He was obstructed on every hand. The Sadducees left Him. The Pharisees left Him. The political party was roused into opposition. The Jews, the great mass of the people, gave Him up. His path was narrowing.

With the third period came the end. The path was very narrow now. When the last act of the drama opens, there are but twelve left to Him. They are gathered on the stage together for the last time. But it must narrow still. One of the disciples goes out after receiving the sop of bread. Eleven are now left to Him. Peter soon follows. There are but ten. One by one, they leave the stage, until all forsake Him and flee, and He is left to die alone. Well might He cry, as He hung there in that awful solitude—as if even God had forgotten Him—*"My God, my God, why hast thou forsaken me?"* (Matthew 27:46; Mark 15:34).

But this experience is not reserved for Jesus. It is typical of the life of every Christian. His path, too, must narrow. As he grows in grace, he grows in isolation. He feels that God is detaching his life from everything around it, and drawing him to Himself for a more intimate fellowship. But as the communion is nearer, the chasm that separates him from his fellow men must widen. Indeed, the degree of a person's religion is to be gauged by the degree of his rejection by the world. With the early Christians, was not this the commonest axiom, and did Paul not warn them, "*We told you before that we should suffer...*" (1 Thessalonians 3:4)? Paul also wrote, "*Unto you it is given in the behalf of Christ, not only to believe on him, but also to suffer for his sake*" (Philippians 1:29). It was the position of honor, as it were, in the family of God to be counted worthy of being persecuted for the sake of Christ.

It is a sad reflection that, as in the case of Christ, the keenest suffering may still sometimes come from one's own family circle. Among our friends, there may be one on whom we all look askance—one who is growing up in the beauty of holiness—and we are unaware of what makes him strange. Again, death is needed to teach us the beauty of a life that has been lived beside our own; and we know the worth of it only when God proves it by taking it to Himself.

Godly Eccentricity Versus All Other Eccentricity

Finally, in regard to all the above, someone may argue that if eccentricity is a virtue, it is easily purchased. Anyone can create an eccentric character. And if that is the requirement of religion, we will have candidates enough for the office. But it remains to define the terms on which a Christian shall be eccentric—Christ's own terms. And let them be guides to us in our eccentricity, for, without them, we will be not Christians but fanatics.

Three qualities distinguish the eccentricity of godliness from all other eccentricity. We gather these qualities from the life of Christ.

1. Godly Eccentricity Is Not Destructive

Note that Christ's eccentricity was not destructive. He took the world as He found it, and He left it as it was. He had no quarrel with existing institutions. He did not overthrow the church—He went to church. He said nothing against politics—He supported the government of the country. He did not denounce society—His first public action was to go to a marriage. In fact, outwardly, and all along, His great aim was to be as normal—as little eccentric—as possible. The true fanatic always tries the opposite. The Spirit alone was singular in Jesus; a fanatic always spoils his cause by extending it to the letter. Christ did not come to destroy but to fulfill. (See Matthew 5:17.) A fanatic comes not to fulfill but to destroy. If we would follow the eccentricity of our Master, let it not be in asceticism, in denunciation, in punctiliousness, and in scruples about trifles, but in largeness of heart, singleness of eye, true breadth of character, true love to men, and heroism for Christ.

2. Godly Eccentricity Is Perfectly Composed

Second, Christ's eccentricity was perfectly composed. We think of eccentricity as associated with frenzy, nervousness, excitableness, and ungovernable enthusiasm. But the life of Jesus was calm. It was a life of marvelous composure. The storms were all around it—tumult and tempest, tempest and tumult, waves breaking over Him all the time, until the worn body was laid in the grave. But the inner life was as a sea of glass. It was a life of perfect composure. To come near it even now is to be calmed and soothed. Go to it at any moment, and the great calm is there. The request to "come" at any moment was a standing invitation all through His life. "Come unto Me at My darkest hour, in My heaviest trial, on My busiest day, and I will give you rest." And when the very bloodhounds were gathering in the streets of Jerusalem to hunt Him down, did He not turn to the quaking group around Him and bequeath to them a last legacy—*"my peace"* (John 14:27)?

There was no frenzy about His life, no excitement. In quietness and confidence, the most terrible days sped past. In patience and composure, the most thrilling miracles were worked. When men came to Him, they did not find restlessness but rest. Composure is necessary for faith. We would be worse than fanatics if we attempted to go along the lonely path with Christ without this spirit. We would do harm, not good. We would leave work half-done. We would wear out before our time. Do not say, "Life is short." Christ's life was short; yet, He finished the work that was given Him to do. He was never in a hurry. And, if God has given us anything to do for Him, He will give time enough to finish it, with a repose like Christ's.

3. Godly Eccentricity Is Consistent

Third, Christ's life was consistent. From the Christian standpoint, a consistent life is the only sane life. It is not worthwhile being religious without being thorough. An inconsistent Christian is the true eccentric. He is the true phenomenon in the religious world; to his fellow Christian, he is the only madman. For, in a sense, madness is inconsistency; madness is incoherency, irrelevancy, disconnectedness. Surely, there is nothing more disconnected than a belief in God and eternity with no corresponding life. That person is certainly beside himself who assumes the name of Christ; who pledges, perhaps in sacramental wine, to be faithful to His name and cause; but who from one year to the next never lifts a finger to help it. The individual who is really under a delusion is he who bears Christ's name but has no uneasiness about the quality of his life, nor any fear for the future, and whose true creed is that

> He lives for himself, he thinks for himself,
> For himself, and none beside;
> Just as if Jesus had never lived,
> As if He had never died.

Yes, a consistent eccentricity is the only sane life. "An enthusiastic religion is the perfection of common sense." To be beside oneself for Christ's sake is to be beside Christ, which is man's chief end, for time and eternity.

"TO ME TO LIVE IS CHRIST"
(*In connection with Acts 9:1–18.*)

"For to me to live is Christ, and to die is gain."
—Philippians 1:21

There is no more significant sign of the days in which we live than the interest society seems to be taking in the biographies of great men. Almost all the more recent popular books, for instance—the books that everyone is reading and has to read—come under the catalogue of biography. And, to meet the demand, two or three times in each season, the market has to be supplied with the lives—in minute detail—of men who but for this current interest would perhaps have lain in unnoticed graves.

This thirst for memoirs and lives and letters is not at all, in every case, to be put down to the hero worship that is natural to every heart. It means, perhaps, a higher thing than this. In the first place, it means that great living is being appreciated for its own sake; and, in the second, that great living is being imitated. If it is true that any of us are beginning to appreciate greatness for its own sake—greatness, that is to say, in the sense of great and true living—it is one of the most hopeful symptoms of our history. And, further, if we are going on from the mere admiration of great men to try to live like them, we are obeying one of the happiest impulses of our being. Indeed, there is no finer influence abroad than the influence of great men in great books, and all that literature can do in supplying the deformed world with worthy and well-formed models is entitled to gratitude and respect.

But a shadow sometimes comes over this thought of the magnetic attraction that greatness is having upon our age—the thought of how hard it is to get our greatness pure. It may be that the well is deep, and the fountain sparkles to the eye; but, perhaps, we ask for a guarantee of quality in vain. Each new ideal that we adjust our life in order to copy turns out to have its adulteration of selfishness or pride, until the pattern we sought to follow surprises us by becoming a beacon for us to shun.

Paul's Motto

There are a few biographies, however, where we may find the subject's greatness to be pure. Among them is one familiar writing that, though seldom looked at as biographical in this sense, really contains the life and letters of probably the greatest man of human history. That man was Paul. The life of Paul the man, apart from the theology of Paul the apostle, is a legitimate and fruitful study from the mere standpoint of the biography of a great and successful life. Judging by his influence on human history, no single life is entitled to more admiration for what it has done, or indeed is more worthy of imitation for what it was. And in our quest after a true life, a worthy and satisfying life, there may be some light for us in this ancient biography that we perhaps have missed in the lives of later men.

If we were to begin by seeking an appropriate motto for Paul's life, we would not need to go further than the quotation that forms our text. This fragment from one of Paul's own letters lets us in at once on the whole secret of his life. The true discovery of a character is the discovery of its ideals. Paul spared us any speculation in his case. "To me to live," he said, "is Christ." This was the motto of his life, the ruling passion of it, which, at the same time, explains the nature of his success, and accounts for it. Paul lived for Christ. *"To me to live is Christ."*

At the outset, a valuable practical point is settled in this biography. When we turn to the biographies of most great men, we find either no key or a very complex one; and we rise from the perusal with nothing more than a vague desire to do better, but with no discovery as to *how*. We gain stimulus, indeed, but no knowledge, which is simply injurious. We are braced up enthusiastically for a little while, but then do nothing. At the end of it all, we are not better; we are only exhausted. This is the reason why biography-hunters, after long dogging the footsteps of greatness, often find that they are perhaps no further on the road to it themselves, but rather more inclined than before to lie down where they were.

The Working Principle of Paul's Life

But Paul explicitly announced to us the working principle of his life. If the lines are great lines, there is nothing mysterious about them. If we want to live like Paul, we simply have to live for Christ—on one side, Christ our life; on the other side, our life for Christ. Both are summed up together in Paul's epitome, *"To me to live is Christ."*

This being the clue to Paul's life, the instructive question next arises, "What exactly did Paul mean by this principle, and how did he come to discover it?" But the question "What is this object of life?" is so closely bound up with how Paul came to have this object of life that the answer to the last question will form at once an explanation and an illustration of the first.

Therefore, let us go at once to the life itself for the answer. Great principles are always best and freshest when studied from the life, and it so happens that a circumstance in Paul's life makes it particularly easy to act on that rule here.

Paul's Two Lives

That circumstance was that Paul had two lives. Many men besides Paul have had two lives, but the line is more clear-cut in Paul's case than in almost any other biography we have.

Both lives were about the same length, as far as we know, but they were so distinct in their general features and details that Paul not only had two lives but, as if to mark the distinction more strikingly, two names. Let us look for a moment at the first of these lives, in which he was known as Saul. The reason will appear presently.

Paul's First Life

As we all know, Paul's first life was spent under the most auspicious circumstances. And, for certain reasons, it will be worthwhile to go over it. Born of a family that belonged to the most select theological school of that day, the son was looked upon early as not only the promise of his parents but also the hope of their religion. They sent him to Jerusalem as a mere lad, and enrolled him as a student in the most distinguished college of the time. (See, for example, Acts 22:3.) After running a brilliant college career, and sitting for many years at the feet of the greatest learning the Jewish capital could boast, we find him bursting upon the world with his splendid talents, and immediately taking a place in the troubled political movements of the day. It was impossible for such a character, having youthful enthusiasm and a Pharisee's pride, to submit to the tame life of a temple rabbi, and he saw his opportunity in the rise of the Christian sect. Here, at last, he would match his abilities in a contest that would, simultaneously, gain him a field of exercise and a name. So far, doubtless, he thought his first life *great*.

He seemed to have next entered into his work of persecution with all the zest of an inquisitor. His conspicuous place among the murderers of the first martyr stamped him at once as a leader. (See Acts 7:1–8:1.) It also gave him the first taste of a popularity that, if it hadn't been for the interruption of the hand of God, would perhaps have resulted in disaster for the struggling Christian church. The young man's success as an inquisitor was recognized in the highest quarters of the land, and his fortune was made. Perhaps no young man of that time had such prospects then as Saul. "He was a man raised up for the emergency," said all Jerusalem; and, henceforth, the Jewish world was at his feet. Courted as the rising man of his day, and flushed with success, he left no stone unturned to find fresh opportunities to add to his influence and power. And as he climbed each rung of the ladder of fame, we can imagine, as a great student of Paul has said, how his heart swelled within him as he read these words at night from the book of Wisdom: "…I shall have estimation among the multitude, and honor with the elders, though I be young. I shall be found of a quick conceit in judgment, and shall be admired in the sight of great men. When I hold my tongue, they shall abide my leisure, and when I speak, they shall give good ear unto me."[8] Such was the man who later said, *"To me to live is Christ."*

Saul had already wreaked his vengeance to the full upon the little church in Jerusalem. At last, the town and neighborhood were well-nigh rid of the pest. Dispersed in all directions, members of the little band had found their way in secret through Judea and Samaria, through Syria and Phoenicia, even into strange cities. Saul's achievement had been accompanied by an unlooked-for calamity—at the height of his triumph, he found his occupation gone. Around Jerusalem, he found no fuel to feed the martyrs' fire or to add more luster to his name.

But Saul did not pause in the pursuit of human fame. The young lawyer's reputation could never end in an anticlimax like this. With an ambition that did not know how to rest, and in the pride of his Pharisee's heart, he pursued the idea to reverse the maxim of the crucified Leader of the hated sect, and to go into all the world to suppress the gospel in every creature. He applied to the high priest for commission and authority; and, *"breathing out threatenings and slaughter"* (Acts 9:1), the man who was going to live for Christ started out on his Christless mission to make havoc of the church.

Paul's Transition to a New Life

This was the last act of Paul's first life. Let us note it carefully. We are on the bridge that separates his two lives. What marks the transition is this fact: Up to this time, his life had been spent in public. It had been one prolonged whirl of excitement and applause. But no sooner had the gates of Jerusalem closed upon Saul than he began to think. The echoes of the people's praises had died away one by one. He had gone out into the great desert. It was strangely silent and soothing, and a lull had come upon his soul at last. It had perhaps been a long time since he had had time to think; but Saul was far too great a man to live an unthinking life for long. His time for reflection had come. And as he wandered with his small escort along the banks of the

Jordan, or through the solitary hills of Samaria, his thoughts were busy with the past.

And if Saul was far too great a man to live an unthinking life, he was also too great a man to think well of his life when he did think about it. Each new day, as he journeyed away from the scene of his triumph, and looked back upon it all from a distance—which always gives the true perspective to a person's life—his mind must have filled with many a sad reproach. And as he lay down at night in the quiet wilderness, his thoughts must often have turned to the true quality of the life to which he was sacrificing his talents and his youth. With his quick perception; with his keen, trained intellect; with his penetration; he must have seen, after all, that this life was a mistake.

Minds of lesser caliber in the applauding world that he had left had told him he was great. Now, in his calmer moments, he knew he was not great. The eternal heavens stretching above him pointed to an infinity that lay behind it all; and the stars and the silence spoke to him of God. And he felt that his life was miserably small. Saul's thoughts were greater than his life. He must have seen how he had been living beneath himself; how he had wasted the precious years of his youth; how he had sold his life for honor and reputation, and had bartered the talents God had given him for a name. He had been dazzled, and that was all. He had nothing really to show for his life, nothing that would stand the test of solid thought. It had all been done for himself. He, Saul of Tarsus, the rising man of his time, was the center of it all. Perhaps he cried in agony, "After all, to me, to live is Saul. To me, to live is myself."

As we have seen, Saul's first great discovery—and it is the discovery that precedes every true reformation of life—was the discovery of himself. When he said, "To me, to live is myself," his conversion began. There was then no retreat for a man like him. He was too great to have such a little center to his life; or, rather, he felt life was too great to be absorbed with even such a personality as his.

But the next element in the case was not so easily discovered, and it is of much more importance than the first. His first achievement was only to discover himself. His second was to discover someone better than himself. He wanted a new center to his life. Where was he to find it? The unseen hand that had painted his own portrait in its true colors on the dark background of his mind had painted every other life the same. The high priests at Jerusalem, the members of the Sanhedrin, his own father at Tarsus—all the men he knew were living lives like his own. They were no better—most of them worse. Must the old center of Saul's life remain there still? Was there nothing better in the entire world than himself?

It may be conjecture, or it may be nearer truth, that while such questionings passed through the mind of Saul as he journeyed, there came into his thoughts some influences from a life—a life like that for which his thoughts had longed. Paul's best known journeys are his missionary tours, and we generally associate him in our thoughts with the countries of Asia and Italy and Greece. But, this time, his way leads through the Holy Land. He has entered the land of Christ. He is crossing the very footsteps of Jesus. The villages along his route are still fragrant with what Jesus said and did. They are not the bitter things that Saul had heard before. Kind words are repeated to him, and tender acts that Jesus did are told. The peasants by the wayside and the shepherds on the hills are full of stories of a self-denying life that used to pass that way a year or two ago, but now will come no more. And the mothers at the cottage doors remember the stranger who allowed their little children to come to Him, and perhaps got them to repeat to Saul the children's blessing that He left behind. Perhaps, in passing through Samaria, the traveler met a woman at a well who told her strange tale, for the thousandth time, of a weary Man who had sat there once and said He was the Christ. And Galilee, and Capernaum, and Bethsaida, and the lakeshore at Gennesaret, are full of memories of the one true Life that surely even then had begun to cast a sacred influence over Saul.

At any event, there seemed to be a strange preparedness in his mind for the meeting on the Damascus road, as if the interview with Jesus then was not so much the first of his friendship as the natural outcome of something that had gone before. And, no doubt, the Spirit's silent working had been telling on his mind during all those quiet days, leading his thoughts up to the revelation that was to come, and preparing a pathos for the memorable question, with its otherwise unaccountable emphasis, "*Why persecutest thou me?*" (Acts 9:4).

We do not know what went on between Saul's heart and God. We do not know how deep repentance ran; nor where, or how, the justifying grace came down from heaven to his soul. We do not know whether just then he went through our formula of conversion—the process that we like to watch and describe in technical words. But we know this: There came a difference into his life. His life was changed. It was changed at its most radical part. He had changed centers. During the process, whatever it was, this great transfer was effected. Saul deliberately removed the old center from his life and put a new one in its place. Instead of "To me, to live is Saul," it was now *"To me to live is Christ."*

Of course, when the center of Saul's life changed, he had to take his whole life apart and build it up again on a totally different plan. This change, therefore, was not a mere incident in a man's life. It was a revolution—a revolution of the most sweeping sort. Never before was a life so filled up with anti-Christian thoughts and impulses brought so completely to a halt. Never before was there such a total eclipse of the most brilliant worldly prospects, nor such an abrupt transition from a career of dazzling greatness to humble and obscure ignominy.

Let those who define conversion as a certain colorless experience that is thought to occur in the feelings blind themselves to the real transition in this life, if they want to. Let them ask themselves if there ever was a more sweeping revolution in any life, for any cause, than in Saul's, when he abandoned himself, literally abandoned himself, and subordinated everything, and evermore, to this one supreme passion—to live for Christ.

Two Stages of Transformation

The stages by which this transcendent standpoint is to be reached are now plainly before us. They are the discovery of self and the discovery of Christ. Between them, these two discoveries exhaust the whole of life. No one truly lives until both these discoveries are made, for many people have discovered themselves who have not yet discovered Christ. *"He that hath not the Son of God hath not life"* (1 John 5:12). Whatever he has—*existence, continuity*—he does not have *life*. The condition for living at all is to live for Christ. *"He that hath the Son"* and Him alone, and no one else, *"hath life"* (1 John 5:12).

1. The Discovery of Self

Paul takes special care, indeed, that we should fully understand the altogether different quality of the two lives that a person may live. In his view, the first life, the ordinary life of men, was altogether a mistake. *"What things were gain to me,"* he tells us, *"those I counted loss for Christ"* (Philippians 3:7). That brilliant career of his was loss; that mission, once noble and absorbing, was merely a waste of energy and misspent time. And he goes further still. His life was death. It was selfishness, pure and simple; it was the carnal mind, pure and simple; and *"to be carnally minded is death"* (Romans 8:6). We will understand the theology of Paul's letters better if we think of the writer as a man escaping death. And with this horrible background to his life, we can see the fuller significance of his words, that, for him, to live is Christ.

Another thing is made plain to us. The ceaseless demand of the New Testament for regeneration also becomes clear to us when we study the doctrine in such a life as this. It was not Saul who wrote the letters; it was a different man altogether—Paul. It was one who was in a totally different world from the other. If it was Saul, he must have been born again before he could have done it. Nothing less could account for it. His interests, his standpoint, his resources, and his friendships were new. All old things, in fact, had passed away. All things had become new. In short, he was a *"new creature"* (2 Corinthians 5:17). The pool, polluted and stagnant, had found its way at last into the wide, pure sea; the spirit, tired of its narrow prison, disgusted with ambition that ended with itself, reached out to the eternal freedom, and found a worthy field of exercise in the great enterprise of Christ.

Finally, there is a group of people to whom this biography of Paul has a special message. The people who most need a change like Paul's are not always those who are most thought to need it. The really difficult cases—to others, but especially to themselves—are the people who cannot really see that their life could be much better. There are thousands who do not see exactly what conversion could do for them. And their great difficulty in changing their life has been just this: "What, after all, would we really have to change? Our lives at present can scarcely be distinguished from the real Christians around us. If we had been irreligious, or profane, or undutiful, or immoral, conversion might do something for us; but we belong to the class of people who feel how well we have been brought up, how much our interests are gathered around religion, and, generally, how circumspect and proper our entire outward life has been. We do not really see, indeed, what change conversion could make."

Now this is a class that seldom gets any sympathy, and none deserves it more. Religious people and religious books are always saying hard things of the "religiously brought up"—bitterly hard and undeserved things—until they almost come to feel as if their goodness were a crime. But there are secret rendings of the heart within these ranks—longings after God that are perhaps purer than anywhere else outside God's true family. And there are those who feel the difficulty of changing in surroundings so Christian-like as theirs; who feel it so keenly that their despair sometimes leads them to the dark thought of almost envying the prodigal and the open sinner, who seem to have more chance of finding the kingdom than they.

The change in Paul's life is exactly the case in point for them. Paul himself was one of those individuals who wonder what use conversion could ever be to them. He was one of the "religiously brought up." In all Jerusalem, there was no man stricter with his religion than he; no man took his place more regularly in the temple, or kept the Sabbath with more scrupulous care. With respect to the law, he was blameless—just the man whom you would have said would never be changed, who was far too good to be susceptible to a change. But this is the man—not far from the kingdom of God, as everyone thought he was—who found room in his most religious heart for the most sweeping reform that ever occurred in a life.

Let those who really do not know very well what religion could do for them have a time of quiet thought, as Paul did. Let them look once more—not at the circumference of their life, but at the center of it. Let them ask one question about it: "Is it Christ?" There is no middle way in religion—there is self or Christ. The quality of the selfishness—the fact that the center of our self may be of a superior order of self, such as intellectual, literary, or artistic—does nothing to destroy this grave distinction. It is between all self and Christ. For that matter, no center could have been more disciplined or cultured than Paul's. In its place, it was truly great and worthy, but its place was anywhere else than where Paul had it for the first half of his life.

This question of centers, then, is the vital question. "To me to live is"—what? "To me to live is myself!" Suppose that it is so. What kind of a purpose to life is that? How much nobler a center our life is worthy of—our one life, a life that is to live forevermore; that is to live with a great center or a mean one—meanly or greatly forevermore! Think of living with oneself forever and forever. Think of having lived, living now, and living evermore, living only for this. *"Consider him that endured such contradiction of sinners"* (Hebrews 12:3) for our sake, who *"made himself of no reputation"* (Philippians 2:7), who gave up form and comeliness (see Isaiah 53:2), who humbled Himself and emptied Himself for us (see Philippians 2:8). Then look with complacency on such a life, if you can.

> I lived for myself, I thought for myself,
> For myself, and none beside;
> Just as if Jesus had never lived,
> As if He had never died.

2. The Discovery of Christ

This leads naturally to the other point—the discovery of Christ. And here, once more, we draw abundant encouragement from our biography of Paul. And it brings us not only to a hopeful thought but also to a very solemn thought. We have all, in some way, made the discovery of Christ—we know more about Christ than Paul did when he became a Christian. Yes, when Paul made Christ the center of his life, he perhaps knew less about Him than most of us. It is a startling truth, in any case, that we are as near the center of life—the center of the universe—as Paul was. We have heard of Christ from our infancy; the features of His life are as familiar as our own. We have no hatred of Him, as Paul once had. And, if the few days' quietness in the Holy Land that Paul had on the threshold of his change were in any way a preparation for the crisis of his life, how much more has our past life been a preparation for a change in ours! We call Paul's change a sudden conversion—we do not know how sudden it was. But if our life were changed today, it would not be a sudden conversion. Our whole past has been leading up to these two discoveries of life. Our preparation, as far as knowledge of the new center goes, is complete. The change, as far as that is concerned, might happen now. We have the responsibility of being so near to eternal life as that.

The question finally comes to be, then, simply a question of transfer. To me to live is myself, or to me to live is Christ. To live for Christ is not simply the sublime doctrine that it includes of "Christ our life." (See Colossians 3:4.) It is not so much Christ our life, but rather *our life for Christ.*

Will it be, then, our life for Christ? *"To me to live is Christ."* Contrast that purpose with all the other purposes of life; take all the centers out of all the great lives, and compare them one by one. Can you match the life-creed of Paul—*"To me to live is Christ"*?

"To me to live is…business." "To me to live is…pleasure." "To me to live is…myself." We can all tell in a moment what our religion is really worth. "To me to live is"—what? What are we living for? What rises naturally to our heart when we press it with a test like this: "To me to live is"—what? First thoughts, it is said, are best in matters of conscience. What was the first thought that came into our heart just then? What word trembled first on our lip just now? "To me to live is"—was it business, was it money, was it ourselves, was it Christ?

"To me to live is business." "To me to live is pleasure." "To me to live is myself." What kind of an end to an immortal life is that? How much nobler a center our life is worthy of—our life, our one precious life, which is to live forevermore; which is to live with a mean center or a great one—meanly or greatly forevermore.

The time will come when we will ask ourselves why we ever crushed this infinite substance of our life within these narrow bounds, and centered what lasts forever on what must pass away. In the perspective of eternity, all lives will seem poor and small and lost and self-condemned beside a life for Christ. There will be plenty of people then to gather around the cross. But who will do it now? Who will do it now? There are plenty of people who will die for Him; there are plenty to spend eternity with Christ; but where is the person who will *live* for Christ? Death and eternity in their place, Christ wants *lives.* There will be no fear about death being gain if we have lived for Christ. So, let it be, *"To me to live is Christ."*

There is but one alternative—the putting on of Christ; Paul's alternative, the discovery of Christ. Indeed, we have all, in some sense, already made the discovery of Christ. We may be as near it now as Paul was when he left Jerusalem. He was given no notice that he was to change masters. The new Master simply crossed his path one day, and the great change came. How often has the Master crossed our path? We know what to do the next time: We know how our life can be made worthy and great—how only. We know how death can become gain—how only. Many, indeed, tell us death will be gain. Many long for life to be over so that they may rest, as they say, in the quiet grave. Let no cheap sentimentalism deceive us. Death can be gain only when to have lived was Christ.

6

CLAIRVOYANCE

*"We look not at the things which are seen,
but at the things which are not seen: for the things which are seen are
temporal; but the things which are not seen are eternal."*
—2 Corinthians 4:18

"Everything that is, is double."
—Hermes Trismegistus

How can we *"look not at the things which are seen"*? If they are seen, how can we help looking at them? *"Look at the things that are not seen."* How can we look at things that are not seen? Does religion have some magic wishing-cap, making the solid world invisible? Or does it supply some strange clairvoyant power to see what is unseen?

This is one of those alluring paradoxes that all great books delight in, which baffle thought while courting it, but which disclose to whoever picks the lock the rarest and profoundest truth.

The surface meaning of a paradox is either nonsense or false. In this case, it is false. At first sight, one would gather that we had here another of these attacks upon the world of which the Bible is supposed to be so fond. It reads as a withering contrast between the things of time and the things of eternity—as an unqualified disparagement of this present world. The things that are seen are temporal—they are nowhere, not worth a moment's thought, not even to be looked at.

In reality, this is neither the judgment of the Bible nor of reason.

Why We Should Look at What Is Seen

There are four reasons why we should look at the things that are seen. First, *because God made them*. Anything that God makes is worth looking at. We do not live in a chance world. It has all been thought out. Everywhere, work has been spent on it lavishly—thought and work—loving thought and exquisite work. All its parts together, and every part separately, are stamped with skill, beauty, and purpose. As the mere work of a Great Master, we are driven to look—deliberately and long—at the things that are seen.

Second, *God made us to look at them*. He who made light made the eye. It is a gift of the Creator on purpose, so that we may look at the things that are seen. The whole mechanism of man is made with reference to the temporal world—the eye for seeing it, the ear for hearing it, the nerve for feeling it, and the muscle for moving around on it and getting more of it. He who harbors even a suspicion of the things that are seen acts contrary to his own nature.

Third, God has not merely made the world, but *He has made it conspicuous*. So far from lying in the shade, so far from being constituted to escape observation, the whole temporal world *clamors* for it. Nature is never and nowhere silent. If you are apathetic, if you will not look at the things that are seen, they will summon you. The bird will call to you from the treetop, the sea will change her mood for you, the flower will look up appealingly from the wayside, and the sun, before he sets with irresistible coloring, will startle you into attention. The Creator has determined that, whether He is seen or not, no living soul will tread His earth without being spoken to by these works of His hands. God has secured that. And even those things that have no speech or language, whose voice is not heard, have their appeal going out to the entire world, and their word to the end of the earth. (See Psalm 19:1–4.) Had God feared that the visible world would be a mere temptation to us, He would have made it less conspicuous. Certainly, He has warned us not to love it (see 1 John 2:15), but nowhere not to look at it.

The fourth reason is the greatest of all. Hitherto, we have been dealing simply with facts. Now we come to a principle. Look at the things that are seen, because *it is only by looking at the things that are seen that we can have any idea of the things that are unseen.* Our whole concept of the eternal is derived from the temporal.

Take any unseen truth, or fact, or law. The proposition is that it can be apprehended by us only by means of the seen and temporal. Take the word *eternal* itself. What do we know of eternity? Nothing that we have not learned from the temporal. When we try to realize that word, there rises up before us the spaceless sea. We may glide swiftly over it day after day, but the infinite expanse recedes before us, knowing no end. On and on, week and month, there stretches the same vague and infinite horizon, the far-off circle we can never reach. We stop. We are far enough. This is eternity!

In reality, this is not eternity; it is mere water—the temporal, liquid and tangible. But, by looking at this thing that is seen, we have beheld the unseen. Consider a river. It is also water. But its different shape mirrors a different truth. As we look, the opposite of eternity rises up before us. There is time, swift and silent; or life, fleeting and irrevocable. So, one might run over all the material of his thoughts, all the groundwork of his ideas, and trace them back to things that are temporal. They are really material, made up of matter, and in order to think at all, one must first of all see.

Nothing could illustrate this better, perhaps, than the literary form of our English Bible. Leaving out for the present the language of symbol and illustration that Christ spoke, there is no great eternal truth that is not borne to us upon some material image. Look, for instance, at its teaching about human life. To describe that, it does not even use the words derived from the temporal world. It brings us face-to-face with the temporal world, and lets us abstract them for ourselves. It never uses the word *fleeting* or *transitory*. It says life is *"a vapour, that appeareth for a little time, and then vanisheth away"* (James 4:14). It likens it to a swift runner (see Job 9:25), a swift ship (see Job 9:26), and *"a tale that is told"* (Psalm 90:9).

It never uses the word *irrevocable*. It speaks of "*water spilt on the ground, which cannot be gathered up again*" (2 Samuel 14:14), or a thread cut by a weaver (see Isaiah 38:12). Nor does it tell us that life is *evanescent*. It suggests evanescent things—"*a dream*" (Job 20:8), "*a sleep*" (see, for example, Psalm 90:5), "*a shadow*" (see, for example, 1 Chronicles 29:15), and a shepherd's tent removed (see Isaiah 38:12). And even to convey the simpler truth that life is short, we find references only to short things that are seen—"*an handbreadth*" (Psalm 39:5), a "*pilgrimage*" (Genesis 47:9), "*a flower*" (Job 14:2), "*a weaver's shuttle*" (Job 7:6).

In these instances, the Bible is not trying to be poetic; it is simply trying to be true. And it distinctly, unconsciously, recognizes the fact that truth can be borne into the soul only through the medium of things. We must refuse to believe, therefore, that we are not to look at the things that are seen. It is a necessity, for the temporal is the husk and framework of the eternal. And the things that are not seen are made of the things that do appear. "All visible things," said Thomas Carlyle, "are emblems; what thou seest is not there on its own account; strictly taken, is not there at all: Matter exists only spiritually, and to represent some Idea, and *body* it forth."[9] And so John Ruskin: "...the more I think of it I find this conclusion more impressed upon me—that the greatest thing a human soul ever does in this world is to *see* something, and tell what it *saw* in a plain way. Hundreds of people can talk for one who can think, but thousands can think for one who can see. To see clearly is poetry, prophecy, and religion—all in one."[10]

How to Look at What Is Unseen

From this point, we can now move on from the negative of the paradox to the second and positive term—"*Look...at the things which are not seen*" (2 Corinthians 4:18). We now understand how to do this. Where is the eternal? Where are the unseen things, that we may look at them? And the answer is: in the temporal. Look, then, at the temporal, but do not pause there. You must penetrate it. Go through it, and see its shadow, its spiritual shadow, on the further side. Look upon this shadow long and earnestly until what you look through becomes the shadow, and the shadow merges into the reality. Look through until the thing you look through becomes dim, then transparent, and then invisible, and the unseen beyond grows into form and strength. For, truly, the first thing seen is the shadow; the thing on the other side, the reality. The thing you see is only a solid, and people mistake solidity for reality. But the eternal that lies behind—that alone is the reality. Look, then, not at the things that are seen, but look through them to the things that are unseen.

The great lesson that emerges from all this is the religious use of the temporal world. Heaven lies behind earth. We see that this earth is not merely a place to live in but to see in. We are to pass through it as "clairvoyants," holding the whole temporal world as a vast transparency through which the eternal shines.

Seeing the Unseen in Daily Life

Let us now briefly apply this principle to daily life. To the majority of us, the most practical division of life is threefold—the working life, the home life, and the religious life. What do these three areas yield us of the eternal—and how?

1. In the Working Life

To most people, work is just work—manual work, professional work, office work, household work, public work, intellectual work. A yellow primrose is just a yellow primrose; a ledger is a ledger; a lexicon is a lexicon. To a worker who has this mind-set (a Christian businessman, perhaps), therefore, as far as spiritual uses are concerned, work is vanity—an unaccountable squandering of precious time. He must earn his success by the sweat of his brow; that is all he knows about it. It is a curse, lying from the beginning upon man as man. So, six days of it each week, he bends his neck to it doggedly; the seventh, God allows him to think about the unseen and eternal.

Now, God would never unspiritualize three-fourths of mankind's active life by work, if work were work—and nothing more.

A second type of workman sees a little further. His work is not exactly a curse; it is his appointed life, his destiny. It is God's will for him, and he must go through with it. No doubt, its trials are good for him; in any case, God has appointed him this sphere, and he must accept it with Christian resignation.

It is a poor compliment to the divine arrangements if they are simply to be acquiesced in. The all-wise God surely intends some higher outcome from three-fourths of life than ailment and resignation.

Next, for the spiritual man, something lies behind this temporal work that explains all. He sees more coming out of it than the year's income, or the employment of his allotted time, or the benefiting of his species. If violins were to be the only product, there is no reason why Stradivarius would spend his life in making them. But work is an incarnation of the unseen. In this loom, man's soul is made. There is a subtle machinery behind it all, working while he is working, making or unmaking the unseen in him. Integrity, thoroughness, honesty, accuracy, conscientiousness, faithfulness, patience—these unseen things that complete a soul are woven into it through work. These things are not found apart from work.

As the conductor leads into our nerves the invisible electric force, so work conducts into our spirit all high forces of character, all essential qualities of life, *"truth in the inward parts"* (Psalm 51:6). Ledgers and lexicons, business letters, domestic duties, the striking of bargains, the writing of examinations, the handling of tools—these are the conductors of the eternal. The conductors of the eternal matter so much that, without them, there is no eternal. No one *dreams* integrity, accuracy, and so on. He cannot learn them by reading about them. These things require their wire as much as electricity does. The spiritual fluids and the electric fluids are under the same law; and messages of grace come along the lines of honest work to the soul like the invisible message along the telegraph wires. Spiritually, patience will travel along a wire as truly as electricity.

Therefore, a workshop, or an office, or a school of learning, is a gigantic conductor. An office is not a place for making money—it is a place for making character. A workshop is not a place for making machinery, for turning wood, for fitting engines, for founding cylinders—it is a place for making men. To God's eye, it is a place for founding character; it is a place for fitting in the virtues to one's life, for turning out honest, modest-tempered, God-fearing men. A school of learning is not so much a place for making scholars as place for making souls; and he who would ripen and perfect the eternal element in his being will do so by attending to the religious uses of his daily task, recognizing the unseen in its seen, thereby turning three-fourths of each day's life into an ever-acting means of grace.

We say some kinds of work are immoral. A person who is turning out careless, imperfect work is turning out a careless, imperfect character for himself. He is touching deceit every moment; and this unseen thing rises up from his work like a subtle essence, and enters and poisons his soul. We say piecework is immoral—that it makes a man only a piece of a man, shuts him out from variety and originality and adaptation, narrowing and belittling his soul. But we forget the counter-truth, that honest and good work make honesty and goodness, integrity and thoroughness—not only this, but also that these alone make them. Again, he who would ripen and perfect his soul must attend to the religious uses of his daily work—seeing the unseen in its seen—heeding it, not with a dry punctiliousness, but lovingly. In this way, he turns the active life of each working day into a means of grace, recognizing its dignity, not as a mere making of money but as an elaborate means of grace that occupies three-fourths of his life.

2. In the Home Life

Next, life is so ordered that another large part of it is spent in the family. Therefore, family life, also, has its part to play in the completing of the soul. The working life could never teach a person all the lessons of the unseen. A whole set of additional messages from the eternal has to be conducted into his soul at home. This is why it is not good for a man to be alone. (See Genesis 2:18.) A lonely man is insulated from the eternal—inaccessible to the subtle currents that ought to be flowing hourly into his soul.

Additionally, home life is a higher source of spirituality than work. It is here that life dawns, and that the first mold is given to the plastic substance. Home is the cradle of eternity.

It has been secured, therefore, that the first laws stamped there, the first lines laid down, the permanent way for the future soul, should be at once the lines of the eternal. Why do all men say that the family is a divine institution? Because God instituted it? But what guided Him in constituting it as it is? Eternity. Home is a preliminary heaven. Its arrangements are purely the arrangements of heaven. Heaven is a father with his children. The parts we will play in that great home are just the parts we have learned in the family here. We will go through the same life there, only without the substance of matter. Matter is a mere temporary quality on which to practice the eternal—as wooden balls are hung up in a schoolroom to teach children numbers until they can think them for themselves.

When a parent wishes to teach his child form and harmony, the properties of matter, beauty, and symmetry—all these unseen things—what does he do but give his child things that are seen, through which he can see them? He gives him a box of "matter," bricks of wood, as playthings; and the child, in forming and transforming them, in building with them lines and squares, arches and pillars, has borne into his soul regularity and stability, form and symmetry. God does the same with us. The material universe is a mere box of bricks. We exercise our growing minds upon it for a time, until, in the hereafter, we become men, and childish things are put away. (See 1 Corinthians 13:11.) The temporal is but the scaffolding of the eternal; and when the last immaterial souls have climbed through this material world to God, the scaffolding will be taken down, and the earth will be dissolved with fervent heat (see 2 Peter 3:10)—not because it is wrong, but because its work is done.

The mind of Christ is to be learned in the family. Strength of character may be acquired at work, but beauty of character is learned at home. There the affections are trained—especially the love that is to abide when tongues have ceased and knowledge fails. (See 1 Corinthians 13:8.) There the gentle life reaches us, the true heaven life. The family circle is the supreme conductor of Christianity. Tenderness, humbleness, courtesy, self-forgetfulness, faith, sympathy—these ornaments of a meek and quiet spirit are learned at the fireside, around the table, in commonplace houses, in city streets.

Daily, in the ordinary intercourse of life, each of us either embodies these principles in our soul or tramples them out of it. As an actor in a drama, each day, each member of the house, consciously or unconsciously, acts a word. The character is the seen; the word is the unseen. And whether he thinks of the word at night or not, the souls of all around have guessed it silently; and when the material mask and costume are put away, and the circumstance of that day's life are long years forgotten, that word of eternity lives on to make or to mar the player, and all the players with him, in that day's game of life.

To awaken a person to all that is involved in each day's life, in even its insignificant circumstances and casual words and looks, surely you have but to tell him all this—that in these temporals lie eternals; that, in life, not in church, lies religion; that all that is done or undone, said or unsaid, of right or wrong, has its part, by an unalterable law, in the eternal life of all.

3. In the Religious Life

We now come to religion. And we will see further how God has put even that into the temporal for us. Reflect, for a moment, upon the teachings of Christ. All that He had to say of the eternal, He put in images of the temporal world. What are all His parables, His allusions to nature, His illustrations from real life, His metaphors and similes, but disclosures to our blind eyes of the unseen in the seen? In reality, the eternal is never nearer to us than in a material image. Reason cannot bring religion near us; only things can. So, Christ never demonstrated anything. He did not appeal to the reasoning power in mankind but to the seeing power—that power of imagination that deals with images of things.

That is the key to all Christ's teaching—that He spoke not to the reason but to the imagination. Incessantly, He held up *things* before our eyes— things that in a few days or years would molder into dust—and told us to look there at the eternal. He held up bread. "I am Bread," He said. (See John 6:35.) And if you think over that statement for a lifetime, you will never get nearer to the truth than through that thing, bread. That temporal object is so perfect an image of the eternal that no reading, thinking, or sermonizing can get us closer to Christ.

Hence, the triumphant way in which Christ ransacked the temporal world, and marked off for us all its common and familiar things as mirrors of the eternal—something that we, with our false views of spirituality, had never dared to do. So, light, life; vine, wine; bread, water; physician, shepherd; and a hundred other things have all become transformed with a light from the other world. Observe that Christ did not say He is *like* these things; He *is* these things. Look through these things—right through—and you will see Him. We disappoint our souls continually in trying, by some other way than through these simple temporals, to learn the spiritual life.

The danger to those who pursue the intellectual life as a specialty is that they will miss this tender and gracious influence. Suppose a student, by a generous, though perilous, homage paid to learning, is allowed to be an exception in the life of the family. He dwells apart, goes his own way, lives his own life; and, unconsciously, and to his pain, he perhaps finds himself gradually looking down on the homelier tasks and less transcendent interests of the family. In society, it is for the scholar that we make allowances; but the eccentricities we condone on account of their high compensations often mark an arrested development of what is really higher. And there is nothing so much to fear in oneself, and to check with more resolute will, than the unconscious tendency in all who pursue culture to get out of step with humanity, and not be at home at home.

A very remarkable example of Christ's use of this principle is the sacraments. His design there was to perpetuate, in the most luminous and arresting way, the two grandest facts of the spiritual world. How did He proceed? He made them visible. He associated these facts with the commonest things in the world—*water* and *bread and wine*—the everyday diet at every peasant's table. By these sacraments, the souls of men are tied down at the most sacred moments of life to the homeliest temporal things. In this way, the highest spirituality, by Christ's own showing, comes to God's children through lowly forms of the material world. Transcendentalism in religion is a real mistake. True spirituality is to see the divinity in common things.

But, yet again, there is a more wonderful exhibition of this law than the sacraments. God furnished the world with a temporal thing for every eternal thing but one. Every eternal truth had its material image in the world, and every eternal law had its working model among the laws of nature. But there was one thing lacking. There was no temporal for the eternal God Himself. And man missed it. He wished to see even this unseen in something seen. In the sea, he saw eternity; in space, infinity; in the hills, sublimity; in the family, love; in the state, law. But there was no image of God. One speaks of what follows with bated breath. *God gave it!* God actually gave it! God made a seen image of Himself—not a vision, not a metaphor—an "*express image of his person*" (Hebrews 1:3). He laid aside His invisibility; He clothed Himself with the temporal; He took flesh and dwelt among us. (See John 1:14.) The incarnation was the eternal become temporal for a little while, so that we might look at it.

It was our only way of beholding it, for we can see the unseen only in the seen. The word *God* conveyed no meaning; there was no seen thing to correspond to that word, and no word is intelligible until there is an image for it. So God gave religion its new word in the intelligible form—a word in flesh—so that, henceforth, all men might behold God's glory; not in itself, for that is impossible, but in the face of Jesus. This is the crowning proof of the religious use of the temporal world. Such, then, are some of the eternal uses of the temporal world.

In recent years, three types of people have taken up their positions with reference to this principle. One will not look at the unseen at all—the materialist. He is utterly blind to the eternal. The second does not look for the unseen in the seen but apart from the seen—the mystic. He is utterly blind to the temporal. He works, or tries to work, by direct vision. The third is not blind either to the unseen or to the seen but is shortsighted toward both— the ritualist. The ritualist selects some half dozen things from the temporal world and tries to see the unseen in them. As if there were only some half dozen things—crosses and vestments, music and stained glass—through which the eternal shone! The whole world is a ritual—that is the answer. If a person means to evade God, let him look for Him in some half dozen forms; he will evade Him. He will not see Him anywhere else. But let him who wishes to get near God, and to always be with God, always move in a religious atmosphere; let him take up his position beside this truth. Worldliness has been defined as a looking at the things that are seen, but only closely enough to see their market value. Spirituality is that further look that sees their eternal value, that realizes that...

Earth's crammed with heaven,
And every common bush afire with God.[11]

7

THE THREE FACTS OF SIN

"Who forgiveth all thine iniquities; who healeth all thy diseases;
who redeemeth thy life from destruction."
—Psalm 103:3–4

There is one theological word that has found its way lately into nearly all the newer and finer literature of our country. It is not only one of the words of the literary world at present; it is perhaps *the* word. Its reality, its certain influence, and its universality have at last been recognized, and, in spite of its theological name, have forced it into a place where nothing but its felt relation to the wider theology of human life could ever have earned for a religious word. That word, it need hardly be said, is *sin*.

Even in the lighter literature of our country, and this is altogether remarkable, the ruling word just now is *sin*. Years ago, it was the blithe term *chivalry* that held the foreground in poem and ballad and song. Later still, the word that held court in novel and romance was *love*. But now a deeper word heads the chapters and begins the cantos. A more exciting thing than chivalry is descried in the arena, and love itself fades in interest before this small word that has wandered out of theology and changed the face of literature, and made many a new book preach.

It is not for religion to complain that her vocabulary is being borrowed by the world. There may be pulpits where there are not churches; and it is a valuable discovery for religion that the world not only has a mind to be amused but also a conscience to be satisfied.

But religion has one duty in the matter when her words are borrowed— to see that they are borrowed whole. Truth that is to pass into such common circulation must not be mutilated truth; it must be strong, wringing, decided, whole; it must be standard truth. In short, it must be Bible truth.

Now, the Bible truth about this word is in itself interesting and very striking. In the works of David, especially, where the delineations are most perfect and masterful, the reiteration and classification of the great facts and varieties of sin form one of the most instructive and impressive features of the sacred writings. The Psalms will ever be the standard work on sin— the most ample analysis of its nature, its effects, its shades of difference, and its cure.

And yet, although sin is such a common thing, I daresay that many of us, perhaps, do not know anything about it. Somehow, it is just the common things we are apt not to think about. Take the commonest of all things—air. What do we know about it? Or, what do we know about water—that great mysterious sea, on which some of you spend your lives, which moans all the long winter at your very doors? Sin is a commoner thing than both of these; it is deeper than the sea, and more subtle than the air; it is mysterious, indeed, moaning in all our lives, through all the winter and summer of our past. It will last, in the undying soul of man, when there is no more sea. To say the least, it is most unreasonable that a person would live in sin all his life without knowing in some measure what he is about.

And, regarding the higher bearings of the case, it is clear that without the fullest information about sin, no one can ever have the fullest information about himself, which he ought to have. And, what is of greater importance, without understanding sin, no one can ever understand God. Even the Christian who has only the ordinary notions of sin in general can neither be making very much of himself or of his theology; for, as a general rule, a person's experience of religion and of grace is in pretty exact proportion to his experience of sin.

No doubt, the intimate knowledge that the Old Testament writers had of themselves had everything to do with their intimate knowledge of God. David, for instance, who had the deepest knowledge of God, also had the deepest knowledge of his own heart; and if there is one thing in the writings he has left us that is more conspicuous than another, it is the ceaseless reiteration of the outstanding facts of sin—the cause, the effects, the shades of difference, and the cure of sin.

In the clause that forms our text, David has given us in a nutshell the whole of the main facts of sin. And, for anyone who wishes to become acquainted with the great pivots on which all human life turns, and on which his own life turns; for anyone who wishes to understand the working of God's grace; for anyone who wishes to examine himself on the other great fact of human sin; there is no more admirable summary than these words: *"Who forgiveth all thine iniquities; who healeth all thy diseases; who redeemeth thy life from destruction."*

These facts of sin, which it is necessary for us to know, may be said to be three in number:

1. The guilt of sin
2. The stain of sin
3. The power of sin

And these three facts correspond roughly with the natural division of the text:

1. *"...all thine iniquities"*—the guilt of sin.
2. *"...all thy diseases"*—the stain of sin.
3. *"...destruction"*—the power of sin.

1. *The Power of Sin*

Perhaps the best fact of sin to start with is the last of these, because the word *life* is contained in the text that describes it: *"Who redeemeth thy life from destruction."*

We all have a personal interest in anything that concerns life. We can understand things—even things in theology—if they will only bear upon our life. And we are always ready, for our life's sake, to give a patient hearing to anything that comes home to life, in influencing it, or bettering it, or telling upon it in any way whatever.

We feel prepared to take kindly to almost any doctrine if it will only bear upon our life. And, surely, in the whole range of truth, none has more of a point of contact with the heart of man than the doctrine of the power of sin. In the first place, then, let us notice that sin is a power, and a power that concerns life.

There is an old poem that bears the curious title of "Strife in Heaven," the idea of which is something like this: The poet supposes himself to be walking in the streets of the New Jerusalem, when he comes to a crowd of saints engaged in a very earnest discussion. He draws near and listens. They are discussing the question of which of them is the greatest monument of God's saving grace. After a long debate, in which each states his case separately, and each claims to have been by far the most wonderful trophy of God's love in all the multitude of the redeemed, it is finally agreed to settle the matter by a vote. Vote after vote is taken, and the list of competition is gradually reduced until only two remain. These are allowed to state their cases again, and the company stands ready to join in the final vote. The first to speak is a very old man. He begins by saying that it is a mere waste of time to go any further; it is absolutely impossible that God's grace could have done more for any man in heaven than for him. He tells again how he had led a most wicked and vicious life—a life filled up with every conceivable indulgence, and marred with every crime. He had been a thief, a liar, a blasphemer, a drunkard, and a murderer. On his deathbed, at the eleventh hour, Christ came to him, and he was forgiven.

The other is also an old man. He says, in a few words, that he was brought to Christ when he was a boy. He had led a quiet and uneventful life, and had looked forward to heaven as early as he could remember.

The vote is taken; and, of course, you would say it results in favor of the first. But no, the votes are all given to the second. We might have thought, perhaps, that the one who led the reckless, godless life—he who had lied, thieved, blasphemed, murdered; he who was saved by the skin of his teeth, just a moment before it might have been too late—had the most to thank God for. But the old poet knew the deeper truth.

Truly, it required great grace to pluck that old brand from the burning. It required depths, absolutely fathomless depths, of mercy to forgive that veteran in sin at the close of all those guilty years. But it required more grace to keep that other life from guilt through all those tempted years. It required more grace to save him from the sins of his youth, and to keep his Christian boyhood pure, to steer him unscathed through the tempted years of riper manhood, to crown his days with usefulness, and his old age with patience and hope. Both started in life together; to one, grace came at the end; to the other, at the beginning. The first was saved from the guilt of sin; the second from the power of sin, as well. The first was saved from dying in sin. But he who became a Christian in his boyhood was saved from living in sin. The one required just one great act of love at the close of life; the other had a life full of love—it was a far greater salvation. His soul was forgiven, like the other, but his life had been redeemed from destruction.

The lesson to be gathered from the old poet's parable is that sin is a question of power as much as a question of guilt—that salvation is, perhaps, a question of life far more than a question of death. There is something in every person's life that he needs saving from, something that would spoil his life and run off with it into destruction if let alone. This principle of destruction is the first great fact of sin—its power.

Anyone who watches his life from day to day, and especially if he is trying to steer it toward a certain moral mark that he has determined in his mind, has abundant and humiliating evidence that this power is busily working in his life. He finds that this power is working against him in his life, defeating him at every turn, and persistently opposing all the good he tries to do. He finds that his natural bias is to break away from God and from good. Then he is clearly conscious that there is an acting ingredient in his soul that not only neutralizes the inclination to follow the path that he knows to be straightest and best, but also works continually and consistently against his better self, and urges his life onward toward a broader path that leads to destruction. (See Matthew 7:13.)

It was this road that David had in mind when he thanked God that his life had been redeemed, or kept back from destruction. We may be sure that, in those times, it was a beaten path, as it is today. And David knew perfectly well when he penned these words that God's hand had veritably saved him from ending his life along that road. In summing up his life in his old age, and calling upon his soul to bless the Lord for all His benefits, it was not enough to thank Him simply for the forgiveness of his sins. God had done far more for him than forgive him for his sin. He had redeemed his life from destruction. He had saved him from the all-but-omnipotent power of sin.

Let those who remember the times when it did break loose in David's life recall what that power was and what that power might have become; how it might have broken up and wrecked his life a thousand times. How little might we have guessed that there was anything in the psalmist's life to make him thank God at its close for keeping it back from destruction. Brought up in the secluded plains of Bethlehem, and reared in the pure atmosphere of country innocence, where could the shepherd lad get any taint of sin that could develop in after years to a great, destroying power? And yet he got it—somehow, he got it. And even in his innocent boyhood, the fatal power lurked there, able enough, willing enough, vicious enough, to burst through the early boundaries of his life and wreck it before it reached its prime. All the time he was walking with God; all the time he was planning God's temple; all the time he was writing his holy psalms, which make all men wonder at the psalmist's grace; while he was playing their grave, sweet melody upon his harp in the ear of God; the power of sin was seething and raging in his breast, ready to quench the very inspiration God was giving him, and to ruin his religion and his soul forevermore. We may be sure that, throughout David's life, God kept His hand on the springs of David's sin; and there was nothing as much to thank God for, in taking the retrospect of his eventful course, than that his life had been redeemed from this first great fact of sin.

To round off the point with an analogy from the old poet, David's salvation was a much more wonderful thing than, for example, the dying thief's salvation. David cost grace far more than the dying thief did. The dying thief needed only dying grace. David needed living grace. The thief needed only forgiving grace; David needed forgiving grace and restraining grace. He needed grace to "keep in" his life, to keep it from running away. But the thief needed no restraining grace. The time for that was past. His life had run away. His wild oats had been sown, and the harvest was heavy and bitter. Destruction had already come upon him in a hundred forms. He had had no antidote to the power of sin, which runs so fiercely in every vein of every person, and he had destroyed himself. His character was ruined, his soul was honeycombed through and through with sin. He could not have joined in the thanksgiving of David's psalm that his life had been saved from destruction. His death had been, and the wreck of his soul had been, but his life had been lost to God, to the world, and to himself. His life had never been redeemed, as David's had been. So, David was the greater debtor to God's grace, and few men have had greater reason than he to praise God in old age for redeeming their life from destruction.

Yes, there is more to salvation than forgiveness. Why? Because there is more to sin than guilt. "If I were to be forgiven today," people say who do not know this fact, "I would be as bad as ever tomorrow." That idea is based on the fallacy, it is based on the heresy, that there is no more for a person in religion than forgiveness of sins. If there were not, it would be little use to us. It would have been little use to a man like David. And David's life would have been incomplete, and David's psalm would have been impossible, if he had not been able to add to the record of God's pardon the record of God's power in redeeming his life from destruction.

"If I were to be forgiven today, I would be as bad as ever tomorrow." No, that's founded on the notion that there's nothing more in religion than forgiveness. If there were not, I say this with all solemnity, it would be very little use to me. We have all thanked God for the dying thief—have we ever thanked God for redeeming our life from destruction? Destruction is the natural destination of every human soul. It is as natural for our soul to go downward as for a stone to fall to the ground. Do we ever thank God for redeeming our soul from that? And when we thank God that we are saved, do we mean that we are saved from hell, or do we sometimes think about how He has rescued our life from the destroying power of sin?

2. The Stain of Sin

The power of sin could never run through a person's life without leaving its mark behind. Nothing in the world ever works without friction. A mountain torrent digs a glen in the mountainside; the sea cuts a beach along the shore; a hurricane leaves a thousand fallen witnesses behind to mark its track. And, as the great river of sin rolls through a human life, it leaves a pile of ruins here and there as melancholy monuments to show where it has been. Nature, with all its strength, is a wonderfully delicate machine, and everything has its reaction somewhere and at some time. Nothing is allowed to pass. And nothing has so appalling a reaction upon everyone and everything as sin.

History is an undying monument of human sin. The most prominent thing on its pages are the stains—the stains of sin that time has not rubbed out. For the most part, the history of the world has been written in the world's blood; and all the reigns of all its emperors and kings will one day be lost in one absorbing record of one great reign—the one long reign of sin. As it has been with history, so it is in the world today. The surface of society is white with leprosy. If we were to take away the power of sin tomorrow, the stain of sin would remain. Whatever the world may suffer from lack of conviction of the guilt of sin, it will never be without conviction of its stain. We see it in one another's lives. We see it in one another's faces.

It is the stain of the world's sin that troubles the world's conscience. It is the stain of the world's sin that troubles philanthropy; that troubles the parliament of the country; that troubles the press of the country. It is the stain of the world's sin that is especially making a place in literature for this word *sin*. It is this side of sin that is absorbing the finest writing of the day; that is filling our modern poetry; that is making a thousand modern books preach the doctrine of retribution, which simply means the doctrine of the stain of sin.

Society cares nothing for you; it is not wise enough to see the power of sin, or religious enough to see the guilt of sin; but it cannot fail to see the stain of sin. It does not care for the power or the guilt of sin; it cares for the stain of sin, because it must. That troubles society. The stain of sin lies down at its doors, and is an eyesore to it. It is a loathsome thing for it to be lying there, and society must do something. So, this is what it does with it: In one corner, it builds a prison—this will rid the world of its annoyance. In another corner, it plants an asylum—the sore may fester there unseen. In another, it raises a hospital; in a fourth, it lays out a graveyard. Prisons, asylums, hospitals—these are just so much roofing that society has put on to hide the stain of sin. In some ways, it is a good thing that sin always has its stain. Just as pain is a good thing to tell that something is wrong, so the stain of sin may be a good thing to tell that the power of sin has broken loose. Society might never trouble itself if it were not for the stain.

And, in dealing with the stain of sin, it sometimes may do a little bit to maim its power. But it is a poor, poor remedy. If it could only see the power and try to deal with that—try to get God's grace to act on that—the world might be redeemed from destruction after all. But it sees the stain only when it is too late—the stain that has dropped from the wound after the throat of virtue has been cut. Surely, when the deed is done, it is the least it could do to remove the traces of the crime.

But one need not go to society or to history to see the stains of sin. We see it in one another's lives, and in our own lives. Our conscience, for instance, is not as quick as it might have been—the stains of sin are there, between us and the light. We have ignored conscience many a time when it spoke, and its voice has grown husky and indistinct. Our intellectual life is not as true as it might have been—our intellectual sins have stained it and spoiled our memory, taken the edge off our sympathy, filled us with suspicion and one-sided truths, and destroyed the delicate power of faith.

There are few sights more touching than to see someone in mature life trying to recover from the stains of a neglected past. The past itself is gone; but it remains upon his life in accumulated dark stains, and he tries in vain to remove them. There was once a time when his robe was white and clean. "Keep your garment unspotted from the world," the kind home-voices said to him as he went out into life. He remembers well the first spot on that robe. Even the laden years that lie between have no day so dark; no spot now lies so lurid red upon his soul as that first sin. Then the companion stain came, for sins are mostly twins. Then another, and another, and many more, until count was lost, and the whole robe was patterned with sin stains. The power of God has come to make a new man of him, but the stains are sunk so deeply in his soul that they are living parts of him still. It is hard for him to give up the world. It is hard for him to be pure. It is hard for him to forget the pictures that have been hanging in the galleries of his imagination all his life—to forget them when he comes to think of God; to forget them when he kneels down to pray; to forget them even when he comes to sit in church. The past of his life has been all against him; and even if his future is religious, it can never be altogether unaffected by the stain of what has been. It is the stain of sin that makes repentance so hard in adult life, that yields the most impressive argument to the young to remember their Creator in their youth. (See Ecclesiastes 12:1.) "For [even] the angels," says Ruskin, "who rejoice over repentance cannot but feel an uncomprehended pain as they try and try again in vain, whether they may not warm hard hearts with the brooding of their kind wings."[12]

But if the stain of sin is invisible in moral and intellectual life, no one can possibly be blind to it in bodily life. Again, we see it in one another's lives; but, more than that, we see it in one another's faces. Vice writes in plain letters, and all the world is its copybook. We can read it everywhere and on everything around, from pole to pole. To take the conspicuous example, the drunkard so stains his bodily life with his sin that the seeds of disease are sown that—long after he has reformed—will germinate in his death. If all the drunkards in the world were to be changed tomorrow, the stains of sin in their bodies would doubtless bring a large majority—in a few years, less or more—to what was, after all, really a drunkard's grave.

There is a physical demonstration of sin, as well as a religious one; and no sin can come in among the delicate faculties of the mind, or among the coarser fibers of the body, without leaving a stain, either as a positive injury to the life, or, what is equally fatal, as a predisposition to commit the same sin again. This predisposition is always one of the most real and appalling accompaniments of the stain of sin. There is scarcely such a thing as an isolated sin in a person's life. Most sins can be accounted for by what has gone before. Every sin has its own pedigree, so to speak, and is the result of the accumulated force, which means the accumulated stain, of many a preparatory sin.

Thus, when Peter began to swear in the high priest's palace, it was probably not the first time Peter had sworn. A person does not suddenly acquire the habit of uttering oaths; and when it is said of Peter, "*Then began he to curse and to swear*" (Matthew 26:74), it does not at all mean by "*then*" and "*began*" that he had not begun it long ago. The legitimate inference is that in the rough days of his fisherman's life, perhaps when the nets got entangled, or the right wind would not blow, Peter had come out with an oath many a time to keep his passion cool. And now, after years of devoted fellowship with Christ, the stain is still so black upon his soul that he curses in the very presence of his Lord. An outbreak that meets the public eye is generally the climax of a series of sins that, until then, discretion has been able to keep out of sight. The doctrine of the stain of sin has no exceptions; and few men, we may be sure, can do a suddenly notorious wrong without knowing something in private of the series to which it belongs.

But the most solemn fact about the stain of sin is that so little can be done for it. It is almost indelible. There is a very solemn fact about this stain of sin—it can never be altogether blotted out. The guilt of sin may be forgiven, the power of sin may be broken, but the stains of sin abide. When it is said that He heals our diseases, it indeed means that we may be healed; but the ravages that sin has left must still remain. Smallpox may be healed, but it leaves its mark behind. A cut limb may be cured, but the scar remains forever. An earthquake may be over in three minutes, but, centuries later, the ground is still split into gulfs and chasms that ages will never close. So, the scars of sin—on body and mind and soul—live with us in silent retribution of our past, and go with us to our graves.

And the stain does not stop with our lives. Every action of every person has an ancestry and a posterity in other lives. The stains of life have the power to spread. The stains of other lives have crossed over into our lives, and stains of our lives into theirs. "I am a part," says the Laureate, "of all that I have met."[13] A hundred years hence, we all must live again—in thoughts, in tendencies, in influences, and perhaps in sins and stains in other lives. The sins of the father will be visited on the children. (See, for example, Exodus 34:7.) The blight on the vicious parent will be visited on the insane offspring. The stain on the intemperate mother will reappear in the wrecked lives of her drunken family. It is the same with finer forms of sin—of companion on companion, of brother on sister, of teacher on pupil. For God Himself has made the law that the curse must follow the breach; and even He who heals our diseases may never interfere with the inevitable stain of a sinful life.

"Take my influence," cried a sinful man who was dying; "take my influence and bury it with me." He was going to be with Christ, but his influence had been against Him; he was leaving it behind. As a conspirator called by some act of grace to his sovereign's table remembers with unspeakable remorse the assassin whom he left in ambush at his king's palace gate, so he recalls the traitorous years and the influences that will plot against his Lord when he is in eternity. Oh, it is worth being washed from sin, if only to escape the possibility of a treachery like that. It is worth living a holy and self-denying life, if only to "join the choir invisible of those immortal dead who live again in minds made better by their presence."[14]

3. The Guilt of Sin

Last, we come to the third great fact of sin—its guilt. And we find ourselves face-to-face with the greatest question of all: "What has God to say about all this mass of sin?"

Probably everyone will acknowledge that his life bears witness to the first two facts of sin. Starting with this admission, a moment's thought lands us in a greater admission. We all acknowledge sin; therefore, we must all acknowledge ourselves to be guilty. Whether we feel guilty or not, guilt is inseparable from sin. Physical evil may make a person sorry, but moral evil makes him guilty. Again, it may not make him *feel* guilty, but we are speaking of facts— he *is* guilty. In the same way, we are guilty for our past lives. We may be sorry for the past. But it is not enough that we are sorry; we are guilty for the past. We are more than sinners—we are criminals.

This is where the literary concept of sin is altogether defective and must be supplemented. It knows nothing, and can teach nothing, of the guilt of a sinner's soul. We learn this when we come to God. God is our Father, but God is also our Judge. And when we know that fact, our sin takes on a darker coloring. It grows larger than our life, and suddenly seems to be infinite. The whole world, the whole universe, is concerned in it. Before, sin only made us recoil from ourselves; now it makes God recoil from us. We are out of harmony with God. Our iniquities have separated us from God; and, in some mysterious way, we have come to be answerable to Him. We feel that the

Lord has turned and looked upon us, as He looked at Peter, and we can only go out and weep bitterly. (See Luke 22:61–62.)

If these experiences are foreign to our souls, we must feel our sense of guilt when we come to look at Christ. Christ could not move through the world without the mere spectacle of His life stirring, to its very depth, the heart of everyone whose path He crossed. And Christ cannot move through the chambers of our thoughts without the dazzling contrast to ourselves startling into motion the sense of burning shame and sin. But, above all, Christ could not die upon the cross without witnessing to all eternity of the appalling greatness of human guilt. And, it is the true climax of conviction that the prophet speaks of: *"They shall look upon me whom they have pierced, and they shall mourn…"* (Zechariah 12:10).

The conviction of sin, in the deepest sense, is not a thing to talk about, but to feel; and when it is felt, it cannot be talked about; it is too deep for words. It comes as an unutterable woe upon the life, and rests there, in dark sorrow and heaviness, until Christ speaks peace.

What the Three Facts of Sin Teach Us

Such, in outline, are the three facts of sin. They are useful in two ways: They teach us ourselves, and they teach us God. You will find salvation along these three lines. Run your eye along the first—the power of sin—and you will understand Jesus. *"Thou shalt call His name Jesus: for he shall save his people from their sins"* (Matthew 1:21). Look at the second—the stain of sin—and you will understand the righteousness of Christ; you will see the need of the one pure Life. You will be glad that there has been One who has kept His garment unspotted from the world. (See James 1:27.) Look at the third, and you will see the Lamb of God taking away the sin of the world. (See John 1:29.) You will understand the atonement, and you will pray,

> Let the water and the blood,
> From Thy riven side which flowed,
> Be of sin the double cure;
> Cleanse me from its guilt and power.[15]

8

THE THREE FACTS
OF SALVATION

Supplement to "The Three Facts of Sin"

"Who forgiveth all thine iniquities; who healeth all thy diseases;
who redeemeth thy life from destruction."
—Psalm 103:3–4

Last Sabbath, we were engaged in a discussion of the three facts of sin.
Today, we come to the three facts of salvation.

The three facts of sin were:

1. The guilt of sin—*"Who forgiveth all thine iniquities."*

2. The stain of sin—*"Who healeth all thy diseases."*

3. The power of sin—*"Who redeemeth thy life from destruction."*

Now we come to the three facts of salvation, the emphasis being on the first words of each clause, instead of the last words.

1. *"Who forgiveth...."*
2. *"Who healeth...."*
3. *"Who redeemeth...."*

Everyone who comes into the world experiences more or less of the three facts of sin; and everyone is allowed to live on in the world mainly that he may also experience the three great facts of salvation. God keeps most of us alive from day to day with this one object. Sin has gotten ahold of us, and He is giving us time—time for grace to get the upper hand of it, time to work out the three facts of salvation in our lives *"with fear and trembling"* (Philippians 2:12) against the three facts of sin. Our being, therefore, lies between these two great sets of facts, the dark set and the bright set; and life is just the battlefield on which they fight it out. If the bright side wins, it is a bright life—saved. If the dark side, it is a dark life—lost.

1. *Christ Redeems Our Life from Destruction*

We have seen how the three dark facts have already begun to work upon our life, and that they are not only working at our life but also sapping it and preying upon it every hour of the day. And now we stand face-to-face with the question that is wrung out from our life by the very sin that is destroying it: "What must I do to be saved?"

The Fact of the Power of Sin

The first fact about which we would ask this question—to begin once more with the fact that most conspicuously concerns life—is the fact of the power of sin. "What must I do to be saved from the power of sin?" What most of us feel we really want religion to do for us, though it is not the deepest experience, is to save us from something that we feel in our life—a very terrible something that is slowly dragging us downward to destruction. This something has gained an unaccountable hold upon us; it seems to make us go wrong, whether we want to or not; and, instead of exhausting itself with all the attempts it has made upon our life in the past, it seems to get stronger and stronger every day. Even the Christian knows that this strange, wild force is right at his very door, and if he does not pray tomorrow morning, for instance, before the day is out, it will have worked some mischief in his life. If he does not pray, in the most natural way in the world, without any effort of his own, without his even thinking about it, it will necessarily come to the front and make his life go wrong. Now, wherever this comes from, or whatever it is, it is a great *fact*. And the first practical question in religion that rises to many a mind is this: "What must I do to be saved from this inevitable, universal, and terrible fact of sin?"

We have all probably made certain experiments upon this fact already, and we could all give some explanation, at least, of what we are doing to be saved.

If we were asked, for instance, what our favorite fact of salvation is for resisting the power of sin, some of us might say it is the fact that we are doing our best. Well, it is a great thing for anyone to be doing his best. But two questions will test the value of this method of resisting the power of sin. In the first place, "How is your best doing?" In the second place, "Do you think you could not do better?" As to how your best is doing, you would probably admit that, on the whole, it was not doing very well. In fact, if you were to be candid, your best has not been much to boast of, after all. And regarding your not doing better, you might also admit that, in some ways, perhaps, you could. This particular method of salvation—of our "doing our best"—is therefore evidently a poor one, as far as results are concerned, and may be judiciously laid aside.

Then, another experiment people try in order to break the power of sin is to get thoroughly absorbed in something else—business, literature, or some favorite pursuit. Sin comes to us in our spare hours, so we try to have no sin by having no spare hours. But our very preoccupation may then be one continuous sin. And, besides, if an individual has no spare hours, he will have spare minutes; and sin generally comes on in a minute. Most sins, indeed, are done in minutes. It may be that they take hours to execute; but, in a moment, the plot is hatched, the will consents, and the deed is done. Preoccupation, then, is clearly no savior.

Then there are other people who withdraw from the world altogether and live the solitary life of the recluse in order to break with sin. But they forget that sin is not in the sinful world outside but in the sinful heart within, and that it enters the hermit's solitary cell as persistently as the wicked world around. So, solitude comes to be no savior.

And there are others still who take refuge in religiousness. In going to church, for instance, and in religious society and books. But there is not necessarily any more power to resist sin within the four walls of a church or in the pages of a religious book than between the walls of a theater or between the covers of a novel. There may be less temptation there, but not necessarily more power. For there is no strength in mere religious ceremonies to cancel the power of sin; and many people prove this, after years and years of church, by wakening to find the power of sin in their breast unchanged and breaking out, perhaps, in every form of vice. Neither is religiousness, therefore, any escape from the dominion of sin.

Last, some of us have resorted to doctrines. We have gotten the leading points of certain doctrines worn into our minds, and because these have a religious name, we are apt to think they also have a religious power. In reality, while dealing with the theory of grace and of sin, we may leave the power to resist sin untouched. And many a pen has been busy with a book on the doctrine of sin, while the life that employed it was going to destruction for lack of salvation from its power.

There is one doctrine, especially, with which the word *salvation* is most often connected and to which many look for their deliverance from the power of indwelling sin. It may seem a startling statement to make, but it will emphasize a distinction that cannot be too clearly drawn, that even the atonement itself is not the answer to the question "What must I do to be saved from the power of sin?" The answer depends entirely on the atonement, but it is not the atonement. The atonement is not the fact of salvation that saves the sinner from the power of sin. If you believed in the atonement today, if you were absolutely assured that your past sins were all forgiven, that would be no criterion that you would not again be as bad as ever tomorrow. The atonement, therefore, is not the fact that deals with the power of sin. The atonement deals with a point. We are coming to that. Right now, we are talking about a life. We are looking out for something that will deal with something in our life—something that will redeem our life from destruction. And a person may believe the atonement but not have his life redeemed from destruction.

We Are Saved by Christ's Life Within Us

Suppose you have gone out into the country on a summer morning, and, as you passed some little rustic mill, you saw the miller come out to set his simple machinery going for the day. He turned on the sluice, but the water-wheel would not move. Then, with his strong arm, he turned it once or twice, then left it to itself to turn busily all day. It is a sorry illustration in detail, but its principle means this: The atonement is the first great turn, as it were, that God gives in the morning of conversion to the wheel of the Christian's life. Without it, nothing more would be possible; but, alone, it would not be enough. The water of life must flow in a living stream all through the working day and keep pouring its power into it ceaselessly until the life and the work are done.

Now, in salvation, practically everything depends upon the clearness with which this great truth is recognized. Sin is a power in our life; let us fairly understand that it can be met only by another power. The fact of sin works all through our life. The death of Christ, which is the atonement, reconciles us to God, makes our religion possible, and puts us in the way of the power that is to come against our sin and to deliver our life from destruction. But the power itself is the water of life, which flows from the life of Christ. By His life, He redeems my life from destruction. This is the power, Paul says, that redeemed his life from destruction. Christ's life—not His death—living in his life, absorbing it, impregnating it, transforming it. As he confessed, "Christ in me." (See Galatians 2:20.) And this, therefore, is the meaning of a profound sentence in which Paul states the true answer to the question "What must I do to be saved?" He records this first great fact of salvation and pointedly distinguishes it from the other. *"If, when we were enemies, we were reconciled to God by the death of his Son, much more, being reconciled, we shall be saved by his life"* (Romans 5:10).

"We shall be saved by his life," says Paul. Paul meant no disrespect to the atonement when he said, *"We shall be saved by his life."* He was bringing out in relief one of the great facts of salvation. If God gives atoning power with one hand, and power to save the life from destruction with the other, there is no jealousy between them. Both are from God. If you call the one justification and the other sanctification, God is the author of them both. If Paul seems to take something from the one doctrine and add it to the other, he takes

nothing from God. Atonement is from God. Power to resist sin is from God. When we say we will be saved by the death of Christ, it is true. When Paul says, "We shall be saved by his life," it is true. Christ is all and in all, "the beginning and the end" (Revelation 21:6; 22:13). Only, when we are speaking of one fact of sin, let us speak of the corresponding fact of grace. When the thing we want is power to redeem our life from destruction, let us apply the gift that God has given us for our life, and for guilt the gift for guilt.

When an Israelite was bitten by a fiery serpent in the wilderness, he never thought of applying manna to the wound. The manna was for his life. But he did think of applying the bronze serpent. (See Numbers 21:4–9.) The manna never would have cured his sin; nor would the bronze serpent have kept him from starving. Suppose he had said, "Now I am healed by this serpent. I feel cured, and I do not need to eat this manna anymore. The serpent has done it all, and I am well." The result would have been, of course, that he would have died. To be sure, the person was cured, but he has to live; and if he eats no manna, his life must languish, go to destruction, die. Without taking any trouble about it, simply by the inevitable processes of nature, he would have died. The manna was God's provision to redeem his life from destruction, after the serpent had redeemed it from death. And if he did nothing to stop the natural progress of destruction, in the natural course of things, he would die. Again, there is no jealousy between these two things— the manna is from God, and the serpent is from God. But they are different gifts for different things. The serpent gave life, but it could not keep life; the manna kept life, but it could not give life. Therefore, the Israelites were saved by looking at the serpent, but they did not try to eat the serpent.

Let us apply this example to the case at hand. The atonement of Christ is the bronze serpent. Christ's life is the manna—the Bread of Life. Our sins are not forgiven by bread, nor are our lives supported by death. Our life is not redeemed from destruction by the atonement, nor kept from day to day from the power of sin by the atonement. Our life is not redeemed from destruction by the death of Christ, nor kept from day to day by the death of Christ. But we are "saved," as Paul says, "by his life" (Romans 5:10). We cannot live upon death. *Mors janua vitae*—"death is the gate of life." And, after we have entered the gateway by the death of Christ, we will be saved by His life.

To sum up: It is one thing, therefore, to be saved by the death of Christ, and another to be saved by His life. And while both expressions are correct, to talk of being saved by the death of Christ is not as scriptural as to talk of being saved by the life of Christ. With his invariable conciseness on important points, Paul has brought out the facts of salvation with profound insight in the pregnant antithesis already quoted: "When we were enemies, we were reconciled by the death of Christ. Now we will be saved by His life." (See Romans 5:10.)

The first fact of salvation, therefore, that is to be brought to bear upon the first great fact of sin is not our own efforts, our own religiousness, our own doctrine, the atonement, or the death of Christ, but the power of the life of Christ. He redeems my life from destruction. How? By His life. This is the fact of salvation. It takes life to redeem life—power to resist power. Sin is a ceaseless, undying power in our life. Thus, a ceaseless, undying power must come against it. And there is only one such power in the universe—only one—that has a chance against sin: the power of the living Christ. God knew the power of sin in a human soul when He made such a great provision. He knew how powerful it was; He calculated it. Then, He sent the living Christ against it. It was the careful and awful estimate of the power of sin. God saw that nothing else would do. It would not do to start our religion and then leave us to ourselves. With hearts like ours, yearning to sin, it would not do to leave us with religiousness or moral philosophy or doctrine. Christ Himself must come and live with us. He must come and make His abode with us. He cannot trust us from His sight; so that, when we live, it will not be we who live but Christ living in us. And the life that we are now living in the flesh must be lived by the power of the Son of God. (See Galatians 2:20.)

What, then, must I do to be saved? Receive the Lord Jesus Christ, and you will be saved. Slave of a thousand sins, receive the Lord Jesus Christ into your life; then, your life, your far-spent life, will yet be redeemed from destruction. Receive the Lord Jesus Christ, and you who have lived in the far famine land will return and live once more by your Father's side. You do not seek a welcome to your Father's house—of your welcome you have never been afraid. But you seek a livelihood; you seek power. You seek power to be pure, to be true, to be free from the power of sin. "What must I do to be saved from that? What power will free me from that?" The answer is: "The power of the living Christ!" *"As many as received him, to them gave he power to become the sons of God"* (John 1:12). *"Power to become the sons of God"*—the great fact of salvation. Receive the Lord Jesus Christ, and you will be saved.

Christ, therefore, is *"the power of God unto salvation"* (Romans 1:16)—the counter-fact to the power of sin unto destruction. Christ is the way—He is also the truth and the life. (See John 14:6.) This power, this life, is within our reach each moment of our life; it is as near, as free, and as abundant as the air we breathe. A breath of prayer in the morning, and the morning life is sure. A breath of prayer in the evening, and the evening blessing comes. Thus, our life is redeemed from destruction. Breath by breath, our life comes into us. Inch by inch, it is redeemed from destruction. So much prayer today—so many inches redeemed today. So much water of life today—so many turns of the great wheel of life today. Therefore, if we want to be saved: *"Whosoever will, let him take the water of life freely"* (Revelation 22:17). If you want to be saved, breathe the breath of life. And, if you cannot breathe, let the groans that cannot be uttered go up to God (see Romans 8:26), and the power will come. To all of us alike, if we but ask, we will receive. (See John 16:24.) For God makes surpassing allowances, and He will do unto the least of us *"exceeding abundantly above all that we ask or think"* (Ephesians 3:20).

2. Christ Heals All Our Diseases

The second fact of sin is the stain of sin; and the second fact of salvation is *"he healeth all thy diseases."* The stain of sin is a very much more complicated thing than even the power of sin, for this reason: most of it lies outside our own life. If it lay only in dark blotches upon our own life, we might set to work to rub it out. But it has crossed over into other lives all through the years that have gone by, and has left its awful mark—*our* mark—on every soul we have touched since the most distant past.

Previously, we discussed the situation of a young man who lay upon his deathbed. He was a Christian, but for many days a black cloud had gathered upon his brow. Just before his last breath, he beckoned to the friends around his bed. "Take my influence," he said, "and bury it with me." He stood on the very threshold of glory. But the stain of sin was burning hot upon his past. Bury his influence with him! No, his influence will remain. His life has gone to be with God, who gave it; but his influence—he has left no influence for Christ. His future will be forever with the Lord. The unburied past remains behind, perhaps, forever to be against him. The black cloud that hangs over many a dying brow means the stain of an influence lost for Christ. With many an individual who dies a Christian, it means that although his guilt has been removed and his life has been redeemed from destruction, the infection of his past still lurks in the world, and his diseases fester in open sores among all the companions of his life.

What must I do to be saved from the stain of sin? Gather up your influence, and see how much has been for Christ. Then, undo all that has been against Him. It will never be healed until then. This is the darkest stain upon your life. The stain of sin concerns your own soul, but that is a smaller matter. That can be undone—in part. There are enough open sores in our past life to make even heaven tremble. But God is healing them. He is blotting them from His own memory, and from ours. If the stains that were there had lingered, life would have been a long sigh of agony. But salvation has come to our soul. God is helping you to use the means for repairing a broken life. He restores your soul; He heals all your diseases.

But your brother's soul, and your brother's diseases? The worst of your stains have spread far and wide outside yourself; and God will heal them, perhaps, only by giving you grace to deal with them. You must retrace your steps over that unburied past and undo what you have done. You must go to the other lives that are stained with your bloodred stains and rub the stains out. Perhaps you did not lead them into their sin, but you did not lead them out of it. You did not show them you were a Christian. You left a worse memory with them than your real one. You pretended you were just like them—that your sources of happiness were just the same. You did not tell them you had a power that kept your life from sin. You did not take them to the prayer closet you had at home and let them see you on your knees, nor tell them of your Bible that was open twice a day. And all these negatives were stains and sins. It is a great injustice to do to anyone we know—the worst turn we could do a friend, to keep the best secret back, and let him go as calmly to hell as we are going to heaven.

If we cannot bury our influence, thank God if, here and there, we can undo it still. The other servant in the kitchen, the clerk on the next stool, the lady who once lived in the next house—we must go to them, by the grace of God, and take the stain away. And let the thought that much that we have done can never be undone—that many whose lives have suffered from our sins have gone away into eternity with the stains still not removed; that when we all stand around the throne together, even from the right hand of the judgment seat of Christ, we may behold on the left among the lost the stains of our own sin, still livid on some soul—let this quicken our steps as we go to obliterate the influence of our past, and turn our fear into a safeguard as we try to keep our future life for Christ.

The second fact of salvation, therefore, is to be effected in part by God and in part by ourselves—by God as regards ourselves; by God and ourselves as regards others. He is to heal our diseases, and we are to spread the balm He gives us wherever we have spread our sin.

3. Christ Forgives All Our Iniquities

The third great fact of sin is guilt, and the third fact of salvation is forgiveness: *"He forgiveth all thine iniquities."* The first question we asked came out of our life; the second mostly from our memory; but the third rises up out of our conscience.

As we looked at our future, our first cry was, "Where can I get power?" Now we are looking at our past, and the question is, "Where can I get pardon?" The questions that conscience sends up to us are always the deepest questions. And the person who has never sent up the question "Where can I get pardon?" has never been into his conscience to find out the deepest need he has. It is not enough for him to look life-ward; he must also look God-ward. And it is not enough for him to discover the stain of his past and cry out, "I have sinned." He must also see the guilt of his life and cry, "I have sinned *against* God." Although it is the most stupendous fact of all, the fact of salvation that God has provided to meet the fact of guilt comes home to a person only when he feels that he is a criminal, and stands like a guilty sinner for pardon at God's bar.

It is not enough for him then to invoke God's strength against the power of sin. As we have seen, just as the fact that meets the guilt of sin can never meet the power of sin, so the fact that meets the power of sin can never meet the fact of guilt. Manna was what was required for a person's life; but it is no use against his guilt. It is nothing that he makes a good resolution not to do wrong anymore, that he asked Christ to come and live with him and break the power of sin, and redeem his life from destruction. God has something to say to him before that. Something must happen to him before that. He must come and give an account of himself.

A good resolution is all very laudable for the days to come, but what about the past? God wants to know about the past. It may be convenient for us to forget the past, but God cannot forget it. We have done wrong, and wrongdoing must be punished. Wrongdoing must be punished—*must*; this is involved in one of the facts of sin. Therefore, the punishment of wrongdoing must be involved in one of the facts of salvation. It is not in the first two facts we have discussed. It must be somewhere in this one.

Now, the punishment of sin is death. *"In the day that thou eatest thereof thou shalt surely die"* (Genesis 2:17). Therefore, death is the punishment that must be in one of the facts of salvation. Again, it was not in the other two; it must be somewhere in this one. It will not meet the case if the sinner professes his penitence and promises humbly never to do the like again. It will not meet the case if he comes on his knees to apologize to God and ask Him simply to forget that he has sinned, or to beg Him to have pity on the misfortunes of his past. God did not say, "In the day thou eatest thereof I will pity thy misfortunes," "In the day thou eatest thereof thou shalt surely apologize," or "…thou shalt surely repent" but *"In the day that thou eatest thereof thou shalt surely die."* So death, and nothing less than death, must be in the fact of salvation from the guilt of sin, if such salvation is to be.

With this fact—this most solemn necessity—understood and felt, the rest is plain. We all know that Someone died. We all know who *deserved* to die. We all know who *did* die. We know we were not wounded for our transgressions; we were not bruised for our iniquities. But we know who was. (See Isaiah 53:5.) The Lord has not dealt with us according to our iniquities, but we know with whom He has. (See Psalm 103:10.) We know who "[bore] *our sins in his own body on the tree"* (1 Peter 2:24)—One who had no sin of His own. We know who was lifted up like the serpent in the wilderness (see John 3:14–15)—He who died, the just for the unjust (see 1 Peter 3:18). If we know these things, we know the great fact of salvation.

It remains only to answer one more question: "How is a poor sinner to make this great fact his?" And the answer is: by trusting Christ. He has nothing else with which to make it his. The atonement is a fact. Forgiveness is a fact. Let him believe it. He does not understand it. He is not asked to understand it. The proper way to accept a fact is to believe it; and *"whosoever believeth in him should not perish, but have everlasting life"* (John 3:16). It is well to understand it, and you may try to understand it, if you can; but, until then, you must believe it. For it is a fact, and your understanding it will not make it less or more a fact. The death of Christ will always be a fact. Forgiveness of sins will always be a fact. Accept the facts of sin; accept the facts of grace. The atonement, you say, confuses you. You do not understand its bearings; the more you think and hear and read, the more mysterious it becomes. And well it may, well it may!

Not long ago, a student went to a professor of theology and asked him how long it had taken him to understand the atonement. He answered, "All my life." Thinking perhaps that there might be some mistake, the young man went to another professor, who taught the very doctrine in his class. "How long did it take you, sir," he asked, "to understand the atonement?" The professor thought a moment, then looked him in the face. "*Eternity*," he said. "*Eternity*; and I won't understand it then."

We have been dealing today with facts; we need not be distressed if we do not understand them. God's love—how could we understand it? God's forgiveness—how could we understand it? "He forgives all my iniquities." That is a fact. What proof could commend itself if God's fact will not do? Verify the fact as you may; find out as much about it as you may. Only, accept it—accept it first. You are keeping your life waiting while you are finding out about it. You are keeping your salvation waiting. And it is better to spend a year in ignorance than to live a day unpardoned. You are staining other lives while you are waiting; your influence is against Christ while you are waiting. And it is better to spend your life in ignorance than to let your influence be against Christ.

Most things in religion are matters of simple faith. But when we come to the atonement, somehow, we all become rationalists. We want to see through it and understand it—as if it were finite like ourselves, as if it could ever be compassed by our narrow minds, as if God did not know that we could never fathom it when He said, "Believe it," instead of "Understand it." We are not rationalists when we come to the love of God, or to faith, or to prayer. We do not ask for a theory of love before we begin to love, or a theory of prayer before we begin to pray. We just begin. Well, just begin to believe in forgiveness.

Once, when some people brought a sick man to Jesus, He just said, *"Man, thy sins are forgiven thee"* (Luke 5:20), and the man just believed it. The sick man did not ask, "But why should You forgive me?" or "How do You mean to forgive me?" He did not say, "I don't see any connection between Your forgiveness and my sin." No; he took the fact. *"Immediately he rose up…, and departed to his own house, glorifying God"* (Luke 5:25). The fact is, if we would come to Christ just now, we would never ask any questions. Our minds would be full of Him. We would be in the region of eternal facts, and we would just believe them. At least, we should believe *Him*; He is the Savior, the sum of all the facts of salvation—the one Savior from all the facts of sin. If you will not receive salvation as a fact, then receive the Lord Jesus Christ as a gift—we ask no questions about a gift. Receive the Lord Jesus Christ as a gift, and you will be saved from the power and the stain and the guilt of sin. For to Him are the power and the glory. Amen.

"WHAT IS YOUR LIFE?"

"For what is your life?"
—James 4:14

Tomorrow, the first day of a new year, is a day of wishes. Today, the last day of an old year, is a day of questions. Tomorrow is a time of anticipation; today is a time of reflection. Tomorrow our thoughts will go out to the coming opportunities and the larger vistas that the future is opening up to even the most commonplace of us. Today, our minds wander among buried memories, and our hearts are full of self-questioning thoughts of what our past has been.

But if tomorrow is to be a day of hope, today must be a day of thought. If tomorrow is to be a time of resolution, today must be a day of investigation. And if we were to search through the Bible for a basis for this investigation, nowhere would we find a better question than *What is your life?*

We must notice, however, that *"life"* is used here in a particular sense—a narrow sense, some would say. The question does not mean the following: "What quality is your life?" "What are you making of life?" "How are you getting on with it?" "How much higher is the tone of it this year than last?" It has a more limited reference than this. It does not refer so much to quality of life as to quantity of life. It means: "How much life do you have?" "What value do you set upon your life?" "How long do you think your life will last?" "How does it compare with eternity?"

And there are reasons that make this form of the question particularly appropriate, not only to this last day of the year, but, apart from that altogether, to the state of much religious thought upon the subject at the present moment. The reasons are mainly these two:

1. There is a large school of thought right now that utterly ignores this question.

2. There is a large school of thought that utterly spoils it.

There may be said to be two ways of looking at life, each of which finds favor right now with a wide circle of people:

1. The theory that life on earth is everything.

2. The theory that life on earth is nothing.

Or, adding the converse to each of these:

1. The theory that life on earth is everything and that eternity is nothing.

2. The theory that life on earth is nothing and that eternity is everything.

The Theory That Life on Earth Is Everything

Now, those who hold to the first of these theories object to the time view of life altogether. There can be no doubt that this is the favorite of the two. For one thing, it is decidedly the fashionable view. It is the view that the culture takes, as well as many thinking men and many thoughtful and modern books. "Life," these say, "is the great thing. We know something about life. We are in it—it is pulsating all around us. We feel its greatness and reality. But the other does not press upon us in the same way. It is far off and mystical. It takes a kind of effort even to believe it. Therefore, let us keep to what we know, what we are in, what we are sure of."

The strength of this school is in their great view of life; their weakness and great error is in their small view of time. Their enthusiasm for the quality of life makes them rush to the opposite extreme and ignore its quantity. The thought that life is short has little influence with them. They simply refuse to let it weigh with them; and, when pressed with thoughts of immortality, or time views of human life, they affirm, with a kind of superiority, that they have too much to do with the present to trouble themselves with sentimentalisms about the future.

The Theory That Life on Earth Is Nothing

The second view is the more antiquated, and perhaps the more illiterate. In this view, earthly life is nothing at all. It is a bubble, a vapor, a shadow. Eternity is the great thing. Eternity is the significant thing. Eternity is the only thing. Life on earth is a kind of unfortunate preliminary—a sort of dismal antechamber, where a person must wait and be content for a little while with a view of eternity from the windows. His turn to go is coming; in the meantime, let him fret through the unpleasant interval as resignedly as he can and pray for God to speed its close.

The strength of this school is that it recognizes time and eternity for themselves. Its weakness, and its great error, is that it refuses to think of earthly life, and spoils the thought of eternity for those who do. The first school needs to be told that life is short. The second school, far from having to be told that life is short, has to be told that life is long.

There Is Truth in Each Theory

It is clear, of course, that each of these views is the natural recoil from the other. The mistake is that each has recoiled too far. The "life is something" theory cannot help recoiling from the "life is nothing" theory; but it need not recoil into "life is everything." Similarly, the "eternity is something" theory cannot help recoiling from the "eternity is nothing" theory; but it need not recoil into "eternity is everything."

It is plain, then, that both these theories are wrong, and yet not altogether wrong. There is a great deal of truth in each—so much, indeed, that if the parts of the truth that each contains were joined into one, they would form a whole: the truth. And if the sides were nearly equal, so that there were as many people who thought that life is nothing as thought that life is everything, there could be nothing more useful than to attempt to strike the harmony between. But the sides are not equal, and hence the better exercise will be to deal with the side that has the truth the furthest in arrears.

This, undoubtedly, is the "life is everything" school. The other is, comparatively, a minority. At least, those who hold the extreme form of it are a minority. It is a more obvious and striking truth that life is something. And it is not difficult to convince the person who makes eternity everything to allow something to life. But to get the individual who makes life everything to grant a little to eternity is a harder thing to attempt; for the power of the world to come may be yet unfelt and unproved, and the race of life so swift, that the rival flight of time may still remain unseen.

Why We Must Think About Eternity and the Brevity of Life

Besides, there are mainly two great classes that swell the ranks of the majority, that refuse to think about time:

1. The great, busy working and thinking class. Those in this class are *too careful* of time ever to think of eternity as its successor. They have too little time to think of time.

2. The great, lazy worldly class. Those in this class are *too careless* of time ever to think that it will cease. They have too much time to think of time—so much of it that they think there will always be much of it.

It is to these two classes that this old year's question, *"What is your life?"* comes home with special power. And the majority has no reason to decline to face the question just because a fanatical minority has nauseated the subject by an exaggeration of eternity. For, if the people in the minority suffer in their lives by treating life as a thing of no importance, the other classes certainly suffer more by exaggerating life at the tremendous expense of eternity.

The great objection to thinking about eternity, or to considering the brevity of life, is that it is not practical. The "life is everything" school professes to be eminently utilitarian. It will have nothing to do with abstractions, nothing that does not directly concern life on earth. Anything that is outside the sphere of action is of little consequence to practical men. The members of this school feel themselves in the rush of the world's work, and it is something to think (to *think*) of that. It is something to live in the thick of it, to yield to the necessities of it, to share its hopes, and to calmly endure its discipline of care. But when you leave life, they protest, you are away from the present and the real. You are off into poetry and sentiment, and the meditations you produce may be interesting for philosophers and dreamers, but they are not for men who take their stand on the greatness of life and crave to be allowed to leave the mystical alone.

Now the answer to that—and it may be thoroughly answered—may be succinctly given. First of all, who told you eternity was nothing? Who told you it was an unpractical, unprofitable dream? Who told you to go on with your work and let time and other abstractions alone? It was certainly not God. God takes exactly the opposite view. He is never done insisting on the importance of the question. *"O that they were wise,…that they would consider their latter end!"* (Deuteronomy 32:29)—this is what God says. *"Lord, make me to know mine end, and the measure of my days, what it is…"* (Psalm 39:4)— that is what David, the man after God's own heart, says. (See 1 Samuel 13:14; Acts 13:22.) *"Teach us to number our days…"* (Psalm 90:12)—that is what Moses, the friend of God, says. (See Exodus 33:11.)

Note the reason God gives for thinking about these things. It was enough, indeed, for Him to say it, without any reason; but He has chosen to give us one. Why are we to number our days? *"…that we may apply our hearts unto wisdom"* (Psalm 90:12). That is the reason for thinking about time. It is to make us wise. Perhaps you have thought this is merely a piece of sentiment;

a flower of rhetoric for the poet's lyric; a harmless, popular imagination for ignorant people who cannot discourse upon life; a dramatic truth to impress the weak to prepare their narrow minds for death. But no, it is not that. God never uses sentiment. And if you think for a moment, you will see that it is not the narrow mind that needs this truth, but his who discourses on life.

The person who discourses most on life should discourse the most on time. When you discourse solely on life, you plead that it is in the interests of life. You despise the time view as impractical in the interests of life—in the interests of the new life school, whose proponents care too much for life to spend their strength upon the sentiment of time. Ah! But if you really cared for life, this sentiment would make you love it all the more. For time is the measurement of life. And everything in life must be profoundly affected by its poor, scant quantity.

Your life on earth is a great thing, a rich and precious possession. It is true that it is full of meaning and issues that no man can reckon. But it is ten thousand times greater for the thought that it must cease. One of the chief reasons why life is so great is precisely that life is so short. If we had a thousand years of it, it would not be as great as if we had only a thousand hours. It is great because it is little. Suppose a man is to be executed, and the judge has given him a month to prepare for death. One short month. How rich every hour of it would become, how precious the very moments would be! But suppose the man has only five minutes. Then how unspeakably solemn! How much greater is the five minutes of life than the month of life! Consider eternity to be a month and earthly life five minutes—if such a tremendous exaggeration of life could be conceived. How much greater does life become for being so very short!

How precious time is to a short-lived man! Suppose I am to die at thirty, and you at sixty; a minute is twice as dear to me, for each minute is twice as short. So, a day to me is more than a day to Methuselah, for he had many days (see Genesis 5:27), and I but few. Oh! If we really felt the dignity of life, we would wonder no less at its brevity than at its dignity. If we felt the greatness of life at this moment, how much keenness would this further thought add to it: that we might be dead before this sermon was done! How many things we permit ourselves on the theory that life is great would be most emphatically wrong on the theory that time is also great! How many frivolous things—yes, how many even great things—would we have to turn out from our lives this moment for just this thought, if we believed it, that time is short! For there is no room among the crowded moments of our life for things that will not live when life and time are past. So, no one who does not feel the keen sense of time flying away at every moment with the work he has done and the opportunities he has lost can know the true greatness of life and the inexpressible value of the self-selected things with which he fills its brief and narrow span. At every point, the thought of death must change the values of the significant things of earth no less than the thought of life, and we must ever feel the solemn relations given to our life and work from the overwhelming thought that the working life is brief.

In strangely suggestive words, a modern poet has described the point when the idea of time and death first began to dawn upon this earth. The scene is laid in some Eastern land, where a great colony had risen from the offspring of Cain, the murderer of his brother. Cain knew what death was. He had seen it. But, of all his scattered family, he alone knew about death, for he had kept his burning secret to himself. Cain's family grew and spread throughout the land, but no thought of death came in to check the joyous waste and exuberance of life—until, one day, in boyish pastime, a hurled stone strikes Lamech's son, and the lad falls to the earth. Friends gather around him as he lies, and bring him toys and playthings to wake him from his sleep. But no sleep like this had ever come to Lamech's son before; and soft, entreating words bring no responsive sound to the cold lips, or light to the closed eyes. Then Cain comes forward, whispering, "The boy is dead," and tells the awestruck family of this mystery of death. And then the poet describes the magic of this message, how "a new spirit from that hour came o'er the race of Cain." How time, once vague as air, began to stir strange terrors in the soul, and lend to life a moment that it had not known before. How even the sunshine had a different look. How "Work grew eager, and Device was born." How...

It seemed the light was never loved before,
Now each man said, "Twill go and come no more."
No budding branch, no pebble from the brook,
No form, no shadow, but new dearness took
From the one thought that life must have an end.[16]

So the thought that life will be no more, that each day lived is hastening on the day when life itself must stop, makes every priceless hour of ours a million times greater, and tinges every thought, word, and act with the shadow of what must be. From all this, it must now be clear that the individual who is really concerned about living well must possess himself continually of the thought that he is not to live long. And it is in the highest interests of great living to stimulate life, not to paralyze it, that God asks us all today, "*What is your life?*"

The Bible's Answer to Its Question "What Is Your Life?"

But the Bible has done more than ask this question. It has also answered it. And when the Bible answers a question, it always gives the best answer. We could do no better, therefore, than to consult it a little further, for it so happens that there are few subjects that the Bible goes into as thoroughly as this one; there are few thoughts that rise more often or more urgently to the surface of the lives of the great men and women of the Bible than "*What is your life?*"

Moreover, there is a trait in the Bible answers that makes them particularly valuable; one that has tended, more than anything else, to impress them profoundly upon the deeper spirit of every age. That trait is this: The answer is never given in hard, bare words but is presented—wrapped up, as it were—in some figure of such exquisite beauty that no mind could refuse to give it a place, if only for the fineness of its metaphor.

Take, as an example, the answer that follows the question in the text, "*What is your life?*" The answer given is this: "*It is even a vapour, that appeareth for a little time, and then vanisheth away*" (James 4:14). Who could afford to forget a thought like that, when once its beauty had struck root within the mind? And if God did not rather choose a few hard, solid sentences of truth to perpetuate an answer to one of the most solid thoughts of life, is it not just because He wanted it to be remembered evermore—because He wanted the thought of the shortness and uncertainty of life to live in every living soul, and haunt the heart in times when other thoughts were passionless and dull? In childhood, before deeper thoughts had come, He would paint this truth, in delicate tints, on every opening soul; and in riper years, when trouble and sickness came and weaned the broken mind from sterner thoughts, He would have the soul still furnished with these ever-preaching pictures of the frailty of its life.

Why is it that, in many hearts, there is such strange attraction to the Bible thoughts of time, and why the particular charm with which the least religious minds will linger over the texts that speak of human life? It is because God has thrown an intensely living interest around these truths by carrying His images of the thoughts He most wanted remembered into the great galleries of the imagination, where the soul can never tire. Had such thoughts been left to reason, that faculty of the mind would have stifled them with its cold touch; had they been sunk in the heart, the heart would have consumed itself and them in hot and burning passion. But in the broad region of the imagination, there is expansiveness enough for even such vast truths to wander at their will, and power and mystery enough to draw both heart and reason after them in wondering, trembling homage. And if no day almost passes over our heads without some silent visitation to remind us what we are, it is because the Bible has utilized all the most common things of life to bring home these lessons to the soul, so that every shadow on the wall, and every blade of withered grass, is full of meanings that every open heart can read.

Now, in this connection, it is a remarkable fact that the Bible has used up almost every physical image that is in any way appropriate to the case. And if we were to examine the concepts of life that have been held by great men in succeeding ages of the world, we would find scarcely anything new, scarcely anything the Bible had not used before.

There lie scattered throughout this Book no fewer than eighteen of these answers—all in metaphor—to the question *"What is your life?"* And anyone who has not previously gathered them together cannot but be surprised at the singular beauty and appropriateness of the collection. To begin with, let us run over their names. What is your life? It is…

+ *"A tale that is told"* (Psalm 90:9)
+ *"A sleep"* (see, for example, Psalm 90:5)
+ A *"pilgrimage"* (Genesis 47:9)
+ *"A vapour"* (James 4:14)

- A swift *"post,"* or runner (see Job 9:25)
- *"A shadow"* (see, for example, 1 Chronicles 29:15)
- A swift ship (see Job 9:26)
- *"A flower"* (Job 14:2)
- *"An handbreadth"* (Psalm 39:5)
- *"A weaver's shuttle"* (Job 7:6)
- A shepherd's tent removed (see Isaiah 38:12)
- *"Water spilt on the ground"* (2 Samuel 14:14)
- A thread cut by a weaver (see Isaiah 38:12)
- *"Grass"* (see Psalm 90:5–6)
- *"A wind"* (Psalm 78:39)
- *"A dream"* (Job 20:8)
- *"Nothing"* (see, for example, Psalm 39:5)

Generally speaking, the first thing to strike one about these images is that they are all quick things—there is a suggestion of brevity and evanescence about them, and this feeling is so strong that we might fancy there was only one answer to the question *"What is your life?"*—namely, your life is *short*. But if we look at them more closely for a moment, shades of difference will begin to appear, and we will find the hints of other meanings just as great and striking, and quite as necessary to complete the conception of *"your life."*

1. Life Is a Very Little Thing

First of all, *three* of the above metaphors give this answer: Your life is a very little thing. We have admitted that life is a very great thing. It is also a very little thing. Measure it by its bearing on eternity, and there is no image in God's universe that can be compared to it for majesty and dignity. It is a sublime thing—Life. But measure it by its bearing on time, by its results in the world, and on other lives, and there is no image too small to speak of its lowliness and narrowness, for *"your life"* is a little thing. It is *"a shadow"*; it is a shepherd's tent removed; it is *"a tale that is told."*

A shadow: It is unreal; it is illusory. It falls across the world without affecting it; perhaps it only darkens it. Then, it rises suddenly and is gone. It leaves few impressions; and, if it could, a shadow cannot act much on other shadows. So, at best, life is a poor, resultless, shadowy thing.

A shepherd's tent removed: Just before sunset, the slopes of the Eastern hills would be dotted with Arab tents. And when night fell, as the traveler in these lands lay down to rest, he would see the glimmering of their fires and hear the noisy bleating of their flocks. But, in the morning, when he looked out, herdsmen and herds alike would be gone. Hours ago, perhaps, the tents had been struck, and the hills would be as silent and lonely as if no foot had ever stirred the dew on their slopes. In the same way, the Bible says, man traces out his trackless path through life. He is here today, in the noise of the world's labor; but, when you look for him tomorrow, he is gone. Sometime in the night, his frail tent has been struck, and his place is empty and still. His life has left no track to tell that it was there—except a burnt-out fire to show that there a shepherd's tent had been removed.

A tale that is told: This is the best of these images. Some people think this means a thought or a meditation. "Your life is a meditation," as the marginal note has it. But as the psalm in which the words occur was written by Moses, it is probable that the obvious meaning of the words is the correct one. In their journeys, the children of Israel would have had many weary hours in which they were unoccupied. There would have been no books to relieve the monotony. And, no doubt, the people would have attempted to while away the tedious marches, and the long hours by the campfires at night, with the familiar Eastern custom of narrating personal adventures in the form of stories or tales. Night after night, as this went on, the different tales of the storytellers would begin to get mixed; then, they would start to confuse their audience, and then, perhaps, even to weary them. The first tale, which had once made a great impression, would lose its power; and the second, which had been thought to be more wonderful still, would be distanced by the third. Then, the third would be forgotten, and the fourth and the fifth, until all earlier stories would be forgotten, and last night's tale would be the vivid picture in every mind today. But the storyteller could know that, tonight, another would have his turn and sit in the place of honor, and tell a more vivid tale than he told the night before, and his would be forgotten and ignored.

So do we spend our years as a tale that is told. The dead have told their tales; they have said their say. They thought we would remember what they did and said. But, no; they are forgotten. They have become old stories now. And our turn will come—our turn to stop; our turn for the Angel of Death to close the chapter of our life, whether it is a novel or a psalm, and to write the universal "Finis" at the end. Even though a sentence here and there may linger for a few brief years to find a place—without quotation marks—in some tale better told, the tale itself must end and be forgotten, like the rest— an ill-told, ill-heard, and ill-remembered tale.

2. Life Is Short

Next, there is another set of metaphors that bring out the more common answer to *"What is your life?"* (which, therefore, it will be necessary only to name): life is a short thing. Shortness, of course, is different from littleness. A lightning flash is short but not little. But life is both short and little. And there are two ways in which life may be recognized as short: (1) measured by growth, and (2) measured by minutes. Those who are growing must feel the shortness of time the most. They have started with the wrecks of being to fashion themselves into men, and life is all too short to do it in. Therefore, they work out their salvation *"with fear and trembling"* (Philippians 2:12)— fearful, lest death should come; trembling, lest life should stop before salvation has been worked out. But those who measure life by its minutes have nothing to say of its brevity; for their purpose, it is long enough. They do not want more time but "the more capacious soul," as someone has said, "to flow through every pore of the little which [they] have."[17] But there is no distinction in the Bible's treatment of the two. Time is the same to all. It is *"an handbreadth,"* *"a weaver's shuttle,"* "a swift runner," "a swift ship," and *"nothing."* It is also like *"the eagle that hasteth to the prey"* (Job 9:26).

David used to pray to God to give him a measure for his days. Well, he got it. It was the breadth of his hand. *"My days* [are] *as an handbreadth"* (Psalm 39:5). We continually carry around with us the measure of our days.

The other symbols are familiar enough. The *"weaver's shuttle"*—does this refer to the monotony, the sameness, the constant repetition, of life? Rather, it indicates quickness, the rapid flight through the thin web of time; the shuttle being, at that time, perhaps, the quickest image men had.

In early times, those who lived in the country could know nothing more rapid or sudden than the swoop of an eagle on its prey; those who lived by the seaside could know nothing more fleet than the swift sailing away of a ship driven by the unseen wind, or the hasty arrival of the swift *"post,"* or messenger, with tidings from afar. And it was not for lack of opportunity if they did not learn their lessons well in those simpler days, when the few changes life had were each thus stamped with the thought of the great change into eternity.

The next concept is so closely allied to this that one can scarcely separate it but for convenience. It suggests the idea of transitoriness. Your life is a transitory thing. It is a thing of change. There is no endurance in it, no settling down in it, no real home to it here. Therefore, God calls it a *"pilgrimage"*—a passing on to a something that is to be. Still closely allied to this, too, is the simile of the text—that life is a *"vapour."* It means there is no real substance in it. It is a coming for a moment, then a passing away forever.

And then there are two or three metaphors that advance this idea still further. In their hands, life passes from transitoriness into mystery. This life of ours, they show us, is a mysterious thing. And it is true that life is a mysterious thing. We do not understand life—why it should begin, why it should end. There is some meaning in it somewhere that has baffled every search; some meaning beyond, some more real state than itself. So the Bible calls it *"a sleep," "a dream,"* and *"a wind."* No book but the Bible could have called our life a sleep. The great books of the Greeks have called death a sleep. As the Laureate puts it, "Sleep, Death's twin-brother."[18] But the Bible has the profounder thought: Life is the sleep. Death is but the waking. And the great poets and philosophers of the world since have found no deeper thought of life than this; and the greatest of them all has used the very word: "our little life is rounded with a sleep."[19] It seems to have been a soothing thought to them, and it may be a sanctifying thought to us, that this life is not the end; and therefore it is a wise thing to turn round sometimes in our sleep, and think how there is more beyond than dreams.

3. Life Is Irrevocable and Uncertain

There are but two more thoughts to bring our questions to a close, and they will add a practical interest to what has gone before.

"What is your life?"

First, life is an irrevocable thing. We have just finished an irrevocable year. As we look back upon it, every thought and word and act of it is there in its place, just as we left it. There are all the Sabbaths in their places, and all the well-spent days or ill-spent days between. There is every sin and every wish and every look still in its own exact surroundings, each under its own day of the month, at the precise moment of the day it happened. We are leaving it all at twelve o'clock tonight; but, remember, we leave it exactly as it stands. No single hour of it can be changed now, no smallest wish can be recalled, no angry word taken back. It is fixed, steadfast, irrevocable—set forever on the past plates of eternity.

Our Book has a wonderful metaphor for this idea: *"water spilt on the ground, which cannot be gathered up again"* (2 Samuel 14:14). No, we cannot gather up these days and put them back into time's breaking urn, and live them over again. They are spilled upon the ground, and the great stream of time has sucked them up and has already cast them on the eternal shores among all bygone years. And there they bide until God's time comes, and they come back, one by one, in order as they went, to meet us again and Him before the judgment bar. Tomorrow is to be a time of resolution, is it? Well, let this resolution take the foremost place of all—that, when this day comes next year, and we look once more at the irrevocable past, there will be fewer things to wish undone and words to wish unsaid, and more spots where memory will love to linger still, more steps that, when retraced in thought, will fill the heart with praise.

Second, life is more than an irrevocable thing; it is an uncertain thing—so certainly uncertain, that it is certain we will not all be here to see this next year close. What does the Bible's grim image of the weaver's thread suspended in the air, and the blade of the lifted knife just touching it with its edge, mean? It means that you must die. The thread of your life is to be cut. The knife may be lifted now, the keen blade just touching it; one pressure of the hand, and it is done. One half, left unfinished, still hanging to the past—the other, dropped noiselessly into eternity.

Oh, life is an abruptly closing thing! Is it not as grass? *"In the morning it flourisheth, and groweth up; in the evening it is cut down, and withereth"* (Psalm 90:6). Is your life ready for the swiftly falling knife, for the Reaper who stands at your door? Have you heard that there is another life—a life that cannot die; a life that, linked to your life, will make the past yet bright with pardon and the future rich with hope? *"This life is in* [God's] *Son"* (1 John 5:11).

IO

"MARVEL NOT"

"Marvel not that I said unto thee, Ye must be born again."
—John 3:7

Every person comes into the world wrapped in an atmosphere of wonder—an atmosphere from which his whole life is a prolonged effort to escape. The moment he opens his eyes, this sense of wonder is upon him, and it never leaves him until he closes them on the greatest wonder—death. Between these wonders—the first awaking and the last sleep—his life is spent, itself a long-drawn breath of mystery.

This sense of wonder is not evil, although it is something to escape from. It is one of God's earliest gifts, as well as one of His best gifts; but its usefulness to childhood or to adulthood depends on the mind's escaping from wonder into something else—on its passing from wonder into knowledge. Hence, God has made the desire to escape it as natural to us as the desire to wonder.

Everyone has been struck by the wonderment of a little child; but the child's desire to escape out of wonderment is a more marvelous thing. His wonder becomes a constant and secret craving for an entrance into the rest of information and fact. His eager questionings, his impatience of his own ignorance, and his insatiable requests for knowledge are simultaneously the symptoms of his wonder and the evidences of his efforts to escape it. And although, in adult life, the developed man is too cautious or too proud to display his wonder like the child, it is there in its thin disguise as inquiry, investigation, or doubt. And there is no more exuberant moment in a person's life than when this wonder works until it passes into truth, when reason flashes a sudden light into a groping mind, and knowledge whispers, "Marvel not!"

A Divine Sense of Wonder

Of all the subjects that men have found convenient to banish into the regions of the unknowable, none suffers so frequently as the subject of being born again. The elements of mystery that are supposed to cluster around it are reckoned an ample excuse—even for the most intelligent minds—for *not trying* to understand it, and more than a justification for anyone who makes the attempt and fails.

Indeed, the famous rabbi who was honored with all this immortal discourse on regeneration is a case in point. Nicodemus was just on the verge of losing himself in this most treasonable despair. Never was a man more puzzled than he at the initial statement of this truth. Never was man's sense of wonder more profoundly excited, never more in danger of losing itself in the mazes of mystery, never nearer taking the easy escape by drowning itself in ignorance, than when Jesus rallied the escaping faculties of the Jewish ruler by the message *"Marvel not."*

The background working of that mind during its strange night interview with Christ is full of interest and lesson, and what we do know is full of implication and meaning. Twice already during the conversation, the great Teacher had said, in substance, *"Ye must be born again."* And one of the strongest intellects of its time stands literally petrified before the words. Nicodemus first tries to summon courage and frame a wondering question in reply: "*How can a man be born when he is old?*" (John 3:4). This was less a question, perhaps, than a soliloquy of his own. He has heard the great Teacher's statement, and he thinks upon it aloud, turning it over in his calm Hebrew mind until his very question returns to him and plunges him in deeper wonderment than before: "How can a man be born again when he is old?"

Next time, he will venture no remark, and the Teacher's words fall uninterrupted on the puzzled scholar's ear: "*Except a man be born of water and of the Spirit, he cannot enter into the kingdom of God. That which is born of the flesh is flesh; and that which is born of the Spirit is spirit*" (John 3:5–6). Jesus has given him the key to it. But Nicodemus does not see it. He seems to have plunged into a dream. His reverie has deepened, until he stands absorbed in thought, with down-turned eyes, before his Master. Jesus stands by in silence and reads the wonder and perplexity in the gathering blackness of his brow. Nicodemus is despairing, perhaps. He is going to give it up. He is utterly baffled with the strange turn the conversation has taken. There is no satisfaction to be gotten from this clandestine meeting, after all; and, puzzled, beaten, and crestfallen, he prepares to take his leave. But Jesus will not let the divine sense of wonder be awoken to end like this. It must end in knowledge, not in ignominy. It must escape into spiritual truth, not into intellectual mystery. So He says, "Wonder not; 'marvel not.' There is nothing so very mysterious that I cannot make you know. You will understand it all if you will come and think of it. You need not marvel that I said to you, '*Ye must be born again.*'"

Thus, Jesus saved Nicodemus from relapsing into ignorance of the greatest truth the world had known until then, or from lulling his wonder to sleep forever in mystery or despair.

Why Did Christ Say, "Marvel not"?

For the sake of those of us who have been tempted to pause where Nicodemus so nearly lost himself on the threshold of this truth; for the sake of those of us who have almost felt drawn into the intellectual sin of drowning our wonder at this truth in despair of it; let us ask ourselves why Christ said, "*Marvel not.*"

It may be convenient to divide the answer into three short headings:

1. "Marvel not"—as if It Were Unintelligible
2. "Marvel not"—as if It Were Impossible
3. "Marvel not"—as if It Were Unnecessary

1. "Marvel not"—as if It Were Unintelligible

There is nothing more unintelligible in the world than *how* a soul is born again. And there is nothing more intelligible than that it *is*. We can understand the fact, however, without necessarily understanding the act. The act of being born again is as mysterious as God. All the complaints that have been showered upon this doctrine have referred to the act—the act with which we really have nothing to do, which is a process of God; the agency, the unseen wind of the Spirit; and which Jesus Himself has expressly warned us not to expect to understand. "*Thou...canst not tell*," He said, "*whence it cometh, and whither it goeth*" (John 3:8).

But there is nothing in this to frighten search. For, precisely the same kind of mystery hangs over every process of nature and life. We do not understand the influence of sunshine on the leaves of a flower in the springtime any more than we do the mysterious budding of spiritual life within the soul; botany is a science for all that.

We do not give up the study of chemistry as hopeless because we fail to comprehend the unseen laws that guide the delicate actions and reactions of matter. Nor do we disbelieve in the influence of food on the vital frame because no one has found the point exactly at which it passes from dead nourishment into life. We do not avoid the subject of electricity because electricity is a mystery, or heat because we cannot see heat, or meteorology because we cannot see the wind. Marvel not, then, from the analogy of physical nature, if, concerning this Spirit of regeneration, we cannot tell where it comes from or where it goes. It is not on that account unintelligible that a man should be born again.

If we care again to take the analogy from the moral and intellectual nature, the same may be said with even greater emphasis. The essence of regeneration is a change from one state to another—from an old life to a new one. Spiritually, its manifestation is in hating things once loved, or loving things once hated. God is no longer avoided but worshipped; Christ no longer despised but trusted.

Intellectually, changes that are at least in some way similar are happening every day. Suppose you rose up yesterday bitterly opposed to such and such a scheme. You were so strong in your opinion that nothing would ever shake you. You would *never* change, you said—you could not. But then you met a friend who began to talk with you about it. You listened, then wavered, then capitulated. You allowed yourself to be "talked round," as you expressed it. You were *converted* to the other side. And, in the evening, your change of mind was so complete that you were literally born again—you were literally another person; you were in a new world of ideas, of interests, and of hopes, with all the old dislikes in that special connection reversed, and the old loves turned into hates.

Something like this goes on in the regeneration of the soul, only with a higher agency. Hence, it is called by similar names, such as "a change of heart," or "a turning around," or "a conversion to the other side." And just as talking round will change a person's opinion or convert him intellectually, so turning round by the Spirit of God will change his heart or convert him spiritually. When you are told, therefore, that your heart may be changed by the Spirit, even as your mind was changed by your friend, "marvel not," as if it were unintelligible, that you may be born again. Note what a few hours' conversation could do in making you love the side you had hated, and hate the side you had loved. Do not marvel at what more the power of God could do in turning round your being from the old love to the new. And, one might even press the analogy a little further to add that if a few minutes' conversation with a fellow man could overturn the stubborn mountain of your mind, how much more should a few minutes' conversation with Christ, such as Nicodemus had, change your life the moment it touched His? Nicodemus's time with Christ overthrew his strongest Messianic views and changed the current of his life forever from that hour.

But more than that, to Nicodemus, even the concept itself of being born again should not have seemed a mystery. It was already a familiar thought, in another sense, to every Jewish heart—nothing more nor less, indeed, than one of the common political phrases of the day. At that time, when a foreigner came to reside in a Jewish town, the custom was to regard him as unclean. He was held at arm's length; he was a person of different caste; "the Jew had no dealings with the Samaritan." (See John 4:9.) But if the foreigner wished to leave his gods and share the religious hopes and civil privileges of the Jews, there was one way out of the old state into the new—just one way: He must be born again. He was baptized with water, and he passed through certain other rites, until finally reckoned clean, when he became as truly one of the chosen people as if he had been the lineal son of Abraham.

And the process of initiation from the Gentile world into the kingdom of the Jew was called a regeneration, or a being born again. There was nothing, therefore, in the thoughtful consideration of the new birth—in the higher sense—for the Jew to marvel at. "*Art thou a master of Israel,*" Jesus might well ask, "*and knoweth not these things?*" (John 3:10). A master in Israel stumbling at an everyday illustration, marveling as if it were unintelligible! "*Marvel not that I said unto thee, Ye must be born again.*" What the Jews did to a stranger in admitting him to their kingdom corresponds exactly with what we do in our process of naturalization.

Naturalization—"spiritualization," if we would be exactly accurate—is the idea, then, expressed in the "*born again*" that Christ spoke of. And when we trace the expression back to its setting in Jewish politics, it yields the beautiful concept that God calls people—the foreigner, the stranger, the wanderer—to forsake the far country, and, having been purified by initiatory rites from all uncleanness, to be translated into the kingdom of His dear Son. (See Colossians 1:13.) And though there may, indeed, be reasons why we would be so slow to understand it, and regions of rightful wonder in the deeper workings of the thought that we have not yet explored, at least this much is clear: We do not need to marvel, as if it were unintelligible.

2. "Marvel not"—as if It Were Impossible

In a word or two, let us consider next why we should not marvel as if being born again were impossible. There is a name for God that men in our day are often tempted to forget—God the *Creator* of heaven and earth. It was the name, perhaps, by which we first knew God—He had made our earth, our house; He had made us. He was our Creator—God. At that time, we thought God could make anything, or do anything, or do everything. But we lost our happy faith of early childhood; and now we wonder what things God can do, as if there were many things He could not do.

But there is one thing we have little difficulty in always crediting to the creating hand of God—*life*. No one but God has ever made life. We call Him the Author of life, and the Author of life is a wondrously fertile Author. He makes much life—life in vast abundance. There is nothing as striking in nature as the prodigality—the almost reckless prodigality—of life. It seems as if God delighted Himself in life. So, the world is filled with it. In the woods, in the air, in the ocean bed—everywhere—there is teeming life, superabundance of life, which God has made.

Well, if God can *give* life, He can surely *add* life. In principle, regeneration is nothing but the adding of more life. It is God adding life *to* life—more life to a person who has some life. The person has life that God gave him once; but part of him—the best part of him—is dead. His soul is dead in trespasses and sins. God touches the soul, and it lives. Even as the body was dead, and God breathed upon it until it lived, so God will breathe upon the soul, and more life, and better life, will come.

So there is nothing impossible in being born again, any more than there is impossibility in being born at all. What did Jesus Christ come into the world for? To give life, He said, even more abundant life. (See John 10:10.) And Christ giving life—that is regeneration. Nicodemus did not need more knowledge, though he thought so, but more *life*; and the best proof that life was possible was that life was granted. So, the best proof of Christianity is a Christian; the best proof of regeneration is a person who has been regenerated. "Can a man be born again when he is old?" Certainly. For it has been done. Think of Bunyan the sinner and Bunyan the saint; think of Newton the miscreant and Newton the missionary; think of Saul the persecutor and Paul the apostle; and marvel not, as if it were impossible that a man should be born again.

3. "Marvel not"—as if It Were Unnecessary

Regeneration is more than intelligible and possible—it is necessary to enter the kingdom of God. *"Except a man be born again, he cannot see the kingdom of God"* (John 3:3). Jesus says it is necessary. A person cannot see the kingdom of God unless he is born again. That person not only cannot enter it, but, Jesus says, he cannot *see* it. It is actually invisible to him. This is why the world says of religion, "We do not understand it; we do not make it out; we do not see it." No, of course they do not see it; they *cannot* see it. It is first necessary to be born again.

When men come into the world, they are born outside the kingdom of God, and they cannot see into it. They may go around and around it, and examine it from the outside, and pass an opinion on it. But they are no judges. They are not seeing what they are speaking about. For *"that which is born of the flesh is flesh; and that which is born of the Spirit is spirit"* (John 3:6); and they can give only a criticism that is material about something that is spiritual. Therefore, the critical value of a worldly man's opinion on religious matters is nothing. He is open to an objection that makes his opinion simply ludicrous—he is talking about something that he has never seen. As far as one's experience of religion goes, regeneration makes all the difference.

It is as if someone has been standing outside some great cathedral. He has heard that its windows are of stained glass and exceedingly beautiful. He walks all around it and sees nothing but dull, unmeaning spaces—there is an iron grating over each window, intensifying the gloom that seems to reign within. There is nothing worth seeing there, but everything to repel. But let him go in. Let him see things from the inside, and his eye is dazzled by the gorgeous play of colors; and the miracles and the parables are glowing upon the glass; and the figure of Jesus is there, and the story of His love is told on every pane; and there are choirs of angels, and cherubim and seraphim, and an altar where, in light that is inaccessible, is God.

So let a person enter into the kingdom of heaven—let him be born again and enter—and he will see the kingdom of God. He will see the miracles and the parables that were meaningless, colorless, to him at one time; he will see the story of the cross, which was a weariness and an offense; he will see the person of Christ and the King in His beauty, and, beholding as in a glass the glory of the only begotten, he will be *"changed into the same image from glory to glory"* (2 Corinthians 3:18). Marvel not if it is necessary for him to be born again in order to see all this.

Within this great world, there are a number of little worlds, to which entrance is attainable only by birth. For instance, there is the intellectual world, which requires the birth of brains; and the artistic world, which requires the birth of taste; and the dramatic world, which requires the birth of acting talent; and the musical world, which requires the birth of harmony and ear. A person cannot enter the intellectual world unless he has brains, or the artistic world unless he has taste. And he cannot make or find brains or taste. They must be born in him. A person cannot make a poetical mind for himself. It must be created in him. Hence, "the poet is born—not made," we say. Likewise, the Christian is born, not made.

There remains one other and imperative protest against the idea that regeneration is unnecessary. Human nature demands regeneration as if it *were* necessary.

No one who knows the human heart or human history will marvel as if it were unnecessary that the world must be born again. Every other conceivable measure has been tried to reform it. Government has tried it, philosophy has tried it, and philanthropy has tried it—and failed. The heart—the national heart or the individual heart—remains *"deceitful above all things, and desperately wicked"* (Jeremiah 17:9). Reformation has been of little use to it, for every reformation is but a fresh and unguaranteed attempt to do what has never been done before. Reconstruction has been of little use to it, for reconstruction is an ill-advised endeavor to rebuild a house that has fallen a thousand times already with the same old bricks and beams. Mankind has had every chance from the creation to the present moment to prove that regeneration was not the one necessity of the world—and, again, it has utterly failed.

Indeed, we are still told that all the world needs is just to get a start. Set a person—or a universe—on his feet, with a few good guiding principles; give human nature fair play; and it must win in the end. But no. The experiment has been tried. In a sense, God tried it Himself. It was fairly done, and it failed. The wickedness of man had become great throughout the land. So, God said He would destroy all living flesh, selecting a few of the best inhabitants to start the world afresh. A fair experiment. So, all the world was drowned except for a little nucleus in an ark—the picked few who were to found Utopia, who were to reconstruct the universe, who were to begin human life again, and make everything so much better than it was before. (See Genesis 6–9.) But the experiment failed. The picked few failed. Their children failed. Their children's children failed. Things got no better; only worse, perhaps, and worse; and no one ever really knew the cause until Jesus told the world that it *must*—that it was *essentially* necessary—that it must, absolutely and imperatively must, be born again.

If human nature makes it necessary, much more does the divine nature. When Christ presents His church to God, it must be as a spotless bride. (See, for example, Ephesians 5:25–27.) In that eternal kingdom, saints are more than subjects—they are the companions of the King. They must be a select number. They must be a very highborn company. If you and I are to be there, do not marvel as if it were unnecessary that we must be born again. *"Lord, who shall abide in thy tabernacle? who shall dwell in thy holy hill?"* (Psalm 15:1). *"He that hath clean hands, and a pure heart"* (Psalm 24:4). *"There shall in no wise enter into it any thing that defileth"* (Revelation 21:27). Marvel not as if it were unnecessary that our robes should be washed in white.

Marvel not as if it were unintelligible…

Marvel not as if it were impossible…

Marvel not as if it were unnecessary…that you must be born again.

Marvel if you are. Marvel if you are.

II

THE MAN AFTER
GOD'S OWN HEART
A Bible Study on the Ideal of a Christian Life

"A man after mine own heart, which shall fulfil all my will."
—Acts 13:22

No one who does not have a very definite concept of what he is living for can be making much of his life. And if you ask, at random, a dozen people what is the purpose of their life, you will be surprised to find how few have formed for themselves more than the dimmest idea. The question of the *summum bonum*[20] has ever been the most difficult for the human mind to grasp. What should a person do with his life? What is life for? And why is it given? These questions have composed the one great puzzle for human books and human thoughts; and ancient philosophy, medieval learning, and modern culture alike have failed to give us the answers to them.

No person, no book—except one—has ever told the world what it needs; so each individual has had to face the problem in his own uncertain light, and carry out, each for himself, the life that he thinks best.

One person says literature is the great thing, so he will be a literary man. He lays down for himself his ideal of a literary life. He surrounds himself with the best ideals of style; and with his great ambition working toward great ends, after great models, he cuts out for himself what he thinks is his great life work. Another says the world is the great thing, so he will be a man of the world. A third will be a businessman; a fourth, a man of science.

And the Christian must have a definite aim and model for his life. The above aims are great aims, but they are not great enough for him. His one Book has taught him a nobler life than all the libraries of the rich and immortal past. He may wish to be a man of business, or a man of science; and, indeed, he may be either. But he covets a nobler name than that. He will be the man after God's own heart. He has discovered the secret that philosophy never knew—that the ideal life is this: "*A man after mine own heart, which shall fulfil all my will.*" And just as the man of the world or the literary man lays down a program for the brief span of his working life, which he feels must vanish shortly in the unknown of the grave, much more will the Christian lay down a program for the great span of his life before it arches over the valley into eternity.

A great man has a great plan for his life—the greatest man has the greatest plan, and keeps it. And the Christian should have the greatest plan, as his life is the greatest, as his work is the greatest, and as his life and his work will follow him when all this world's life and work are done.

The Key to the Ideal Life

Let us ask, "What is the true plan of the ideal Christian life?" We need a definition so that we may know it, a description so that we may follow it. And if you look, you will see that both, in a sense, lie on the surface of our text. "*A man after mine own heart*"—here is the definition of what we are to be. "*Which shall fulfil all my will*"—here is the description of how we are to be it. These words are the definition and the description of the model human life. They describe the man after God's own heart. They give us the key to the ideal life.

The general truth of these words is simply this: The purpose of life is to do God's will. Now, that is a great and surprising revelation. No human being ever figured it out. It has been presented to the world since Christ walked on the earth, yet few have discovered it even today. One person will tell you that the purpose of life is to be true. Another will tell you that it is to deny self. Another will say that it is to keep the Ten Commandments. A fourth will point you to the Beatitudes. One will tell you that it is to *do* good, another that it is to *get* good, still another that it is to *be* good. But the aim of life is in none of these things. It is more than them all, and it includes them all. The end of life is not to deny self, nor to be true, nor to keep the Ten Commandments—it is simply to do God's will. It is not to get good, nor to be good, nor even to do good but to do only what God wills, whether that is working or waiting, winning or losing, suffering or recovering, living or dying.

But this concept is too great for us. It is not practical enough for us. It is the greatest concept of mankind that has ever been given to the world. The great philosophers, from Socrates and Plato to Immanuel Kant and John Stuart Mill, have given us their concepts of an ideal human life. But none of these concepts is at all as great as this. Each of them has constructed an ideal human life. They call it a universal life, a life for all other lives, a life for all people and all time to copy. Yet none of them is half as deep, as wonderful, and as far-reaching, as this: "*A man after mine own heart, which shall fulfil all my will.*"

But, for this very reason, it is at first sight impracticable. We feel helpless beside so great and eternal a truth. God must teach us these things. Like little children, we must sit at His feet and learn. And, as we come to Him with our difficulty, we find He has prepared two practical helps for us, so that He may humanize it and bring it near to us; so that, by studying these helps, and following them with willing and humble hearts, we will learn to copy into our lives the great ideal of God.

The two helps that God has given us are these:

1. The model life realized in Christ, the living Word.
2. The model life analyzed in the Bible, the written Word.

The usual method is to deal almost exclusively with the first of these. Today, for certain reasons, we will consider the second. Regarding the first, of course, if a person could follow Christ, he would lead the model life. But what is meant by telling a person to follow Christ? How is it to be done? It is like putting a young artist before a Murillo[21] or a Raphael, and telling him to copy it. But even as the artist, in following his ideal, has colors put into his hand, and brush and canvas, and a hint here from this master, and a touch there from another, so with the pupil in the school of Christ: The great Master Himself is there to help him. The Holy Spirit is there to help him. But the model life is not to be mystically attained. There is spirituality about it, but not unreality. God has therefore provided another great help, our second help: The model life analyzed in the Word of God. Without the one, the ideal life would be incredible; without the other, it would be unintelligible. Hence, God has given us two sides of this model life—the first is realized in the living Word, and the second is analyzed in the written Word.

What the Christian Needs for an Ideal Life

Let us search our Bibles, then, to find this ideal life, so that, by copying it in our lives, reproducing it day by day and point by point, we may learn to make the most of our little life. Then, it will be said of us, as it was said of David, "*A man after mine own heart, which shall fulfil all my will.*"

1. A Reason for Living

The first thing our ideal man needs is a reason for his being alive at all. He must account for his existence. Why is he here? And the Bible's answer is this: "*I come...to do thy will, O God*" (Hebrews 10:7).

That is what we are here for—to do God's will. "*I come...to do thy will, O God.*" That is the object of your life and mine—to do God's will. It is not to be happy, or successful, or famous, or to do the best we can, and to get on honestly in the world. It is something far higher than this—to do God's will. There, at the very outset, is the great key to life. Any one of us can tell in a moment whether our lives are right or not. Are we doing God's will? We do not mean, "Are we doing God's work?"—preaching or teaching or collecting money—but "Are we doing God's will?" A person may think he is doing God's work, when he is not even doing God's will. And a person may be doing God's work and God's will quite as much by hewing stones or sweeping streets as by preaching or praying. So, the question means just this: Are we working out our common, everyday life along the great lines of God's will? This is different from the world's model life. The world's idea of it is, "I come to push my way." The Christian's idea of it is, "Not my way—*not my will, but thine, be done*'" (Luke 22:42). This is what the man after God's own heart says: "I do not seek my own will, but the will of Him who sent me." (See John 6:38.)

2. Sustenance

The second thing the ideal man needs is sustenance. After he has life, you must give him food. Now, what food should you give him? Should you feed him with knowledge, or with riches, or with honor, or with beauty, or with power, or with truth? No; there is a rarer luxury than these—so rare, that few have ever more than tasted it; so rich, that they who have will never live on other fare again. It is this: *"My meat is to do the will of him that sent me"* (John 4:34).

Again, to do God's will is what a man lives for; it is also what he lives on. Meat is strength, support, nourishment. The strength of the model life is drawn from the divine will. Man has a strong will. But God's will is everlasting strength—almighty strength. Such strength the ideal man receives. He grows by it, he assimilates it—it is his life. *"Man shall not live by bread alone, but by every word that proceedeth out of the mouth of God"* (Matthew 4:4; see also Luke 4:4). Nothing can satisfy his appetite but this—he hungers to do God's will. Nothing else will fill him.

Everyone knows that the world is hungry. But the hungry world is starving. It has many meats and many drinks, but there is no nourishment in them. It has pleasures and gaiety and excitement, but there is no food there to satisfy the immortal craving of the soul. It has the theater and worldly society, and worldly books, and worldly lusts. But these things merely intoxicate. There is no sustenance in them. So, our ideal life turns its eye from them all with unutterable loathing. "My meat is to do God's will." To do God's will! No possibility of starving on such wonderful fare as this. God's will is eternal. The Christian lives upon eternal food. In springtime, it is not sown; and in summer drought, it cannot fail. In harvest, it is not reaped, yet the storehouse is ever full. Oh, what possibilities of life it opens up! What possibilities of growth! What possibilities of work! How a soul develops on God's will!

3. Friendship

The next thing the ideal man needs is society. Man is not made to be alone. He needs friendships. Without society, the ideal man would be a monster, a contradiction. You must give him friendship. Now, whom will you give him? Will you compliment him by calling upon the great men of the earth to come and minister to him? No. The ideal man does not want compliments. He has better food. Will you invite the ministers and the elders of the church to meet him? Will you offer him the companionship of saint or angel, or of seraphim or cherubim, as he treads his path through the wilderness of life? No; for none of these will satisfy him. He has a better friendship than saint or angel, seraphim or cherubim. The answer trembles on the lips of everyone who is trying to follow the ideal life: "*Whosoever shall do the will of my Father which is in heaven, the same is my brother, and sister, and mother*" (Matthew 12:50; see also Mark 3:35).

Yes. *My* brother and *My* sister and *My* mother. Mother! The path of life is dark and cheerless to you. There is a smoother path just by the side of it—a forbidden path. You have been tempted many a time to take it. But you knew it was wrong, and you paused. Then, with a sigh, you struck along the old weary path again. It was the will of God, you said. Brave mother! Oh, if you knew it, there was a voice at your ear just then, as Jesus saw the brave thing you had done, that said, "*My* mother!" "He who does the will of My Father, the same is *My* mother." Yes, this is the consolation of Christ—"My mother." What society to be in! What does the darkness of the path matter, if we have the brightness of His smile? Oh! It is better, as the hymnist says:

> It is better to walk in the dark with God,
> Than walk alone in the light;
> It is better to walk with Him by faith,
> Than walk alone by sight.[22]

Some young man here is suffering fierce temptation. Today, he feels strong; but tomorrow, his Sabbath resolutions will desert him. What will his companions say if he does not join them? He cannot face them if he is to play the Christian. Companions! What are all the companions in the world to this? What are all the friendships, the truest and the best, to this dear and sacred brotherhood of Christ? "He who does the will of My Father, *the same is my brother.*"

My mother, My brother, and My sister. Christ has a sister—some sister here. Sister! Your life is a quiet and even round of common and homely things. You dream, perhaps, of a wider sphere, and sigh for a great and useful life, like some women whose names you know. You question whether it is right that life is such a little bundle of very little things. But nothing is little that is done for God, and it must be right if it is His will. And if this common life, with its homely things, is God's discipline for you, be assured that in your small corner, your unobserved, your unambitious, your simple woman's lot is very near and very dear to Him who said, "Whoever does the will of My Father, the same is My sister."

Now we have found the ideal man a Friend. But he needs something more.

4. Language

The ideal man needs language. He must speak to his Friend. He cannot be silent in such company. And speaking to such a Friend is not mere conversation. It has a higher name. It is communion. It is prayer. Well we listen to hear the ideal man's prayer. It must be something about God's will, for that is what he is sure to talk about. That is the object of his life. That is his meat. In that, he finds his society. So, he will be sure to talk about it. Everyone knows what his prayer will be. Everyone remembers the words of the ideal prayer: "*Thy will be done*" (Matthew 6:10).

Note the emphasis on "*done.*" He prays that God's will may be done. It is not that God's will may be "borne," "endured," "put up with." There is activity in his prayer. It is not mere resignation. How often is this prayer intoned with mere endurance, tolerance, passivity. "Thy will be done," people say resignedly. "There is no help for it. We might as well submit. God evidently means to have His way. Better to give in at once and make the most of it."

This is far from the ideal prayer. It is a great thing to say this, but not in this spirit. It may be nobler to suffer God's will than to do it; perhaps it is. But there is nothing noble in resignation of this sort—this resignation under protest, as it were. And it disguises the meaning of the prayer "Thy will be done." Again, this prayer is intensely active. It is not an acquiescence simply in God's dealing. It is a cry for more of God's dealing—God's dealing with me, with everybody, with the whole world, with everything. It is an appeal to the mightiest energy in heaven or earth to work, to make more room for itself, to energize. It is a prayer that the almighty energies of the divine will may be universally known, felt, and worshipped.

The ideal man has no deeper prayer than this. It is the truest language of his heart. He does not want a bed of roses, nor his pathway strewn with flowers. He wants to do God's will. He does not want health or wealth, nor does he covet sickness or poverty—just what God sends. He does not want success—even success in winning souls—or lack of success. All he wants is what God wills for him. He does not want to prosper in business, or to barely keep struggling on. God knows what is best. He does not want his friends to live; himself to live or die. God's will be done. The currents of his life are deeper than the circumstances of things. There is a deeper principle in it than to live to gratify himself. And so, he simply asks that, in the ordinary round of his daily life, there may be no desire of his heart more deep, more vivid, more absorbingly present than this: "Thy will be done" (Matthew 6:10).

He who makes this the prayer of his life will know that of all prayer it is the most truly blessed, the most nearly in the spirit of Him who sought not His own will, but the will of Him who sent Him.

> My Jesus, as Thou wilt!
> If among thorns I go,
> Still sometimes here and there
> Let a few roses blow.
> But Thou on earth along
> The thorny path hast gone,
> Then lead me after Thee.
> My Lord, Thy will be done![23]

5. Praise

But the ideal man does not always pray. There is such perfect blessedness in praying the ideal prayer that language sometimes fails him. The peace of God passes all understanding (see Philippians 4:7), much less all expression. It comes down upon the soul and makes it ring with unutterable joy. And language stops. The ideal man can no longer pray to his Friend. So, his prayer changes into praise. He is too full to speak, so his heart bursts into song. Therefore, we must find in the Bible the praise of the ideal man's lips.

And who does not remember in the Psalms the song of the ideal man? The huntsmen would gather at night to sing of their prowess in the chase; the shepherd would chant the story of the lion or the bear that he killed as he watched his flocks. But David took down his harp and sang a sweeter psalm than all: *"Thy statutes have been my songs in the house of my pilgrimage"* (Psalm 119:54). He knew no sweeter strain. How different from those who think God's law is a stern, cold thing! God's law is His written will. It has no terrors to the ideal man. He is not afraid to think of its sternness and majesty. "I will meditate on Your laws day and night," he says. (See Psalm 1:2.) He tells us the subject of his thoughts. Ask him what he is thinking about at any time. "God's laws," he says. How he can please his Master. What more he can bear for Him. What next he can do for Him. He has no other pleasure in life than this. You need not speak to him of the delights of life.

"I will delight myself in thy statutes" (Psalm 119:16), he says. You see what amusements the ideal man has. You see where the sources of his enjoyment are. Praise is the overflow of a full heart. When it is full of enjoyment, it overflows; and you can tell the kind of enjoyment from the kind of praise that runs over. The ideal man's praise is of the will of God. He has no other sources of enjoyment. The cup of the world's pleasure has no attraction for him. The delights of life are bitter. Here is his only joy, his only delight: *"I delight to do thy will, O my God"* (Psalm 40:8).

6. Education

The next thing the ideal man needs is education. He needs teaching. He must take his place with the other disciples at his Master's feet. What does he need from the great Teacher? To be taught wisdom? No. Wisdom is not enough. To be taught what truth is? No, not even that. To be taught how to do good, how to love, how to trust? No, there is a deeper need than all these. "*Teach me to do thy will*" (Psalm 143:10). This is the true education. This was the education of Christ. Wisdom is a great study; likewise, truth and good works and love and trust are great studies. But there is an earlier lesson—obedience. So, the ideal pupil prays, "*Teach me to do thy will.*"

7. The Ideal Promise

And now we have gone almost far enough. These are really all the things the ideal man can need. But, in case he should lack anything else, God has given the man after his own heart a promise. God provides for everything. An emergency might arise in the ideal man's life; or, he might make a mistake or lose heart or be afraid to ask his Friend for some very great thing he needs, thinking it is too much; or for some very little thing, thinking it unworthy of notice.

So God has given the ideal promise: "*If we ask any thing according to his will, he heareth us: and…we know that we have the petitions that we desired of him*" (1 John 5:14–15). If he asks anything—no exception, no limit to God's confidence in him. God trusts him to ask right things. If he is a man after God's own heart, God is guiding him, even in what he asks; so, God sets no limit to his power. If anyone is doing God's will, let him ask anything. It is His will that he ask anything. Let him put God's promise to the test.

Notice what the true basis of prayer is. The prayer that is answered is the prayer that is given according to God's will. And the reason for this is plain. What is God's will is God's wish. And when a person does what God wills, he does what God wishes done. Therefore, God will have that done at any cost, at any sacrifice. Thousands of prayers are never answered, simply because God does not wish them. If we pray for any one thing, or any number of things, that we are sure God wishes, we may be sure our wishes will be gratified. For our wishes are only the reflection of God's wishes.

And the wish in us is almost equivalent to the answer. It is the answer casting its shadow backward. Already, the thing is done in the mind of God. It casts two shadows—one backward, one forward. The backward shadow— that is the wish before the thing is done, which sheds itself in prayer. The forward shadow—that is the joy after the thing is done, which sheds itself in praise. Oh, what a rich and wonderful life this ideal life must be! Asking anything, getting everything, willing with God, praying with God, praising with God. Surely, this last promise is too much. How can God trust us with a power so deep and awesome? Ah, He can trust the ideal life with anything. "If he asks anything…." Well, if he does, he will ask nothing amiss. If it is asked, it will be God's will. If it is not asked, it will be God's will. For this man has come *to do God's will.*

8. A Hope for the Future

There is only one thing more that the model man may ever wish to have. As he thinks of the unspeakable beauty of this life—of its angelic purity, its divine glory, its Christlike unselfishness, its heavenly peace—we can imagine him wondering how long this life will last. It may seem too bright and beautiful, for all things fair must soon come to an end. And, if any cloud could cross the true Christian's sky, it would be when he thought that this ideal life might cease. But, in the riches of His forethought, God has rounded off this corner of his life with a great, far-reaching text, which looks above the circumstance of him, and projects his life into the vast eternity beyond. *"He that doeth the will of God abideth for ever"* (1 John 2:17).

May God grant that you and I may learn to live this great and holy life, remembering the solemn words of Him who lived it first, who alone lived it all: *"Not every one that saith unto me, Lord, Lord, shall enter into the kingdom of heaven; but he that doeth the will of my Father which is in heaven"* (Matthew 7:21).

PENITENCE

*"And the Lord turned, and looked upon Peter....
And Peter went out, and wept bitterly."*
—Luke 22:61–62

At some time in his life, every person has fallen. Many people have fallen many times; few have fallen few times. And the more a person knows his life, and watches its critical flow from day to day, the larger the number of these falls seems to grow, and the oftener he reaches out to God with his penitential prayer, "Turn yet again, O Lord!"

We have all shuddered as we have read the tale of Peter's guilt. Many a time, we have watched the plot as it thickens around him, and felt the almost unconscious sympathy that betrayed itself. How similar the story was to what we have sometimes experienced. And as we followed the dreary stages of his fall, we knew that the same well-worn steps have been traced since then by every human foot.

Everyone who has an inner history can understand how Peter could have slept in the garden when he should have watched and prayed. (See, for example, Luke 22:39–46.) The best of us will not challenge the faithlessness that made him follow Christ *"afar off"* (Matthew 26:58; Mark 14:54; Luke 22:54), instead of staying by his Master's side. For we, too, know what it is to sometimes get out of step with Christ. We will be the last to stop and ask his business in that worldly company who warmed themselves by the fire. And none who knows that the heart is *"deceitful above all things"* (Jeremiah 17:9) will wonder that this man who had lived so long in the inner circle of fellowship with Christ, whose eyes were familiar with miracles, who was one of that most select audience who witnessed the glory of the transfiguration—that this man, when his ears were yet full of the most solemn words the world had ever heard, when his heart was warm still with Communion table thoughts—would have turned his back on his Lord and, almost before the sacramental wine was dry upon his lips, cursed Him to His face. Alas! Such things are not strange to those who know the parts in the appalling tragedy of sin.

But there is a greater fact in Peter's life than his sin—a much lesser-known fact: Peter's penitence. The entire world is united with Peter in his sin, but not everyone is with him in his penitence. Sinful Peter is one man, and repentant Peter is another; and many people who have kept his company along these worn steps to sin have left him to trace the tear-washed path of penitence alone. But the real lesson in Peter's life is the lesson in repentance. His fall is a lesson in sin that requires no teacher, but his repentance is a great lesson in salvation. And Peter's penitence is full of the deepest spiritual meaning to all who have ever made Peter's discovery—that they have sinned.

Four Outstanding Characteristics of the State of Penitence

The few words that form the sorrowful sequel to the tale of Peter's sin may be defined as "the ideal progress of Christian penitence." They contain materials for the analysis of the most rare and difficult grace in spiritual experience. And, lying underneath the two simple sentences of our text are the secrets of some of the most valuable spiritual laws. We find there four outstanding characteristics of the state of penitence:

1. *It is a divine thing.* It began with God. Peter did not turn. Rather, *"the Lord turned, and looked upon Peter."*

2. *It is a very sensitive thing.* A look did it. *"The Lord...looked upon Peter."*

3. *It is a very intense thing.* *"Peter went out, and wept bitterly."*

4. *It is a very lonely thing.* *"Peter went out"*—out into the quiet night, to be alone with his sin and with God.

These four qualities are characteristic not only of the penitential state but of all God's operations on the soul.

1. Penitence Is a Divine Thing

We find that the beginning of this strange experience came from God. It was not Peter who turned. The Lord turned and looked upon him. When the cock crowed, that might have recalled Peter to himself; he was just in the very act of sin. (See, for example, Luke 22:34, 61.) And, when someone is in the thick of his sin, his last thought is to throw down his arms and repent. So, Peter never thought of turning, but the Lord turned; and when Peter would rather have looked anywhere else than at the Lord, the Lord looked at him. And this scarce-noticed fact is a great sermon to everyone who sins: The Lord turns first.

The result of this distinction is this: There are two kinds of sorrow for sin. They are different in their origin, in their religious value, and in their influence on our life. The commoner kind is when a person does wrong, and, in the ordinary sense of the word, is sorry that he has done it. We are always more at ease in such a case when sorrow comes. It seems to provide a sort of guarantee that we are not disposed to do the same again, and that our better self is still alive enough to enter its protest against the sin that the lower self has done. And we count this feeling of reproach that treads so closely on the act as a sort of compensation or atonement for the wrong. This is a kind of sorrow that is well-known to all who examine themselves and who in any way struggle with sin. It is a kind of sorrow that is coveted by all who examine themselves; it gives relief to what is called a penitential heart, and lends fervor to many a penitential prayer.

But the startling truth is that there is no religion in such a state. There is no real penitence there. It may not contain even one ingredient of true repentance. It is all that many people know of repentance, and all that many people have for repentance, but it is not true sorrow for sin. It is wounded self-love. It is sorrow that we were weak enough to sin. We thought we were stronger men and women, but when we were put to the test, we found, to our chagrin, that we had failed. And this chagrin is what we are apt to mistake for penitence.

But this penitence is no divine gift or grace—it is merely wounded pride; it is sorrow that we did not do better, that we were not as good as we and our neighbors had thought. It is just as if Peter had turned and looked upon Peter. And when Peter turns and looks upon Peter, he sees what a poor, weak creature Peter is. If God had not looked upon Peter, he might have wept well-nigh as bitterly, not because he had sinned against his God, but because he, the great apostle, had done a weak thing—he was as weak as other men.

The fit of low spirits that comes to us when we find ourselves overtaken in a fault, though we flatter ourselves to reckon it a certain sign of penitence, and a setoff to the sin itself that God will surely take into account, is often nothing more than vexation and annoyance with ourselves that, after all our good resolutions and attempts at reformation, we have broken down again.

Contrast, for a moment, such a penitence with the publican's prayer of penitence in the temple. (See Luke 18:9–14.) It was not chagrin or wounded pride with him. And, as we read the story, we feel that the Lord must have turned and looked upon the publican when he cried, "God"— as if God were looking right down into the man's eyes—"*God be merciful to me a sinner*" (Luke 18:13). Stricken before his God, this publican had little thought of the self-respect he had lost, and he did not feel it to be an indignity to take the culprit's place and to be taught the true divinity of a culprit's penitence.

Now, it will be seen at once that the difference between the publican's penitence and the first-named sorrow is exactly the difference between the human and the divine. The one is God turning and looking upon man; the other is man turning and looking upon himself. There is no wrong in a person's turning and looking upon himself—but there is danger. There is the danger of misinterpreting what he sees and what he feels. What he feels is the mortification and the self-reproach of the sculptor who has made an unlucky stroke of the chisel; the chagrin of the artist who has spoiled the work of weeks by a clumsy touch. Apart from religion altogether, we must feel mortified when we do wrong. Life, surely, is a work of art. Character-building, soul-culture, is the highest kind of art; and it would be strange, indeed, if failure passed by without the mind resenting it.

But what is complained of is not that it passes by without the mind resenting it, but that it passes by without the soul resenting it. There must be penitence of some sort; but, in the one case, it is purely artistic; in the other, it is spiritual. And the danger is the more subtle, because the higher the character is, the more there must necessarily be of the purely artistic penitence.

The effect is that self gets into what ought to be the most genuine experience of life, makes the most perfect imitation of it, and transforms the greatest opportunities for recovery into the basest ministry to pride. The true experience, on the other hand, is a touching lesson in human helplessness; it teaches that God has to come to a person's relief at every turn of his life, and how the same hand that provides his pardon actually has to draw him to the place of penitence.

God looking into the sinner's face has introduced a Christian element into human sorrow. And Paul, in making the Christian vocabulary, had to coin a word that was strange to all the philosophies of the world then, and is so still, when he joined the concepts of God and sorrow into one, and told us of the *"godly sorrow"* that had the marvelous virtue of working repentance not to be repented of. (See 2 Corinthians 7:10.) And it is this new and sacred sorrow that comes to sinful men as often as the Lord turns and looks upon their life; it is this that adds the penitential incense of true penitence to the sacrifice of a broken and contrite heart. As Luke brings out, that was a great distinction in the prodigal's life: between coming to himself and coming to his father. *"He came to himself"* (Luke 15:17), and then, *"he...came to his father"* (Luke 15:20). So, we are always coming to ourselves. We are always finding out, like the prodigal, the miserable bargains we have made. But it is only when we come to our Father that we can get them undone and have the real debt discharged.

2. Penitence Is a Very Sensitive Thing

Second, we come to the sensitiveness of penitence. Or, perhaps, we should rather talk of the sensitiveness of the penitent human soul. *"The Lord turned, and looked upon Peter."* There is nothing more sensitive in the entire world than a human soul that has once been quickened into its delicate life by the touch of the divine. Men seldom estimate aright the exquisite beauty and tenderness of a sinner's heart. We apply coarse words to move it, and coarse, harsh stimulants to beat it into life. And, if no answer comes, we make the bludgeon heavier and the language coarser still, as if the soul were not too fine to respond to weapons as blunt as these. There is coarseness in the fibers of the body, and these may be moved by blows; and there is coarseness in human nature, and that may be roused by threats. But the soul is as fine as a breath; and it will preserve, through misery and cruelty and sin, the marvelous delicacy that shows how near it lies to the Spirit of God who gave it birth.

Peter was naturally, perhaps, the coarsest of all the disciples. Our picture of him is of a strong-built, suntanned fisherman, robust and fearless in disposition, quick-tempered and rash, a man who would bluster and swear—as we know he did—a wild man who had the making of a memorable sinner, if God had not made him a memorable saint. But inside this wild breast, there lay a most lovely and delicate plant—the most tender plant, perhaps, but one that God had growing on the earth. With His own hand, He had placed it there. With His own breath, He nourished it from day to day; and already the storms in the wild breast were calmed and tempered for the holy flower that had begun to send a perfume through even coarse Peter's life. It always purifies a man to have a soul, and there is no such beauty of character as that which comes out in unconscious ways from a life made fine by Christ.

So, God did not thunder and lightning to make Peter hear His voice. God knew that although Peter was blustering and swearing with his lips, there was dead silence in his soul. A whisper at that moment—that moment of high-strung feeling—a whisper, even at that moment, was not fine enough in its touch for this exquisitely sensitive spirit; so, the Lord turned and *looked*. A look, and that was all. But it rent his heart as lightning could not, and melted into his soul.

There is a text in the Psalms that uses the strange expression of the *"gentleness"* of God. (See Psalm 18:35.) When God is so great, so awesome in majesty, we wonder sometimes that He uses so little violence with us, who are so small. But it is not His way. His way is to be gentle. He seldom drives; instead, He draws. He seldom compels; instead, He leads. He remembers that we are dust. (See Psalm 103:14.)

We think it might be quicker work if God were to threaten us and compel us to do right. Yet God does not want quick work but good work. God does not want slave work but free work. Thus, God is gentle with us all, molding us and winning us many a time with no more than a silent look. Coarse treatment never wins souls. Therefore, God did not drive the chariot of His omnipotence up to Peter and command him to repent. God did not threaten him with the thunderbolts of punishment. God did not even speak to him. That one look laid a spell upon his soul that was greater than any voice or language he would hear for the rest of his life.

Here, then, are two great lessons—the gentleness of God, and the gentleness of the soul—the one as divine a marvel as the other. God may be dealing with us in some quiet way right now, and we are unaware of it. So mysteriously has our life been shaped, and so unobtrusive are the fingers that mold our will, that we scarcely believe it has been the hand of God at all. But it is God's gentleness. And the reason why God made Peter's heart sensitive—and yours and mine, too—was to meet this gentleness of His.

Yes, we altogether misunderstand God—and religion—if we think that God deals coarsely with our souls. If we ask ourselves what, primarily, has influenced our life, we find the answer in a few silent voices that have preached to us, and winds that have passed across our soul so gently that we could scarcely tell when they had come or gone. The great physical forces of the world are all silent and unseen. The most ponderous of all—gravity—came down the ages with steps so noiseless that centuries of wise men had passed away before an ear was quick enough to detect its footfall. And the great spiritual forces that startle men into thoughts of God and of what is right; that make men remember, in the rush of the world's life, that they have souls; that bring eternity near to us, when time is yet sweet and young; are not so much the warnings from the dead who drop at our side, nor the threats of judgment to come, nor the retributions of the life that is; rather, they are still, small voices that penetrate, like the look Christ gave Peter, and turn man's sensitive heart to God. The likeness of a long-dead mother's face; the echo of a children's hymn laden with pure memories, coming over the guilty years that lie between; the fragments of an old, forgotten text—these are the messengers that heaven sends to call the world to God. Let those who are waiting for Christ to thunder at their door before they will let Him in remember that the quiet service of the Sabbath day, and the soft whisper of text and psalm, and the pang of conscience, and the deep, deep heart-wish to be whole, are Christ's ways of looking for them. Let workers for Christ remember this. In our soul, let us consider how God may be turning and looking upon us, and searching our hearts, as He did Peter's, for signs of penitence.

Let those who try to keep their influence for Christ ponder Christ's methods of influence. Let those who live in the shade, whose lives are naturally bounded by timidity and reserve, be glad that, in the genius of Christianity, there is a place for even the "gospel of the face." And let those who live in the battle, when coarser weapons fail, discern the lesson of Elijah:

> A great and strong wind rent the mountains, and brake in pieces the rocks before the LORD; but the LORD was not in the wind: and after the wind, an earthquake; but the LORD was not in the earthquake: and after the earthquake a fire; but the LORD was not in the fire: and after the fire a still small voice.   (1 Kings 19:11–12)

3. Penitence Is a Very Intense Thing

We will look at the third point only briefly, for this truth is obvious. We learn from Peter's recovery that spiritual experience is *intense*. "Peter went out, and wept bitterly." This short sentence forever settles the question of emotion in religion. When the Lord turned and looked upon Peter, and memory crushed into one vivid moment the guilt of those never-to-be-forgotten hours, what else could Peter do but weep bitterly? Let memory so work on any of our lives today, and let the eye of the Eternal bring the naked truth out from our past, and then let us ask if "*bitterly*" is too strong a word to express the agony of God's discovery of our sin. Peter had much need, indeed, to weep bitterly; and if, at times, there are no bitter tears in our religious life, it is not because we have less of Peter's sin but little of Peter's grace.

It is vain to console ourselves by measuring, as we try to do, the small size of the slips we make as compared with his. There is such a thing in the world as a great sin, but there is no such thing as a small sin. The smallest sin is a fall, and a fall is a fall from God; and to fall from God is to fall from the greatest height in the universe. The publicity of a sin has nothing to do with its size. Our fall last week, or yesterday, or today, was just as great, perhaps, as Peter's fall, or David's, or Noah's, or Jacob's, or the many private sins that history has made public examples, or that the Bible has placed as beacons for the whole human race.

Every sin that was ever committed demands a bitter penitence. And if there is little emotion in a person's religion, it is because there is little introspection. *Religion without emotion is religion without reflection.* Let a person sit down calmly to think about his life. Let him think about how God has dealt with him since he first spoke God's name. Let him add to that how he has dealt with God ever since he could sin. And, as he turns over the secrets of the past, and forgotten sins come crowding one by one into his thoughts, can he help having a strong emotion rise in his heart and shed itself in tears? Yes, religion without emotion is religion without reflection. And, conversely, the person who gives himself to earnest thought about his ways will always have enough emotion to generate religious fervor in his soul.

However, let religious emotion run in the right channel. Let it work itself out in action and not in excited feeling—let it be something more than nervous agitation or mere fear—and there is no experience more purifying to the soul. No doubt, it was a great thing for Peter that he wept bitterly. And, no doubt, from the bitterness of that night of penitence came much of the sweetness that hallowed his life afterward.

4. Penitence Is a Very Lonely Thing

Last, penitence is a lonely thing. When the Lord turned, He looked upon *Peter*. No one else noticed the quiet glance that was exchanged. But it did its work. In a moment, it singled out one man and cut him off from all the rest of the world. *"And Peter went out...."* There was no man beneath the firmament of God that night as alone as Peter with his sin.

It has been said that men know two kinds of loneliness—a loneliness of space and a loneliness of spirit. The fisherman in his boat on the wide sea knows loneliness of space. Yet that is not true loneliness, for his thoughts have peopled his boat with the forms of those he loves. But Peter had a loneliness of spirit. A distance wider than the wide sea cut off the denier from all fellowship with man, and left him to mourn alone. All this is spiritual truth.

When God speaks, He likes no other voice but His own to break the stillness. Hence the place that has always been given to solitude in all true religious life. It can be overdone, but it can also be grossly underdone. There is no lesson more worth insisting on in days like ours than this: When God wants to speak with a person, He wants that person to be alone. And God develops the germ of the recluse enough in all true Christian hearts to see that it is done. "Talent forms itself in solitude," says the German poet; "character amidst the storms of life."[24] And if religious character is developed and strengthened in the battle of the world, it is no less true that religious talents are cultivated in quiet contemplation and communion alone with God. There are none more profoundly to be pitied than the worshippers who do all their religion in public; and he who does not know what it is to sometimes go out from the crowd and be alone with God is a stranger to the most divine experience that comes to sanctify a Christian's heart.

But what gave beauty to Peter's loneliness was this: He took God's time to be alone. Peter's penitence was not only intense and lonely; it was also immediate. Peter did not have to "go out." He might have stood where he was and braved it out. There have been times when God has looked at us when we were sinning, but we did not do as Peter did. He lost no time between his sin and his penitence. Many times, we spoil the grace of our penitence by waiting until the sin grows old. We do it on purpose. Time seems to smooth the roughness off our sin and take away its bitterness. We postpone our penitence until we think the edge is off the sharpness of the wrong. As if time, as if eternity, could ever make a sinner's sin less black. Sin is always at its maximum. And, no one ever gets off with penitence at its minimum. The time for penitence is exactly the time when we have sinned. And, perhaps, that time is now. Peter's penitence came sharp upon his sin. It was not on his deathbed or in his afterlife, but just when he had sinned. Many a person who postpones his penitence until he cannot help it postpones his penitence until it cannot help him; he will not see the Lord turning until He turns and looks upon him in judgment. Then, indeed, he goes out to weep. But it is out into that night that knows no dawn.

When the Lord Looks at You

Such are the lessons from Peter's penitence. Just one more thought: When God speaks to you, He speaks so loudly that all the voices of the world seem mute. And yet, when God speaks, He speaks so softly that no one hears the whisper but you. Today, perhaps, the Lord has turned and looked at someone here. And the soul of someone has gone out to weep. No one noticed where the Lord's glance fell, and no one in the church knows that it was on *you*. You sit there in your usual place. But your spirit is far away right now, dealing with some old sin, and God Himself is giving you a lesson—the bitterest yet sweetest lesson of your life—in heartfelt penitence. Do not come back into the crowd until the Lord has turned and looked at you again, as He looked at the thief upon the cross (see Luke 23:39–43), and you have beheld "the glory of the love of God in the face of Jesus." (See 2 Corinthians 4:6.)

WHAT IS GOD'S WILL?

*"The God of our fathers hath chosen thee,
that thou shouldest know his will."*
—Acts 22:14

Today, we resume the subject of the will of God. We have already tried to learn two lessons in this regard:

1. That the purpose of Christ's life was to do the will of God. Jesus said, "I came to do the will of Him who sent Me." (See John 6:38.)

2. That the purpose of our life is to do the will of God.

"The Chief End of Man"

To help us recall what we learned earlier, let us compare this description of our purpose in life to another definition of our purpose with which we are all familiar. Of course, the above description is not the most complete statement of the aim of our life, but it is the most practical; and, again, if we will refer to it for a moment, it will help us to remember the conclusions we came to previously.

For instance, our Shorter Catechism[25] puts the purpose of life in quite different words. "Man's chief end," it says, "is to glorify God, and to enjoy Him forever." But this answer is simply too great for us. It is too great to understand. It is wonderfully conceived and put together, but it goes past us. There is too much in it. It is really the same answer, but turned toward God. It is as true as the other answer, but too profoundly true. It expresses the purpose of life God-ward; it determines the quality of all the things we do by the extent to which they make way in the world for the everywhere-coming glory of God. But, again, this is too wonderful for us. We need a principle life-ward as well as God-ward. We need something to tell us what to do with the things beneath us and around us and within us, as well as the things above us.

Our Purpose Is to Do God's Will

Therefore, there is a human side to the Shorter Catechism's answer, which we can state thus:

What is the chief end of man?

Man's chief end is to do the will of God.

In one sense, this is not such a divine answer. But we are not divine. We understand God's will—God's glory—only faintly. We are still only human, and "glory" is a word for heaven.

Ask a schoolboy who is learning the first question in the Catechism to do a certain thing for the glory of God. The opportunity of doing the thing may be gone before the idea can be driven into the boy's head of what the glory of God means. But tell him to do the thing because it is God's will that he should do it—he understands that. He knows that God's will is just what God likes, and what he himself probably does not like. The concept of it from this side is so clear that even a schoolboy need not miss the purpose of life—for that purpose is simply doing what God likes. If our souls are not great enough, then, to think of God's glory as the practical rule of life, let them not be too small to think of God's will. And, if we look after the end of life from this side, God will look after it from the other. If we do the will of God, God will see that it glorifies Him.

Let us suppose, then, that after casting about for an object in life, we have at last come to a stop, because we've found the answer: The purpose of my life is to do the will of God. Let us suppose, also, that we have gotten over the disappointment of finding that there is nothing *higher* for us to do in the world. Or, perhaps, taking the other side, suppose we are beginning to feel the splendid conviction that, after all, our obscure life is not to be wasted; that having this ideal principle within it, it may yet be as great in its homely surroundings as the greatest human life—seeing that no one can do more with his life than the will of God; that though we may never be famous or powerful or called to heroic suffering or acts of self-denial that will vibrate through history; that though we are not intended to be apostles or missionaries or martyrs but to be common people living in common houses, spending the day in common offices or common kitchens; yet, doing the will of God there, we shall do as much as apostle or missionary or martyr—seeing that they can do no more than do God's will where they are, even as we can do as much where we are, and answer the end of our life as truly, faithfully, and triumphantly as they.

Is It Possible to Do God's Will?

Suppose that we feel all this, and we desire, as we stand on the threshold of the truly ideal life, that, God helping us, we will live it, if we may. The chief end of life is to do the will of God. We are met at once with these questions: "How are we ever to know what the will of God is—to know it clearly and definitely? Is it possible? And if so, how?"

Now, to begin with, we probably have an opinion on the matter already. And if you were to express it, it would be this: It is *not* possible. You have thought about the will of God, and read and thought, and thought and read, and you have come to the conclusion that the will of God is a very mysterious thing—a very mysterious thing that some people *may* have revealed to them, though it does not seem in any way possible for you. Your nature is different from other people's; and though you have strained your eyes in prayer and thought, you have never yet seen the will of God. And if you ever have been in the same line with it, it has been only by chance, for you can see no principle in it, nor any certainty of ever being in the same line again. Indeed, you can recall one or two special occasions when you think you were near the will of God, but they must have been special interpositions on God's part. He does not show His will like that every day. Once or twice, alone, in a lifetime—that is enough of this high experience one can ever dare expect.

Now, of course, if this is true—if the thing is impossible—it is clearly no use going on to find out what God's will is. If this experience is correct, and we cannot know God's will due to the mystery of it, we may as well give up the ideal life at once. But if you were to examine this opinion, even cursorily, you would find at once how far away from the point it was.

In the first place, it is based exclusively on your own experience—not on God's thoughts regarding it, but on your own thoughts. The true name for this is *presumption*.

Second, it assumes that, since the purpose of life is to do God's will, and you are unable to know God's will, you are therefore not responsible for fulfilling the purpose of life. This is *self-deception*.

It also suggests the idea that God *could* teach you His will, if He liked, seeing that He has done so once or twice, by your own admission. And yet, although He wants you to do His will, and you want to do it, too, He deliberately refuses to tell you what it is. This is *an accusation against God*.

It is something worse than unreasonable, therefore, to say that we think it is hopeless for us ever to know God's will. Indeed, on the contrary, there is a strong supposition that we would find it out. For, if it is so important a thing that the very purpose of life is involved in it, it would be absurd to imagine that God would keep us even the least in the dark as to what His will is.

And this supposition is changed into a certainty when we balance our minds for a moment on the terms of this text: "*The God of our fathers hath chosen thee, that thou shouldest know his will.*" It is not simply a matter of supposition; it is a matter of *election*. Have you ever thought about this strange, deep calling of God? We are called to salvation—we have thought of that. We are called to holiness—we have thought of that. But this truth is as great as either of the others: We are called to know God's will. We are answering the other parts of our call. Are we answering it in this: What is God's will? *Are* we knowing God's will? How much have we learned of that to which we have been called? And, is it our continual prayer, as it was his who said these words, that we may *be filled with the knowledge of [God's] will* (Colossians 1:9)?

It is a reasonable object of search, then, to find out what God's will for us is. And it is a reasonable expectation that we may find it out so fully as to know, at any moment, whether we are in line with it or not; and when difficulty arises about the next step of our life, we may have absolute certainty about which way God's will inclines. There are many kinds of assurance in religion; and it is as important to have assurance of God's will as it is to have assurance of God's salvation. For just as the loss of assurance of salvation means absence of peace and faith, as well as usefulness, so absence of assurance of God's will means a miserable Christian life, imperfect Christian character, and impaired Christian usefulness.

We start our investigation, therefore, in the belief that God must have light for all of us on the subject of His will, and with the desire to have assurance in the guidance of our life by God as clear and strong as that of our redemption and salvation by Christ.

In one sense, of course, no one can know the will of God, even as, in one sense, no one can know God Himself. God's will is a great and infinite mystery—a thing of mighty mass and volume, which can no more be measured out to hungry souls in human sentences than the eternal knowledge of God or the boundless love of Christ can. But even as there is a sense in which one poor human soul can hold enough of the eternal knowledge of God and the boundless love of Christ, so there is a sense in which God can put as much of His will into human words as human hearts can bear—as much as human wills can will or human lives can perform.

Two Aspects of God's Will for Us

As we put God's will into human words, we find that it divides itself into two great parts:

1. The part of God's will that everyone may know—a universal part for everyone.

2. The part of God's will that no one knows but you—a particular part for you.

1. God's Universal Will

There is a part of God's will that everyone may know. It is written in divine characters in two sacred books, which every person may read. One of them is the Bible, and the other is nature. The Bible is God's will in words, in formal thoughts, in grace. Nature is God's will in matter and tissue and force. Nature is not often considered a part of God's will. But it is a part, and a great part, and the first part. And, perhaps one reason why some people never know the second is that they do not yield full obedience to the first.

Natural Laws

God's law of progress is from the lower to the higher; and scant obedience at the beginning of His will means disobedience with the rest. The laws of nature are the will of God for our bodies. As there is a will of God for our higher nature—the moral laws—there is just as emphatically a will of God for the lower—the natural laws. Therefore, if you want to know God's will in the higher, you must begin with God's will in the lower, which simply means this: If you want to live the ideal life, you must begin with the ideal body. The law of moderation, the law of sleep, the law of regularity, the law of exercise, the law of cleanliness—these are the laws, or will, of God for you. Natural laws are the beginning of God's will for you. And, if we are ambitious to get on to do God's will in the higher reaches, let us respect it as much in the lower; for there may be as much of God's will in minor things, as much of God's will in taking good bread and pure water, as in keeping a good conscience or living a pure life.

Whoever heard of gluttony, or laziness, or uncleanness, or the person who was careless and undisciplined in regard to natural life, doing God's will? If someone disobeys God in these, you have no certainty that he has any true principle for obeying God in anything else. For God's will does not only run into the church and the prayer meeting and the higher chambers of the soul but into the common rooms at home, down to wardrobe and larder and cellar; and into the bodily frame, down to blood and muscle and brain.

This, then, is the first contribution to the contents of the will of God. And, for distinction, these may be called the physical contents.

Moral Laws

Next in order, we come to the moral contents, both of these coming under the same heading as parts of God's will that everyone may know.

These moral contents, as we have seen, are contained in the Word of God. And the Bible has a variety of names for them, such as *"testimonies," "laws," "precepts," "statutes,"* and *"commandments."* This is a much more formidable array than the physical contents. It is one thing to be in physical condition—a prizefighter may be that, though not in a religious way—but it is quite another to be in moral condition. And it is a difficult matter to explain exactly what God's will is in this great sense; for, on the one hand, there is the danger of elevating it so high as to frighten the timid soul from ever attempting to reach it; and, on the other, the insensible tendency to lower it to human standards and aims.

However, it must be fully understood that, as far as its formidableness is concerned, that is absolutely unchangeable. God's moral law cannot be toned down into anything less binding, less absolutely moral, or less infinitely significant. Whatever it means is meant for everyone in its rigid truth as the definite and formal expression of God's will for him.

From the moral side, there are three different departments of God's will. Foremost, and apparently most rigid of all, are the Ten Commandments. Now, the Ten Commandments contain, in a few sentences, one of the largest-known portions of God's will. They form the strictest code of morality in the world; it is the basis of all others, the most venerable and universal expression of the will of God for mankind. After this comes the Beatitudes of Christ. This is another large portion of God's will. It forms the most unique code of morality in the world, the most complete and lovely additional expression of the will of God for Christians. Passing through the human heart of Christ, the older commandment of the Creator becomes the soft and mellow beatitude of the Savior—it passes from the colder domain of law, with a penalty on failure, to the warm region of love, with a benediction on success.

These are the two chief elements in the moral part of the will of God for mankind. But there is a third set of laws and rules that is not to be found exactly expressed in either of these. The Ten Commandments and the Beatitudes take up most of the room in God's will, but there are shades of precept still unexpressed that also have their place. Hence, we must add to all this mass of law and beatitude many more laws and many more beatitudes that lie enclosed in other texts, and in other words of Christ, which have their place like the rest as portions of God's will.

Here, then, we already know a great part of what God's will is, although, perhaps, we have not often called it by this name. And, before going on to discover any more, it may be worthwhile to pause for a moment and find out how to practice it. For, perhaps, when we see how great a thing this will of God is, our impulse for the moment is to wish we had not known it. We were building ourselves up with the idea that we were going to try this ideal life, and that it was easy and smooth compared with the life we left. There was a better future opening to us, with visions of happiness and holiness and even of usefulness to God. But our hopes are dashed now. How *can* we do God's will—this complicated mass of rules and statutes, each bristling with the certainty of a thousand breakages? How can we keep these ten grave laws, with their unflinching scorn of compromise and their exacting obligation, to the uttermost jot and tittle? How can our coarse spirits breathe the exquisite air of these Beatitudes, or fit our wayward wills to the narrow mold of all these binding texts? Can God know how weak we are, and how blind and biased toward the breakages, before we ever thought of Him? Can He think how impossible it is to keep these laws, even for one close-watched, experimental hour? Did Christ really mean it—not some lesser thing than this—when He taught in the ideal prayer that God's will was to be done on earth even as it is done in heaven?

There can be but one answer. "*God…hath chosen thee, that thou shouldest know his will.*" And God expects from each of us neither less nor more than this. He knows the frailty of our frame; He remembers that we are dust. (See Psalm 103:14.) And yet *such* dust that He has given each of us the divinest call to the vastest thing in heaven. There, beside our frailty, He lays down His holy will—lays it down confidingly, as if a child could take it in its grasp. And, as if He intends the child to cradle it and to carry it next to his heart, He says, "*If a man love me, he will keep my words*" (John 14:23).

There must be something, therefore, to ease the apparent hopelessness of doing this will of God—something to give us heart to go on with it, to give us strength to obey God's call. We were not prepared to find it running in to the roots of things like this; but there must be something brighter somewhere than the dark side we have seen. Well, then, let us think for a moment on the following points.

In the first place, there *must be* such laws. God is a King—His kingdom is the kingdom of heaven. His people are His subjects. Subjects must have laws. Therefore, we start with a necessity. Laws must be.

Second, it is a privilege to have these laws. Who is afraid of law? Good subjects? Never. Criminals are afraid of laws. Who dreads the laws of this country; who cries out against them; who would abolish them if they could? Drunkards, thieves, murderers. Who loves the laws of this country? The honest, the wise, and the good. Again, who are afraid of God's laws and would abolish them if they could? The wicked, the profligate, the licentious. But *you* would not. The just and holy, the pure in heart and life, love them and respect them. Even more, they demand them. It would be no kingdom without them—no kingdom worth belonging to. If it were not for its laws of truth and purity, and its promise of protection from unrighteousness and sin, it would have no attraction for them. It is the inaccessible might and purity of will in the kingdom of God that draws all other wills as subjects to its sway. It is not only not hard, therefore, that there should be such elements in God's will as law, but it is also a privilege.

Third, it is more than a privilege to have them—it is also a privilege to *do* them. And this is a particular privilege. It consists partly in forgetting that they are laws—in changing their names, such as *commandment*, *precept*, *testimony*, and *statute*, into this: the will of God. No sternness can then enter with the thought, for God's name is in the phrase, as well as the help of God, the power of God, and the constraining love of Christ. This takes away the hopelessness of trying to keep God's will. It makes it a personal thing, a relation to a living will rather than to didactic law.

Further, there is a wonderful provision near it. When God puts down His great will beside me, telling me to do it, He puts down right beside it something just as great—His love. And, as my soul trembles at the fearfulness of will, love comes with its calm omnipotence and draws it to itself, then takes my timid will and twines it around His, until mine is fierce with passion to serve, and strong to do His will—just as if some mighty task was laid to an infant's hand, and the engine-grasp of a giant strengthened it with his own.

Where God's law is, God's love is. Look at law—it withers your very soul with its stern, inexorable face. But look at love, or look at God's will, which means look at love's will, and you are reassured, and your heart grows strong. No martyr dies for abstract truth. For a Person, for God, he will die a triple death. Likewise, no one will die for God's law. But, for God, he will do it. Therefore, where God's will seems strong to command, God's love is strong to obey. Hence, the profound texts *"Love is the fulfilling of the law"* (Romans 13:10) and *"This is the love of God, that we keep his commandments: and his commandments are not grievous"* (1 John 5:3).

God's will, then, is as great as God and as high as heaven, yet as easy as love. For love knows no hardness and feels no yoke. It desires no yielding to its poverty in anything it loves. Let God be greater, and His will sterner, and love will be stronger and obedience only more true. Let not God come down to my level, slacken truth for me, make His will weaker for me. My interests, as subject to Him, are safer with my King, are greater with the greatness of my King. Only give me love—pure, burning love and loyalty to Him—and I will climb from law to law through grace and glory to the place beside the throne where the angels do His will.

There are two ways, therefore, of looking at God's will—one looking at the love side of it, the other at the law; the one ending in triumph, the other in despair; the one a liberty, the other a slavery. To make this fully clear—for this is the hardest point to hold—we might illustrate it in a simple way, such as the following example.

Suppose you occasionally go into a workshop and watch the workmen at their task. The majority of the workmen do their work in an uninterested, mechanical sort of way. Everything is done with the most proper exactness and precision—almost with slavish precision, a closer observation would reveal. They come *exactly* at the top of the hour in the morning, and they throw down their work *exactly*, to a second, when the closing bell has rung. There is a certain punctiliousness about them, and a scrupulosity about their work; and, as partly the cause of it, perhaps, you observe an uncomfortable turning of their head occasionally, as if some eye was upon them, then a dogged going on of their work again, as if it were always done under some restraint.

But, among the workmen, you also notice one who seems to work on different principles. As he goes about his work, there is a buoyancy and cheerfulness about him that is foreign to all the rest. You will sometimes see him at his place even before the bell has rung; and, if unfinished work is in his hands when closing time has come, he does not mind an extra five minutes when all the others are gone. What strikes you about him is the absence of that punctiliousness that marked the others' work. It does not seem at all a tyranny to him, but even a freedom and a pleasure; and though he is apparently not as mechanical in his movements as his fellow workers, his work seems better done and greater, despite the ease and light-heartedness that characterize him through its course.

Now, the difference between them is this: The first set of men are hired workmen. The man by himself is the master's son. Not that he is outwardly different; he is a common workman in a cotton jacket, like the rest. But he is the master's son. The first group works for wages, comes in at regulation hours—lest anything be kept off their wages—and keeps the laws of the workshop, in terror of losing their place. But the son keeps them, and keeps them better—not for wages but for love.

So, the Christian keeps the will, or the laws, of God because of the love of God. Not because they are workshop regulations framed and hung up in front of him at every moment of his life, but because they are his Master's will. They are as natural to him as air. He would never think of not keeping them. His meat is to do the will of his Father who is in heaven. (See John 4:34.)

There is no room for punctiliousness in this—the true way of doing God's will. A scrupulous Christian is a hired servant and not the Master's son.

2. God's Particular Will for the Individual

Then there is a part of God's will that is known only to you. There is God's will for the world, and God's will for the individual. There is God's will written on tablets of stone for the entire world to read. And there is

God's will carved in sacred hieroglyphic that no one reads but you. There is God's will rolling in thunder over the life of universal man. There is God's will dropped softly on the believer's ear in angel whispers or the still, small voice of God. To distinguish this final element in God's will from the physical and moral contents we discussed earlier, one might call it the more strictly spiritual content.

This is a distinct addition to the other parts of God's will—one that many people ignore, and other people deny. But there is such a region in God's will—a region unmapped in human charts, unknown to human books—a region for the pure in heart, for the upright, for the true. It is a land of mystery to those who do not know it, a land of foolishness, weaknesses, and delusive sights and sounds. But there is a land where the Spirit moves, a luminous land, a walking in God's light. That is where God's own people have their breathing from above, where each saint's steps are ordered by the Lord.

This region of God's will may be distinguished from the other regions in two ways. For one thing, by its secrecy. It is a private thing; it is between God and you. You want to know what to do next—your calling in life, for instance. You want to know what action to take in a certain matter. You want to know what to do with your money. You want to know whether to participate in a certain plan. Then, you enter into this private chamber of God's will, and ask the private question, "Lord, what would You have me do?"

Second, it is distinguished by its action. It concerns a different department of our life. The first part of God's will, all that has gone before, affects our *character*. But this part affects something more. It affects our *career*. And this is an important distinction. A person's career in life is almost as important as his character in life; that is to say, it is almost as important to God, which is the real question. If character is the goal of life, then the ideal career is exactly where character can best be established and developed, which means that a person is to live for his character. But if God's will is the purpose of life, God may have a will for my career, as well as for my character. This does not mean that a person is to live for his career, but rather for God's will in his character *through* his career.

I may want to put all my work into my character. But God may want my work for something else. For instance, He may want to use me; I may not know why, when, how, or for whom. But it is possible that He may need me for something or other at some time or other. It may be that I am needed throughout my life, or at some particular time in my life that may be past now, or may be still to come. Whatever the case, I must hold myself in readiness and let Him trace my path. For, although it does not look now as if He has anything for me to do, the next turn of the road may bring it; so, I must watch the turnings of the road for God. It is worthwhile doing this if there is even a *chance* that God would need me—the chance of His needing me even *once*.

There is a man in Scripture whom God used perhaps only once. This man may have done many other things for God; still, there was one thing God gave him to do that so far overshadowed all other things that he seems to have done only this. Indeed, he seems to have been born, to have lived and died, for this. It is the only thing we know about him. But it is a great thing. His name was Ananias, and he was the instrument in the conversion of Saul, who became the apostle Paul.

What was he doing in Damascus that day, when Saul arrived under conviction of sin? Why was he living in Damascus at all? Perhaps you will say, "Because he was born there, and his father before him." Let it be so. A few will be glad to cherish a higher thought. He was a good man, and his steps were ordered by ordinary means, if you like—by the Lord. Could not Ananias have been as good a man in Jericho, or in Antioch, or in Ephesus? Quite as good. His character might almost have been the same. But his career would have been different. And, possibly, his character might have been different from the touch of God upon his career. For, when God comes into a person's career, it sometimes makes a mighty difference in his character—teaches him to live less for character and for himself, and more for his career and for God; or, rather, to live more for both—more for his character by living more for his career. Gold is gold wherever it is; but it makes *some* difference to the world whether it is made into a Communion cup or gilds the proscenium of a theater.

There is a difference, then, between God in character and God in career. You may have God in your character without having God in your career. Perhaps you would have been in London today, or in China. Perhaps you would have been a missionary; perhaps you will be one yet. Perhaps you would have been in poorer circumstances, or in a different business alto-gether. Perhaps you have chosen a broader path than God would have willed for you. Your character may not *seem* to have suffered; but your career has. You may be doing God's will with one hand consecrated to Christ, and making your own autobiography with the other consecrated to self.

Do you want to know the will of God, then? Consult God about your career. It does not follow that, because He has done nothing with you last week or last year, He may have nothing for you now. God's will in career is mostly an unexpected thing—it comes as a surprise. God's servants work on short notice. On only a few hours' warning, Paul used to have to go off to what was the ends of the earth in those days. And so may you or I. This is not something to startle us, to be alarmed at, or to make us say, "If this might be the upshot, we will let God's will alone." It would be a wonderful privilege if this happened to you or me; yes, a wonderful privilege that He would count us worthy to suffer this or anything more for Him.

But you are old, you say. Ananias was old. Or steeped in a profession. Paul was steeped in a profession. Or, you are inexperienced and young, you say. A lad once came to Jesus with five loaves and two small fishes, but they fed five thousand men. So, bring your lad's experience, your young offer of service, and God may use you to twice five thousand souls. That does not mean that you are to do it. But be in God's counsels, and He will teach you whether you are or not.

How are you to know this secret will of God? It is a great question. We cannot explore it now. Let this suffice: It can be known. It can be known to you. "*The steps of a good man are ordered by the* Lord" (Psalm 37:23). "*I will guide thee with mine eye*" (Psalm 32:8). Unto the upright in heart, He will cause light to arise in darkness. This is not mysticism; it is no visionary's dream. It is not to drown reason with enthusiasm's airy hope, or to supersede the Word of God with fanaticism's blind caprice. No, it is not there. It is what Christ said of the Shepherd of the sheep: "*The sheep hear his voice: and he cal-leth his own sheep by name, and leadeth them*" (John 10:3).

THE RELATION OF GOD'S WILL TO SANCTIFICATION

"This is the will of God, even your sanctification."
—1 Thessalonians 4:3

"As he which hath called you is holy, so be ye holy in all manner of conversation [behavior]; because it is written, Be ye holy; for I am holy."
—1 Peter 1:15–16

"Lo, I come to do thy will, O God....By the which will we are sanctified through the offering of the body of Jesus Christ once for all."
—Hebrews 10:9–10

Two Sabbaths ago, our discussion of the will of God landed us— perhaps in a rather unforeseen way—in the great subject of sanctification. You may remember that we then made the discovery that the end of sanctification, in the sense of consecration, is to do the will of God, and that the proof was based on these words: *"Present your bodies a living sacrifice, holy, acceptable unto God....And be not conformed to this world..."* (Romans 12:1–2). Why? *"...that ye may prove what is that good, and acceptable, and perfect, will of God"* (Romans 12:2). We are to present ourselves to God, not because it is a pleasant and luxurious thing to live in the state of consecration, but to do the will of God. To sum this up in a single sentence: "This is sanctification, even to prove the will of God."

But our first text is apparently the very opposite of this: *"This is the will of God, even your sanctification."* Last time, it looked as if sanctification was for the purpose of the will of God; now, it looks as if the will of God is for the purpose of sanctification.

It is evident, therefore, that there is still something in this part of the subject that demands an explanation. And, in order to gain that explanation, it will be necessary to present the other side of the same question, and complete the view of the subject of holiness itself.

The Meaning of "Sanctification"

In the Bible, there are two great meanings of the word *"sanctification."* The first may roughly be called the Old Testament meaning. The second is identified—though not exclusively—with the New Testament. The Old Testament meaning had this trait: It did not necessarily imply any inward change in the sanctified heart. In fact, it was not even necessarily applied to hearts at all, but to things. A field could be sanctified; a house could be sanctified; an altar, a tabernacle, gold and silver vessels, the garments of the priest, and the cities of refuge, could all be sanctified. In short, anything that was set apart for sacred use was said to be "sanctified."

But in the New Testament, the word had a deeper meaning. It meant not only outward consecration but also inward holiness. It meant an internal purification of the heart from all uncleanness, and an enduement with the holy mind of Christ. It was not a mere separation, like the first, but a *visitation*—a separation from the lower world, and a visitation from the higher, the coming in of God's Spirit from above with a principle of holiness that was to work an inward likeness to the character of God.

The practical purpose of the first process was mainly to put something in a position where God could use it. A golden candlestick was sanctified so that it might be of some use to God. A house was sanctified so that it might be exclusively His—to do with what He liked. In similar manner, a person is consecrated so that God may use him. Consecration is the process by which he is put into position for God. And all that sanctification does for him, in the first sense of the word, is to put him into position in such a way that he will always be within reach of God, and so that he will do what God likes—that is to say, *do what God wills.*

But there is something more to sanctification than man's merely being a tool in the hands of God. If there were not, automatons could do the work far better than people could. They would never oppose God's will, and they would always be in position. But God's will has a reaction upon the instruments whom He employs. God's will does not stop with His will, as it were. It springs back upon the person using it, and benefits him. If the instrument is a sanctified cup, or a sanctified house, God's will does not spring back and make an internal change in it; but if the instrument that does God's will is a person, not only is God's will done, but the person, or doer, is also affected. God never keeps anything all to Himself. Does not He who *"so loved the world, that he gave his only begotten Son"* (John 3:16), *"with him also freely give us all things?"* (Romans 8:32). His Son is for us, His love is for us, and His will is for us. How do we know that His will is for us? Because *"this is the will of God, even your sanctification."* Whatever else may be involved in it, this is in it; whatever else He may get from it, this is something that you get: your sanctification. As Hebrews 10:10 says, *"By the which will we are sanctified."*

God says, "This is My will: not My gain but yours; not My eternal advantage but yours; not My holiness but '*your sanctification.*'" Do you think God wants your body, when He asks you to present it to Him? Do you think it is for His sake that He asks for it, so that He might be enriched by it? God could make a thousand better bodies with a breath. It is for your sake that He asks it. He wants your gift in order to give you His gift—your gift that was just in the way of His gift. He wants your will out of the way in order to make room for His will.

When you give everything to God, God gives it all back again—and more. You present your body as a living sacrifice so that you may prove God's will. You will prove it by getting back your body—a glorified body. You lose the world so that you may prove God's will. God's will is for you to gain heaven. This is the will of God, therefore, that you would gain heaven. Or, this is the will of God, that you would gain holiness, for holiness is heaven. Or, "this is the will of God, even your sanctification."

To sum up these facts, then, we find that they shape themselves into the following two propositions:

1. That our sanctification, or, more strictly, our consecration, is for the purpose of doing the will of God, to prove "what is that good, and acceptable, and perfect, will of God" (Romans 12:2).

2. That God's will reacts upon us, a conspicuous part of His will being that we would be personally holy. "This is the will of God, even your sanctification."

How Can We Become Holy?

We have already discussed the first of the above propositions. Now the question is how we can best fulfill this conspicuous part of the will of God and become holy ourselves. It is God's will for all of us that we would become holy.

"How are we to become holy?" We have probably asked this question many times already in our life. We have thought, and read, and prayed about it, and perhaps have not yet reached a conclusion about how, indeed, we are to become holy. Perhaps, the question has long ago assumed another and evasive form with us: "When are we going to become holy?" Or, perhaps, a hopeless form: "How are we ever to become holy?"

The real way out of the difficulty is to ask a still deeper question: "Why do I want to be holy?" All the great difficulties of religion are centered on our motives. Impurities in a spiritual stream generally mean impurities at the spiritual source. And all fertility or barrenness of soul depends upon which source supplies the streams of the desires. Our difficulties about becoming holy, therefore, most likely lie in our reasons for wanting to become holy. For if you grant the true motive to holiness, you need no definition of holiness. True holiness may be found where there is the true motivation. We will get nearer the true roots of holiness, therefore, if we spend a little time on the root question, "Why do I want to be holy?"

Inadequate Motivations for Holiness

1. The Influence of Someone We Know

The first thing that started some of us to search for a better life was "infection." We caught an "infection" for a better life from someone we knew. We were idling our own way through life when someone crossed our path with high aims and great enthusiasms. We were taken with the principles on which that life was lived. Its noble purpose charmed us; its disregard of the petty troubles and cares of life astonished us. We felt unaccountably interested in it. There was a romance in its earnestness and self-denial that captivated us, and we thought we would like to dismantle our own life and put it together again according to this new plan. Thus, we got our first motive for holiness.

Now, this was not a wrong motive, but it was an imperfect one. It answered its purpose—but only so far. For God takes strange ways to start a person's religion. For instance, there is nothing more remarkable in the history of conversion than the infinite diversity of answers to this question: "What made you first think about your soul?" God does take strange ways to start a person for heaven. The way home is sometimes shown to him by an unexpected fingerpost. And, from a motive so unworthy that he dare not admit it later, there come to many an individual his first impulses toward God. Additionally, long after the person has begun to run the Christian race, God may try to hasten his lagging steps by the spur of a motivation as far beneath an heir of heaven as his spiritual life is beneath what it ought to be.

But the principle to be noted through it all is that the motivations that God allows us to start on are not the ones we are to live on. It may be that adversity in business gives us a fresh start. It may be affliction, ambition, church pride, or a thousand other things. But the impulse cannot last, and it cannot carry us far. And there must come a time of exchange for a higher motivation, if we would grow in grace, or move onward into a holier life. A person's motivation must grow in order for grace to grow. And many a person has to live on old grace, because he lives on an old motive. God allowed us to begin with a lower one; and then, when He gave us more grace, it was so that we might get a higher one. But we spent the grace on something else, and our motivation is no higher than before. So, although we got a start in religion, we were little the better for it, and our whole life has stood still for lack of a strong enough motive to go on.

2. The Influence of a Good Book

But it was not necessary for us to have caught our "infection" from a friend. There is another great source of infection, and some of us are breathing its atmosphere every day—books. We may have gotten our motivation to be good from a book.

In works on ethics, and in the works of all great poets, and perhaps even in some novels, we found that the highest aim of life was to be true and pure and good. We found modern literature ringing with the praises of virtue. Before long, we began to respect it, then to admire it, then to wish for it. Thus, we caught the enthusiasm for purity that has changed our whole lives, in a way, and given us a chief motivation for religion.

Well, we must thank God for having given us a start, anyhow. It is something to have begun. It is a great thing to have an enthusiasm to be true and pure and good. Nor will the Bible ever be jealous of any lesser book that God may use to stir people up to a better life. But all lesser books "sin and come short of God's glory." (See Romans 3:23.) And the greatest motivations of the greatest of the lesser books fall as far short of the glory of God as those who live on only the enthusiasms that are kindled on the altar of modern literature fall short of the life and mind of Christ. God may give these motives to a person to start with. If the individual will not look into God's Book for them, God may see fit to put something remotely like them into mankind's books.

Jesus Christ would come to people right where they were. There is no place on earth so dark that the light of heaven will not come to it; and there is no spot of earth where God may not choose to raise a monument of His love. There is always room, anywhere in the world, for a holy thought. It may come to a person on the roadside, as to Paul (see Acts 9:1–20); or in the fork of a sycamore tree, as to Zacchaeus (see Luke 19:1–10). It may come to someone at his boats, as to Peter (see, for example, Matthew 4:18–20); or through his Bible, as to the eunuch (see Acts 8:26–39).

But, whether it comes to a person at his boats or through his Bible, whatever is good is God's; and we may be thankful that the Giver of all good has "peopled" the whole earth and air and sky with thoughts of His glory, and filled the world with voices that call us near to Him.

At the same time, it must be understood again that the initial motivations are never meant to move us far on the road to God. As a matter of fact, they can never move us thus; and, if an individual does not get higher motivations, his religion must, and his morality may, come to a bitter end. The melancholy proof comes to everyone, at some point, that many of those who inspire us with these almost divine enthusiasms are, and have been, degraded men and women themselves. For if a person's motivations for goodness are not higher than the enthusiasms of his own higher nature, the chances are that, in time, the appeals of his lower nature will either curb or degrade them. The true motivation for holiness, then, is not to be caught from books.

3. Fear

Next, some of us were induced to aim at a better life from motivations of prudence, or from fear. We had read in the Bible this very startling sentence: "Without holiness, no one will see the Lord." (See Hebrews 12:14.) Now, we wished to see God. And we found the Bible full of commands to keep God's law. So, with fear and trembling, we began to try to keep it. Its strictness was a continual stimulus to us. We were kept watching and praying. We lived in an atmosphere of fear, lest we should break it. No doubt, this has done good—great good. As with the other two motivations we have discussed, it was not a bad motive—only an imperfect one. But, also like the others, it will have to be exchanged for a higher one, if true progress in holy living is to be made.

4. Gratitude to God

Then, some of us found our motivation in gratitude. The great love of God in Christ had come home to us with a particular power. We felt the magnitude of His sacrifice for us, of His forgiveness of us. And we would try to return His love. So, we set our hearts with a gracious purpose toward

God. Our life and behavior would be becoming of the gospel of Christ. We would do for His sake what we would never do for our own sake. But, even a noble impulse like this has failed to fulfill our heart's desire, and even our generosity has left us little nearer to God.

5. A Feeling of God's Presence

Last, there is another thought that has sometimes helped us onward for a time—a feeling that comes over us at times of Communion, at times of revival, which Christian workers feel at all times: "Here we are, surrounded by great privileges—singled out from the world for God's particular charge. God comes very close to us; often, the very ground is holy. *'What manner of persons ought* [we] *to be in all holy conversation and godliness'* (2 Peter 3:11)? How different we should be from all the people around us! How much more separate from every appearance of evil! How softly we who bear the vessels of the Lord should walk!"

Why Such Motivations Are Deficient

Now, some of these motivations are very beautiful. They are the gifts of God. Doubtless, many people have attained a certain measure of holiness by employing them. And these motives have at least awakened in us some longings for God. But they are all deficient, and hopelessly inadequate to carry on what they sometimes so hopefully begin.

They are deficient in these three ways:

1. They do not convey the full scriptural truth.

2. They are inadequate to produce more than a small degree of holiness.

3. They never produce the true quality of holiness.

If we have not yet had higher motives than these, then it follows that our spiritual life is being laid down upon principles that can never, in the nature of things, yield the results we had hoped and waited for.

We have been wondering why our growth in grace has been so small—so small, indeed, that sometimes it has almost seemed to cease. And, without looking at books or doctrines, as we look into our hearts, we find one reason, at least—perhaps the principal one: Our motivation is incomplete.

Now, the weaknesses of the initial motive, apart from the error of it, consisted in these: First, it lacked authority; second, it proposed no standard. Regarding the first, there was no reason why one should strive to be better. It was left to one's own discretion. Our friend, or our favorite author, said it, and the sense of obligation rose or fell with the nearness or remoteness of his influence. And regarding the standard, our friend, or our favorite author's favorite hero, was but a poor model, at best, for only a most imperfect spiritual beauty can ever be copied from anything made of clay.

The Right Motivation for Holiness

Well then, what is the right motivation for holiness of life? Hitherto, we have been dealing with ordinary motives; now we must come to extraordinary ones. Holiness is one of the most extraordinary things in life, and it demands only the noblest motives, the noblest impulses. Now we will see how God has satisfied this demand of our nature for an extraordinary motivation for this extraordinary thing, holiness; how He has satisfied it so completely that the soul, when it discovers it, need never feel unsatisfied again. God's motivation for holiness is this: *"Be ye holy; for I am holy"* (1 Peter 1:16).

It is a startling thing when the voice of God comes close to us and whispers, *"Be ye holy"*; but when the question "Why should we be holy?" returns from our lips, it is a more solemn thing to receive this answer: *"For I am holy."* This is the motivation *God* gives us for holiness. Its authority—its divine obligation—is *"Be ye holy."* Its divine motive is *"For I am holy."*

Think of the greatness of the obligation. Long ago, when we began the Christian life, we heard a voice, saying, "Be ye holy." Perhaps, as we have seen, it was an infectious voice, the voice of a friend. Perhaps it was an inspiring voice, the voice of poetry or literature. Perhaps it was a warning voice, the voice of the law. But it was not a commanding voice—the voice of God. And the reason, perhaps, was that we were not thinking of the voice; we were thinking of the *holy*. We had caught sight of a new and beautiful object— something that seemed full of promise, something that was to consecrate even the common hours of our life. The religious world seemed bright to us then, and the individuals and the books that would help us to reach out our hands to this beautiful object were dear.

This fascination with holiness was something new that had come into our life. Had we been asked about the voice that said, "Be ye holy," we would indeed have said it was God's. But, in truth, it was only our own voice, which had caught some far-off echoes from our reading, or our thinking, or our friends. There was no *authority* in the voice, therefore, and it rested with our own poor wills whether or not we would grow in holiness. Sometimes, our will was strong and true, and we were better men and women than ever before in our lives; but there were intervals when we listened to another voice, such as "Be ye prosperous," or "Be ye happy," and then we lost all that we had gained. But with the divine obligation before us, it is no longer optional that we should be holy. We *must* be holy.

And then see how the motivation for holiness is attached to the obligation to be holy. The motive for holiness is *"For I am holy."* The motive accounts for the obligation. God's one desire for the whole earth is that it would be holy, precisely because He is holy. And the best He can do with us is to make us like Himself. The whole earth is His, and He wants it all to be in harmony with Him. God has a right to demand that we would be holy—that everyone would be holy, and everything just, because He Himself is holy and just. To use the simplest illustration, we allow no decorations in our house that are not lovely and pleasant to the eye. We have no business cumbering God's earth with ourselves if we are not holy—no business living in the same world with Him. We are an offense to God; we are discordant notes in the music of the universe.

But God lays this high obligation upon us for our own sake. For this we were made. For this we were born in a Christian land. For this, strange things have happened in our lives—strange pieces of discipline have disturbed its quiet flow—strange troubles, strange providences, strange chastenings. There is no other explanation for the mystery of our life than this: God wants us to be holy. At any cost, God will have us holy. Whatever else we *may* be, this one thing we *must* be. *"This is the will of God, even your sanctification."* It is not necessary that we would be prosperous or famous or happy; but it is necessary that we would be holy. And, the deepest moments of our life sometimes give us glimpses of a still more tender reason why God says, *"Be ye holy"*—for our own sakes, because it would be hell to be unholy.

There is now only one thing lacking in our new motivation for holiness. We have discovered the sources of its obligation far up in the counsels of God, and deep down in the weakness of our own nature. We have found holiness to be an absolutely necessary virtue—to live without which is to contradict our Maker. But we have not yet looked at its *quality*. What is this thing we are to pursue so ardently? Is there any plain definition of it—any form that could be easily stated and easily followed? It may be very easily stated. It is for those who have tried it to say whether it is easily followed.

"As he which hath called you is holy, so be ye holy" (1 Peter 1:15). "Be holy, *as* He is holy." As He who has called you is holy, *so* you yourself be holy. This is the form of holiness we are asked to aim at; this is God's commentary on the motive. This is the standard. *"As he...so...ye."* Think for a moment about the difference between these pronouns: *"he"* and *"ye."* He who has called you—Jesus Christ. He *"who did no sin, neither was guile found in his mouth: who, when he was reviled, reviled not again; when he suffered, he threatened not"* (1 Peter 2:22–23). *He* who was without spot or blemish, in whom even His enemies found no fault.

Ye, the fallen children of a fallen race. *Ye*, with hearts deceitful above all things, and desperately wicked. *Ye* are to become as *He*. The two pronouns are to approach one another. The "cruel-fiers" are to work their way up to the crucified. You are to become *as He*. There is a motive as high as the holiness of God. It makes us feel as if we still had our lifework before us. It seems as if it is all yet to begin. We have scarcely even begun to be like God, for we began, perhaps, with no higher motive than to be like someone else—not like God at all. But the little goodness that we get from books, and the chance impulses that come from other lives, have never fulfilled in us the will of God, and could never sanctify such hearts as ours. They could never make *"ye"* become *"as he."*

No doubt, a great deal of human good is possible to man before he touches the character of Christ. High human motives and human aims may make a noble human life. But they never make a holy life. A holy life is a life like Christ's. And, whatever things may be attained for a better life from the lower motives, one thing must necessarily be absent from them all—a life like Christ's; or rather, a spirit like Christ's. For the life like Christ's can come only from Christ; and the spirit of Christ can be caught only from Christ.

Thus, we come at last to the profound meaning of another text that stands alone in the Word of God and forms the only true climax to such a subject as this. *"Lo, I come…to do thy will, O God"* (Hebrews 10:7), the author of Hebrews quotes from David. Then, he goes on to add, *"By the which will we are sanctified…"* (Hebrews 10:10). Christ came to do God's will, by which we are sanctified. *"This is the will of God, even your sanctification."* But the writer of Hebrews adds another lesson: *"By the which will we are sanctified…."* How? *"…through the offering of the body of Jesus Christ once for all"* (Hebrews 10:10).

Our sanctification is not in books, or in noble enthusiasms, or in personal struggles for a better life. It is in *"the offering of the body of Jesus Christ once for all."* Justification is through the blood of Jesus Christ once for all. Sanctification is through the body of Jesus Christ once for all. It is not something to be generated but to be received. It is not to be generated in fragments of experience at one time and another—it is already complete in Christ. We have only to put on Christ. And, though it may take a lifetime of experience to make it ours, *whenever* the sanctification comes, it can come *only* from Christ. And, if we ever have sanctification, it will be only because of Christ, and inasmuch as we have Him. Our sanctification is not what morality gives, nor even what the Bible gives, nor even what Christ gives—it is what Christ *lives*. It is Christ Himself.

The reason why we resort so much to lower impulses to a Christian life is imperfect union with Christ. We take our *doctrines* from the Bible, and our *assurance* from Christ. But because of a lack of the living, bright reality of His presence in our hearts, we search the entire world for impulses. We search religious books, tracts, and sermons for impulses, but in vain. They are not there. Christ says, *"I am Alpha and Omega, the beginning and the end"* (Revelation 21:6; 22:13). *"Christ is all, and in all"* (Colossians 3:11). The beginning of all things is in the will of God: *"by the which will…."* The end of all things is in sanctification through faith in Jesus Christ: *"by the which will we are sanctified."* Between these two poles, all spiritual life and Christian experience run. And no motive outside Christ can lead a person to Christ. If your motivation for holiness is not as high as Christ, it cannot make you rise to Christ. For water cannot rise above its level.

Beware lest any man spoil you through philosophy and vain deceit, after the tradition of men, after the rudiments of the world, and not after Christ. For in him dwelleth all the fulness of the Godhead bodily. And ye are complete in him, which is the head of all principality and power.
(Colossians 2:8–10)

Of God [Christ Jesus] *is made unto us wisdom, and righteousness, and sanctification, and redemption.* (1 Corinthians 1:30)

As ye have therefore received Christ Jesus the Lord, so walk ye in him.
(Colossians 2:6)

HOW TO KNOW
THE WILL OF GOD

"If any man will do his will, he shall know of the doctrine,
whether it be of God."
—John 7:17

There is an experience that becomes more and more familiar to everyone who is trying to follow Christ—a feeling of the growing loneliness of his Christian life. It comes from a sense of the particularly personal interest that Christ takes in him, which sometimes seems so strong as almost to make him feel that his life is being detached from all the other lives around him, that it is being drawn out of the crowd of humanity as if an unseen arm linked in his were taking him aside for a nearer intimacy and a deeper and more private fellowship.

It is not, indeed, that the rest of the great family of God is to be eclipsed by him, or that he is in any way the favorite of heaven. He has the sanctifying and, in the truest sense, humbling realization that God makes Himself as real to each poor part as if he were the whole. Thus, even as, when he first came to Christ, he felt as if he were the only lost one, so now, in continuing with Christ, he feels as if he is the only found one. And perhaps it is true that, without any loss in the feeling of saintly communion with all those throughout the world who say "Our Father" with him in their prayers, the more he feels that Christ has all of him to Himself, the more he feels that he has Christ all to himself. Christ has died for other men, but in a particular sense for him. God has a love for the entire world, but a particular love for him. God has an interest in the entire world, but a particular interest in him. This is always how it is with a close fellowship, and it is true of the universal fellowship of God with His own people.

God's Specific Will for an Individual's Life

But if there is one thing that is most personal to the Christian, that is more singularly his than God's love or God's interest—one thing that is a finer symbol of God's love and interest—it is the knowledge of God's will— the private knowledge of God's will. And it is most personal, inasmuch as it is most private. For instance, my private portion of God's love is only a private *share* in God's love—only a part; it is the same in quality and kind as all the rest of God's love, as all His other children receive from Him. But God's will is something for myself. There is a will of God for me that is willed for no one else. It is not a share in the universal will, in the same sense as I have a share in the universal love. It is a particular will for me—different from the will He has for anyone else—a private will, a will that no one else knows about, that no one can know about except me.

To be sure, as we have seen, God likewise has a universal will for me and every other person. God tells the entire world His will through the Ten Commandments, the Beatitudes of Christ, and the conscience. There is no secret about that part; it is as universal as His love. It is the will on which the character of every person is to be formed and conformed to God's.

Yet, we have also seen that there is a will for our career as well as for our character. There is a will for *where* I am to become like God—in what place, such as this town or another town—as well as *that* I am to become like God. There is a will for where I am to be, and what I am to be, and what I am to do tomorrow. There is a will for what plan I am to take up, and what work I am to do for Christ, and what business arrangements I am to make, and what money I am to give away. This is God's private will for me, for every step I take, for the path of life along which He points my way. It is God's will for my career.

If I have God's will in my character, my life may become great and good. It may be useful and honorable, and even a monument of the sanctifying power of God. But it will be only a life. However great and pure it may be, it can be no more than a *life*. And it ought to be a *mission*. There should be no such thing as a Christian "life"; each life should be a mission.

God has a life plan for every human being. In the eternal counsels of His will, when He arranged the destiny of every star, every grain of sand and blade of grass, and each of those tiny insects that live for but an hour, the Creator had a plan for you and for me. Our life was to be the slow unfolding of this plan, as the cornstalk from the corn seed, or the flower from the gradually opening bud. It was a plan of what we were to be; of what we might become; of what He would have us to do with our days and years, or to influence with our lives. But we all had the terrible power to evade this plan, if we chose, and to shape our lives from another idea, from another will. The bud could become only a flower, and the star could revolve only in the orbit God had fixed. But it was man's prerogative to choose his path, and his duty to choose it in God. Yet, the divine right to choose at all has always seemed more important to him than his duty to choose in God; so, for the most part, he has taken his life from God and has cut his career from himself.

It Is Possible to Know God's Will

As a result, there are two principal classifications of people in the Christian world today: (1) those who have God's will in their character, and (2) those who have God's will in their character *and* in their career. Those who come under the first classification are in the world to live. They have a life. The second are in the world to minister. They have a mission.

Those who belong to the first class, those who are simply living in the world and developing character, no matter how finely they may be developing their character, cannot understand very clearly that they are not fulfilling God's will. They are really outside a great part of God's will altogether. They understand the universal part; they are molded by it, and their lives as lives are in some sense noble and true. But they miss the private part, the secret whispering of God in the ear, and the constant message from earth to heaven. *"Lord, what wilt thou have me to do?"* (Acts 9:6). They never have the secret joy of asking a question like this, the wonderful sense in asking it, of being in the counsels of God, the overpowering thought that God has taken notice of you and your question, that He will let you do something—something particular, personal, and private—that no one else has been given to do. This is what gives life for God its true sublimity, and makes a perpetual sacrament of all its common things. Life to those in the first class is, at best, a bare and selfish thing, for their truest springs of action are never moved at all; and the strangest thing in human history—the bounding of the career from step to step, from circumstance to circumstance, from tragedy to tragedy—is unexplained and unrelated, and it hangs over life as a perpetual mystery.

Possibly, the chief reason why so few people have thought of taking God into their career is that so few have really taken God into their *life*. No one ever thinks of having God in his career—or need think of it, until his life is fully molded into God's. And no one will succeed in even knowing what having God in his career can mean until he knows what it is to have God in the secret chambers of his heart. It requires a well-kept life to know the will of God, and none but the Christlike in character can know the Christlike in career.

Consequently, some people deny the very fact of God's guidance in an individual's life. They say it gives life an importance quite foreign to the divine intention in making mankind. It is argued that one life is of no greater importance than any other life. To talk of special providences happening every hour of every day is to detract from the majesty and dignity of God; in fact, it reduces religious life to mere religious caprice, and the thought that God's will is being done to a hallucination of the mind.

There is another side to the objection, which, though less pronounced and definite, is still subtly dangerous. That other side is this: There does, indeed, seem to be some warrant in Scripture for coming to know the will of God. However, in the first place, that probably means only on great occasions that happen once or twice in a lifetime. Second, the whole subject is so obscure that, all things considered, a person would do better to walk by his own common sense and leave such mysteries alone.

But the Christian cannot allow the question "What is the will of God for me?" to be put off with poor evasions like these. Every day, indeed, and many times a day, the question rises in a hundred practical forms: "What is God's will for me today—right now?" "What is the will of God for the next step?" "What is the will of God for this arrangement and for that one?" "What is God's will in regard to this amusement?" "What is the will of God for this projected work for Christ?" He feels he must consult the will of God for all these concerns, and he believes that God has a will for him in all such things. It is not only a matter of hope, but a point in his doctrine and creed, that it must be possible *somehow* to know what God's will is.

Instruments for Discovering the Will of God

In order to vindicate the reasonableness of such expectations as these, it may simply be affirmed as a matter of fact that there *are* a number of instruments for finding out the will of God. One of them is a very great instrument, so far surpassing all the rest in accuracy that there may be said to be only one that has never been known to fail. The others are smaller and clumsier—much less delicate, indeed—and often fail. They often fail to come within sight of the will of God at all; and they are so far astray at other times as to mistake some other thing for it. Still, they are instruments and, notwithstanding their defects, have a value by themselves. And, when the greater instrument employs their humbler powers to second its attempts, they immediately become as keen and as unerring as it is.

Some Lesser Instruments

The most important of these minor instruments is *reason*. Although it is a lesser instrument, in many cases, it is great enough to reveal the secret will of God. For example, suppose God is taking your life and character through a certain process. He is running your career along a certain chain of events. Sometimes, the light that He is showing you stops, and you have to pick your way for a few steps by the dimmer light of thought. But it is God's will for you then to use this thought, and to elevate it, through regions of consecration, into faith, and to walk by this light until the clearer beam from His will comes back again.

Another of these instruments is *experience*. There are many paths in life that we all tread more than once. God's light was by us when we first walked them, and it lit a beacon here and there along the way. But the next time He sent our lines along that path, He knew the sidelights would still be burning, and He let us walk alone.

There is also *circumstance*. God closes things in around us until all our alternatives are reduced to one. If we must act, that one is probably the will of God right then.

And then there is the instrument of *other people*. This includes the advice of others—an important element, at least—and a consideration of the welfare of others, and our example to others, and the many other facts and principles that make up the moral person, which, if not always strong enough to discover what God's will is, are often not too feeble to determine what it is *not*.

The Greatest Instrument

Even the best of these instruments, however, has but little power in its own hands. The ultimate appeal is always to the one great instrument, which uses them, in turn, as it requires; and which supplements their discoveries, or even supplants them, if it so chooses, by its own superior light and might and right. It is like some great telescope that can sweep the skies in the darkest night and trace the motions of the furthest stars, while all the rest can see but a faint, uncertain light, which here and there pierces for a moment the clouds that lie between.

This great instrument for discovering God's will can penetrate where reason cannot go, where observation has not been before, where memory is helpless, and where the guiding hand of circumstance has failed. It has a name that is seldom associated with any purpose so great, a name that any child may understand, even as the stupendous instrument itself, with all its mighty powers, is sometimes moved by infant hands when others have tried in vain.

The name of the instrument is *obedience*. Obedience, as it is sometimes expressed, is the organ of spiritual knowledge. As the eye is the organ of physical sight, and the mind is the organ of intellectual sight, so this strange power, obedience, is the organ of spiritual vision.

This is one of the great revelations that the Bible has given to the world. It is purely a Bible thought. Philosophy never conceived a truth so simple and yet so sublime. And, although it was known in Old Testament times, and expressed in Old Testament books, it was reserved for Jesus Christ to make the full discovery to the world, and to add to His teaching another of the profoundest truths that have come from heaven to earth—that the mysteries of the Father's will are hidden in this word *obey*.

The circumstances in which Christ made the great revelation to the world are known to everyone. The Feast of Tabernacles was in progress in Jerusalem when Jesus entered the temple to teach. A circle of Jews who seem to have been spellbound by the extraordinary wisdom of His words were gathered around Him. He made no pretensions of being a scholar. He was not a graduate of the rabbinical schools. He had no access to the sacred literature of the people. Yet here was this stranger from Nazareth, confounding the wisest minds in Jerusalem, and unfolding with calm and effortless skill such truths as even those temple walls had never heard before. *"And the Jews marvelled, saying, How knoweth this man letters, having never learned?"* (John 7:15). What organ of spiritual knowledge could He possess, *"having never learned"*? They did not know that Christ *had* learned. They did not know about the school at Nazareth, whose Teacher was in heaven, whose schoolroom was a carpenter's shop, and whose lesson was the Father's will. They did not know that hidden truths could come from God, or *"wisdom from above."* (See James 3:15, 17.)

What came to them was gathered from human books, or caught from human lips. They knew no organ except the mind, no instrument for knowing the things of heaven except that by which they *learned* in the schools. But Jesus pointed to a spiritual world that lay still farther beyond, and told them of the spiritual eye that reads its profounder secrets and reveals the mysteries of God. *"My doctrine is not mine,"* He said, *"but his that sent me"* (John 7:16). Earlier, He had taught, *"My judgment is just; because I seek not mine own will, but the will of the Father which hath sent me"* (John 5:30). And then, lest men would think this great experience was never meant for them, He applied His principles to every human mind that seeks to know God's will. *"If any man will do [God's] will, he shall know of the doctrine, whether it be of God"* (John 7:17).

The word *"doctrine"* here is not to be taken in our sense of the word *doctrine*. It is not the doctrine of theology. *"Any man"* can *"know,"* if he will do God's will. But it is God's teaching—God's mind—that he will know. If anyone will do His will, he will know God's mind; he will know God's teaching and God's will.

In this sense, or indeed in the literal sense, looking at these words for the first time, it almost appears as if a contradiction were involved. It seems to indicate that to *know* God's will, we must *do* God's will. But how are we to do God's will until we know it? Not knowing God's will is the very dilemma we are in. And it seems no way out of it to say, "Do it, and you will know it." We want to know it, in order to do it; but now we are told to do it, in order to know it! *"If any man will **do**...he shall **know**."*

But that is not the meaning of the words. That is not even the words themselves. It does not say, "If any man do, he shall know," but *"If any man **will** do...."* The whole sense of the passage from John 7 turns upon that word *"will."* It means, "If anyone is *willing* to do, he will know." He does not need to do God's will in order to know it; he needs only to be willing to do it. For *"will"* is not at all the sign of the future tense, as it appears to be. It is not connected with the word *"do"* at all but is a separate verb altogether, meaning "is willing," or "wills." If anyone wills, or is willing, to do, he will know.

Notice the difference this makes in the problem. Before, it looked as if doing God's will was to come first, and then knowing His will; but now, we see that another element is thrown in at the very beginning. Being willing comes first, and then knowing; and, thereafter, the doing may follow—the doing, that is to say, if the will has been sufficiently clear to proceed.

The whole stress of the passage, therefore, turns on this word *"will."* And Christ's answer to the question of how we are to know the will of God may be simply stated thus: "If anyone is willing to do God's will, he will know it"; or, in even plainer language, "If anyone is sincerely *trying* to do God's will, he will know it."

The connection of all this with obedience is just that being willing is the highest form of obedience. It is the spirit and essence of obedience. There is an obedience in the world that is not genuine obedience, because the *act* of obedience is there, but the *spirit of submission* is not.

We read in the Bible,

A certain man had two sons; and he came to the first, and said, Son, go work to day in my vineyard. He answered and said, I will not: but afterward he repented, and went. And he came to the second, and said likewise. And he answered and said, I go, sir: and went not. Whether of them twain did the will of his father?   (Matthew 21:28–31)

Here, obedience comes out in its true colors as something in the will. And if anyone has an obeying will, a truly single and submissive will, he will know if the teaching, or if the leading, is of God.

Discerning God's Will

If we were to apply this principle to a practical situation, it might be found to work something like the following. Suppose that, tomorrow, there is some difficulty before us in our path. It lies across the very threshold of our life, and we cannot begin the work week without at least some notice that it is there. It may be some trifling item of business life, over which unaccountable suspicions have lately begun to gather, and to force themselves, in spite of everything, into our thoughts and conscience, and even into our prayers. Or, it may be that some change of circumstance is opening up, and alternatives are appearing and demanding that we make a choice. Perhaps, it involves some practice in our life that the clearing of the spiritual atmosphere and increasing light from God are hinting is wrong, while our reason cannot coincide exactly with them and condemn it. At any event, there is something on our mind—something to do, to suffer, to renounce—and there are alternatives to distinguish, to choose from, to reject. Suppose, indeed, we made this case a personal one, as well as an illustrative one, and, in view of the solemn ordinance of Communion to which we are shortly called, we ran the lines of our self-examination along it as we proceeded. The question rises, "How are we to separate God's light on the point from our own, to disentangle our thoughts on the point from His, and to be sure we are following His will, not the reflected image of our own will?"

From a natural standpoint, the first process toward this discovery would be one of outlook. We would naturally set to work by collecting all the possible materials for decision from every point of the compass, balancing one consequence against the other, then summing up the points in favor of each, until we chose the one that emerged, in the end, with most of reason on its side. But this would be only the natural man's way out of the dilemma. The spiritual man would go about it in another way. The way just described, he would argue, has no religion in it at all, except perhaps the acknowledgment that reason is divinely given; and though it might be quite possible and even probable that the light would come to him through the medium of reason, yet he would reach his conclusion, and, likely enough, a different conclusion, from quite another side.

And his conclusion would likewise be a better and sounder conclusion. For the insight of the nonreligious method would be impaired; and the real organ for knowing God's will would be so out of order from disuse that even reason would be biased in its choice. A heart not quite subdued to God is an imperfect element in which His will can never live; and the intellect that belongs to such a heart is an imperfect instrument and cannot find God's will unerringly—for God's will is found in regions that obedience alone can explore.

Accordingly, the spiritual man would go to work from the opposite side. He would begin not with outlook but with "in-look." He would not give his mind to observation. He would devote his soul to self-examination—to self-examination of the most solemn and searching kind. For, this principle of Christ is not a concession to an easy life, or a careless method of rounding a difficult point. Rather, it is a summons to learn the highest and most sacred thing in heaven by bracing the heart to the loftiest and severest sacrifice on earth: the bending of an unwilling human will until it breaks in the will of God. It means that the heart must be watched with a jealous care, and kept for God most solemnly. It means that the hidden desires must be taken out one by one and regenerated by Christ. It means that the faintest inclination of the soul, when touched by the Spirit of God, must be prepared to assume the strength of will and to act at any cost. It means that nothing in life should be dreaded as much as that the soul would ever lose its sensitiveness to God; that God would ever speak and find the ear just dull enough to miss what He has said; that God would have some active will for some human will to do, and our heart not be the first in the world to be ready to obey.

When we have attained to this by meditation, by self-examination, by commemoration, and by the Holy Spirit's power, we may be ready to make it our daily prayer that we may know God's will. And when the heart is prepared like this, and the wayward will is drilled in sacrifice and patience to surrender all to God, God's will may come out in our career at every turning of our life, and be ours not only in sacramental aspiration but also in act.

To search for God's will with such an instrument is to scarcely search at all. God's will lies transparently in view at every winding of the path. And if perplexity sometimes comes, in such way as has been supposed, the mind will gather the phenomena into the field of vision, as carefully, as fully, as laboriously, as if no light would come at all, and then stand still and wait until the wonderful discerning faculty of the soul, that eye that beams in the undivided heart and looks right out to God from the willing mind, fixes its gaze on one far distant spot—one spot that is perhaps dark to all the rest of the world—where all the lights are focused in God's will.

How this infinite and this finite are brought to touch, *how* this invisible will of God is brought to the temporal heart, must ever remain unknown. The mysterious meeting place between the human and the divine in the prepared and willing heart—where, precisely, the will is finally moved into line with God's will—of these things no one knows, but only the Spirit of God. (See 1 Corinthians 2:11.)

"The wind bloweth where it listeth, and thou hearest the sound thereof, but canst not tell whence it cometh, and whither it goeth" (John 3:8). When every passion is annihilated, and no thought moves in the mind, and all the faculties are still and waiting for God, the spiritual eye may trace, perhaps, some

delicate motion in the soul, some thought that stirs like a leaf in the unseen air and tells that *God* is there. It is not solely the stillness, nor the unseen breath, nor the thought that stirred, but these three mysteries in one, that reveal God's will to me. It is true that God's light does not supersede our thoughts but rather illuminates them. However, when God sends an angel to "trouble the pool" (see John 5:1–4), let us have faith for the angel's hand, and believe that some power of heaven has stirred the waters in our soul.

Let us but get our hearts in position for knowing the will of God—only, let us be willing to know God's will in our hearts so that we may *do* God's will in our lives—and we will raise no questions as to how His will may come, and feel no fears in case the heavenly light should go.

But let it be remembered, as has already been said, that to will to do God's will requires a well-kept life. It requires a well-kept life to do the will of God, and an even better-kept life to *will* to do His will. To be willing to do the will of God is a rarer grace than to be doing His will. For he who is willing may sometimes have nothing to do, and must be willing to only wait. And it is far easier to be doing God's will than to be willing to have nothing to do—it is far easier to be working for Christ than it is to be willing to cease. No, there is nothing rarer in the world today than the truly willing soul, and there is nothing more worth desiring than the will to will God's will.

There is no grander possession for any Christian life than the transparently simple mechanism of a sincerely obedient heart. And, if we could keep the machinery clear, there would be lives in the thousands doing God's will on earth, even as it is done in heaven. God would be in the career of many a person whose soul is now being allowed to drift with every changing wind of life—a useless thing to God and to the world. And many a noble Christian character would be rescued from wasting all its virtues on itself and be saved for work for Christ.

And, when the time of trial comes, and everything in earth and heaven is dark, and even God's love seems dim, what is there ever left to cling to but this will of the willing heart—a God-given, God-ward bending will that says, amid the most solemn and perplexing vicissitudes of life,

> Father, I know that all my life
> Is portioned out for me,

And the changes that are sure to come
I do not fear to see;
But I ask Thee for a present mind
Intent on pleasing Thee.[26]

MEMORIAL PROFILE BY
W. ROBERTSON NICOLL

P rofessor Drummond's influence on his contemporaries is not to be measured by the sale of his books, great as that has been. It may be doubted whether any living novelist has had so many readers; and perhaps no living writer has been so eagerly followed and so keenly discussed on the Continent and in America. For some reason that is difficult to assign, many who exercise great influence at home are not appreciated elsewhere. It has been said, for example, that no book of Ruskin's has ever been translated into a Continental language. And though such a negative is obviously dangerous, it is true that Ruskin has not been to Europe what he has been to England.

But Professor Drummond had the widest recognition from Norway to Germany. There was a time when scarcely a week passed in Germany without the publication of a book or pamphlet in which his views were canvassed.

In Scandinavia, perhaps, no other living Englishman was so widely known. In every part of America, his books had an extraordinary circulation. This influence reached all classes. It was strong among scientific men, whatever may be said to the contrary. Among such men as Von Moltke, Mr. Arthur Balfour, and others belonging to the governing class, it was stronger still. It penetrated to every section of the Christian church, and far beyond these limits.

Still, when this is said, it remains true that his deepest influence was personal and hidden. In the long series of addresses he delivered all over the world, he brought about what may at least be called a crisis in the lives of innumerable hearers. He received, I venture to say, more of the confidences of people untouched by the ordinary work of the church than any other man of his time. Men and women came to him in their deepest and bitterest perplexities. To such, he was accessible and, both by personal interviews and by correspondence, gave such help as he could. He was an ideal confessor. No story of failure daunted or surprised him. He had a message of hope for everyone; and, while he was the warm friend of a chosen circle and acutely responsive to their kindness, he did not seem to lean upon his friends. He himself did not ask for sympathy, and did not seem to need it. The innermost secrets of his life were between himself and his Savior. While frank and, at times, even communicative, he had nothing to say about himself or about those who had trusted him. There are multitudes who owed to Henry Drummond all that one person can owe to another, and who felt such a shock pass through them at the news of his death as they can never experience again.

Henry Drummond was born at Stirling in 1851. He was surrounded from the first by powerful religious influences of the evangelistic kind. His uncle, Mr. Peter Drummond, was the founder of what is known as the Stirling Tract enterprise, through which many millions of small religious publications have been circulated throughout the world. As a child, he was remarkable for his sunny disposition and his sweet temperament, while the religiousness of his nature made itself manifest at an early period. I do not gather, however, that there were many auguries of his future distinction. He was thought to be somewhat aimless and independent in his work.

In due course, he proceeded to the University of Edinburgh, where he distinguished himself in science, but in nothing else. He gained, I believe, the medal in the geology class. But like many students who do not go in for honors, he was anything but idle. He himself tells us that he began to form a library, his first purchase being a volume of extracts from Ruskin's works. Ruskin taught him to see the world as it is, and it soon became a new world to him, full of charm and loveliness. He learned to linger beside the ploughed field and revel in the affluence of color and shade that were to be seen in the newly turned furrows, and to gaze in wonder at the liquid amber of the two feet of air above the brown earth.

Next to Ruskin, he put Emerson, who, all Drummond's life, powerfully affected both his teaching and his style. Differing as they did in many ways, they were alike in being optimists with a high and noble idea of good, but with no correspondingly definite idea of evil. Mr. Henry James says that Emerson's genius had a singular thinness, an almost touching lightness, sparseness, and transparency about it. And the same was true, in a measure, of Drummond's.

The religious writers who attracted him were Channing and F. W. Robertson. Channing taught him to believe in God, the good and gracious Sovereign of all things. From Robertson, he learned that God is human, and that we may have fellowship with Him, because He sympathizes with us. It is well known that Robertson himself was a warm admirer of Channing. The parallels between Robertson and Channing in thought, and even in words, have never been properly drawn out. It would be a gross exaggeration to say that the contact with Robertson and Channing was the beginning of Drummond's religious life. But it was through them, and it was at that period of his studentship, that he began to take possession for himself of Christian truth. And it was a great secret of his power that he preached nothing except what had personally come home to him and had entered into his heart of hearts. His attitude to much of the theology in which he was taught was not that of denial but of respectful distance. He might have come later on to appropriate it and preach it, but the appropriation would have been the condition of the preaching. His mind was always receptive. Like Emerson, he was an excellent listener. He always stood in a position of hopeful expectancy, and regarded each delivery of a personal view as a new fact to be estimated on its merits. I may add that he was a warm admirer of Mr. R. H. Hutton and thought his essay on Goethe the best critical piece of the century. He used to say that, like Mr. Hutton, he could sympathize with every church but the "Hard Church."

After completing his university course, he went to the New College, Edinburgh, to be trained for the ministry of the Free Church. The timing was critical. The Free Church had been founded in a time of intense Evangelical faith and passion. It was a visible sign of the reaction against Moderatism. The Moderates had done great service to literature, but their sermons were favorably represented by the solemn fudge of Blair. James Macdonell, the brilliant *Times* leader-writer who carefully observed from the position of an outsider the ecclesiastical life of his countrymen, said that the Moderate leaders deliberately set themselves to the task of stripping Scotch Presbyterianism free from provincialism, and so triumphant were they that most of their sermons might have been preached in a heathen temple as fitly as in St. Giles. They taught the moral law with politeness; they made philosophy the handmaiden of Christianity with well-bred moderation, and they so handled the grimmer tenets of Calvinism as to hurt no susceptibilities.

The storm of the Disruption[27] blew away the old Moderates from their place of power, and men like Chalmers, Cunningham, Candlish, Welsh, Guthrie, Begg, and the other leaders of the Evangelicals more than filled their place. The obvious danger was that the Free Church would become the home of bigotry and obscurantism. This danger was not great at first. There was a lull in critical and theological discussion, and men were sure of their ground. The large and generous spirit of Chalmers impressed itself on the church of which he was the main founder, and the desire to assert the influence of religion in science and literature in all the field of knowledge was shown from the beginning. For example, the *North British Review* was the organ of the Free Church, and it did not stand much behind the *Edinburgh* and the *Quarterly*, either in the ability of its articles or in the distinction of many of its contributors. But the Free Church especially showed its wisdom by founding theological seminaries and filling their chairs with its best men. A professorship of divinity was held to be a higher position than the pastorate of any pulpit. As time went on, however, and as the tenets of the Westminster Evangelicanism were more and more formidably assailed, the Free Church came in danger of surrendering its intellectual life. The whisper of heresy would have damaged a minister as effectually as a grave moral charge. Independent thought was impatiently and angrily suppressed. Writing in the *Spectator* in 1874, Macdonell said that the Free Church was being intellectually starved, and he pointed out that the Established Church was gaining ground under the leadership of such men as Principal Tulloch and Dr. Wallace, who, in a sense, represented the old Moderates, though they were as different from them as this age is from the last.

The Free Church was apparently refusing to shape the dogmas of traditional Christianity in such a way as to meet the subtle intellectual and moral demands of an essentially scientific age. There was an apparent unanimity in the Free Church, but it was much more apparent than real. For one thing, the teaching of some of the professors had been producing its influence. Dr. A. B. Davidson, the recognized master of Old Testament learning in this country, a man who joins to his knowledge imagination, subtlety, fervor, and a rare power of style, had been quietly teaching the best men among his students that the old views of revelation would have to be seriously altered. He did not do this so much directly as indirectly, and I think there was a period when any Free Church minister who asserted the existence of errors in the Bible would have been summarily deposed. The abler students had been taking sessions at Germany and had thus escaped from the narrowness of the provincial coterie. Some of them were interested in literature, some in science, some in philosophy. At the New College, they discussed in their theological society the problems of the time with daring and freedom. A crisis was sure to come, and it might very well have been a crisis that would have broken the church in pieces. That it did not was due largely to the influence of one man—the American evangelist Mr. Moody.

In 1873, Mr. Moody commenced his campaign in the Barclay Free Church, Edinburgh. A few days earlier, Drummond had read a paper to the Theological Society of his college on "Spiritual Diagnosis," in which he maintained that preaching was not the most important thing, but that personal dealing with those in anxiety would yield better results. In other words, he thought that practical religion might be treated as an exact science. He had given himself to scientific study with a view of standing for the degree of Doctor of Science. Moody at once made a deep impression on Edinburgh, and attracted the ablest students. He missed in this country a sufficient religious provision for young men, and he thought that young men could best be molded by young men. With his keen American eye, he perceived that Drummond was his best instrument, and he immediately associated him in the work. It had almost magical results. From the very first, Drummond attracted and deeply moved crowds, and the result was that, for two years, he gave himself to this work of evangelism in England, in Scotland, and in Ireland.

During this period, he came to know the life histories of young men in all classes. He made himself a great speaker; he knew how to seize the critical moment. And his modesty, his refinement, his gentle and generous nature, his manliness, and, above all, his profound conviction, won for him disciples in every place he visited. His companions were equally busy in their own lines, and in this way the Free Church was saved. A development on the lines of Tulloch and Wallace was impossible for the Free Church. Any change that might take place must conserve the vigorous evangelical life of which it had been the home. The change did take place. Robertson Smith, who was by far the first man of the circle, won, at the sacrifice of his own position, toleration for biblical criticism, and proved that an advanced critic might be a convinced and fervent evangelical. Others did something, each in his own sphere, and it is not too much to say that the effects have been worldwide. The recent writers of Scottish fiction—Barrie, Crockett, and Ian Maclaren—were all children of the Free Church, two of them being ministers. In almost every department of theological science, with perhaps the exception of church history, Free Churchmen have made contributions that rank with the most important of the day. It is but bare justice to say that the younger generation of Free Churchmen have done their share in claiming that Christianity should rule in all the fields of culture, that the incarnation hallows every department of human thought and activity. No doubt, the claim has excited some hostility. At the same time, the general public has rallied in overwhelming numbers to its support; and any book of real power written in a Christian spirit now has an audience compared with which that of most secular writers is small.

Even at that time, Drummond's evangelism was not of the ordinary type. When he had completed his studies, after brief intervals of work elsewhere, he found his professional sphere as lecturer on natural science in the Free Church College at Glasgow. There, he came under the spell of Dr. Marcus Dods, to whom, as he always testified, he owed more than to any other man.

He worked in a mission connected with Dr. Dods's congregation, and there preached the remarkable series of addresses that were afterward published as *Natural Law in the Spiritual World*. The book appeared in 1883, and the author would have been quite satisfied with a circulation of 1,000 copies. In England alone, it has sold about 120,000 copies, while the American and foreign editions are beyond count.

There is a natural prejudice against premature reconciliations between science and religion. Many would say with Schiller, "Feindschaft sei zwischen euch, noch kommt ein Bündniss zu frühe: Forschet beide getrennt, so wird die Wahrheit erkannt." In order to reconcile science and religion, finally you must be prepared to say what is science and what is religion. Until that is done, any synthesis must be premature, and any book containing it must, in due time, be superseded. Drummond was not blind to this fact, and yet he saw that something had to be done. Evolution was becoming more than a theory—it was an atmosphere. Through the teaching of evolutionists, a subtle change was passing over morals, politics, and religion. Compromises had been tried and failed. The division of territory desired by some was found to be impossible. Drummond did not begin with doctrine and work downward to nature. He ran up natural law as far as it would go, and then the doctrine burst into view.

It was contended by the lamented Aubrey Moore that the proper thing is to begin with doctrine. While Moore would have admitted that science cannot be defined, and that even the problem of evolution is one of which as yet we hardly know the outlines, he maintained that the first step was to begin with the theology of the Catholic Church, and that it was impossible to defend Christianity on the basis of anything less than the whole of the church's creed. Drummond did not attempt this. He declined, for example, to consider the relation of evolution to the fall and to the Pauline doctrine of redemption. What he maintained was that, if you begin at the natural laws, you end in the spiritual laws; and in a series of impressive illustrations, he brought out his facts of science, some of them characteristic doctrines of Calvinism—brought them out sternly and undisguisedly. By many of the orthodox, he was welcomed as a champion, but others could not acquiesce in his assumption of evolution, and regarded him as more dangerous than an open foe. The book was riddled with criticisms from every side. Drummond himself never replied to these, but he gave his approval to an anonymous defense that appeared in the *Expositor*, and it is worthwhile to briefly recall the main points.

(1) His critics rejected his main position, which was not that the spiritual laws are analogous to the natural laws, but that they are the same laws. To this, he replied that if he had not shown identity, he had done nothing. But he admitted that the application of natural law to the spiritual world had decided and necessary limits, the principle not applying to those provinces of the spiritual world most remote from human experience. He adhered to the distinction between nature and grace, but he thought of grace as also forming part of the divine whole of nature, which is an emanation from the recesses of the divine wisdom, power, and love.

(2) His use of the law of biogenesis was severely attacked from the scientific side and the religious side alike. Even Christian men of science thought he had laid dangerous stress on the principle *omne vivum ex vivo*,[28] and declined to say that biogenesis was as certain as gravity. They further affirmed, and surely with reason, that the principle is not essential to faith. From the religious side, it was urged that he had grossly exaggerated the distinction between the spiritual man and the natural man, and that he had ignored the susceptibilities or affinities of the natural man for spiritual influence. The reply was that he had asserted the capacity for God very strongly. "The chamber is not only ready to receive the new life, but the Guest is expected, and until He comes is missed. Until then, the soul longs and yearns, wastes and pines, waving its tentacles piteously in the empty air, or feeling after God if so be that it may find Him."

(3) As for the charge that he could not reconcile his own statements as to divine efficiency and human responsibility, it was pointed out that this was only a phase of the larger difficulty of reconciling the exercise of the divine will with the freedom of the human will. What he maintained, in common with Augustinian and Puritan theology, was that in every case of regeneration, there is an original intervention of God.

(4) The absence of reference to the atonement was due to the fact that the doctrine belonged to a region inaccessible to the new method, lying in the depths of the divine Mind, and to be made known only by revelation.

(5) The charge that he taught the annihilation of the unregenerate was repudiated. The unregenerate had not fulfilled the conditions of eternal life; but that does not show that they may not exist through eternity, for they exist at present, although in Mr. Drummond's sense, they do not live.

There is no doubt that many of the objections directed against his book applied equally to every form of what may be called evangelical Calvinism. But I think that the main impression produced on competent judges was that the volume, though written with brilliant clearness of thought and imagination, and full of the Christian spirit, did not give true place to personality, freedom, and conscience—terms against which physical science may even be said to direct its whole artillery, as far as it tries to depersonalize man, but terms in which the very life of morality and religion is bound up. Perhaps Drummond himself came ultimately to take this view. In any case, Matthew Arnold's verdict will stand: "What is certain is that the author of the book has a genuine love of religion and a genuine religious experience."

Drummond's lectureship in Glasgow was constituted into a professor's chair, and he occupied it for the rest of his life. His work gave him considerable freedom. During a few months of the year, he lectured on geology and botany, and he also gave periodic discourses on biological problems and the study of evolution. He had two examinations in the year. The first, which he called the "stupidity" examination, was to test the men's knowledge of common things, asking such questions as, "Why is grass green?" "Why is the sea salty?" "Why is the heaven blue?" "What is a leaf?" and so forth. After this Socratic inquiry, he began his teaching, and he examined his students at the end. He taught in a classroom that was also a museum, always had specimens before him while lecturing, and introduced his students to the use of scientific instruments, besides taking them for geological excursions. In his time of leisure, he traveled very widely. He paid three visits to America and one to Australia. He also took the journey to Africa commemorated in his brilliant little book *Tropical Africa*, a work in which his insight, his power of selection, his keen observation, his fresh style, and his charming personality appear to the utmost advantage. It was praised on every side, although Mr. Stanley made a criticism to which Drummond gave an effective and good-humored retort.

During these journeys, and on other occasions at home, he continued his work of evangelism. He addressed himself mainly to students, on whom he had a great influence. For years, he went every week to Edinburgh for the purpose of delivering Sunday evening religious addresses to university men. He was invariably followed by crowds, the majority of whom were medical students. On several occasions, he also delivered addresses in London to social and political leaders, the audience including many of the most eminent men of the time. The substance of these addresses appeared in his famous booklets, beginning with *The Greatest Thing in the World*, and it may be worthwhile to say something of their teaching.

Mr. Drummond did not begin in the conventional way. He seemed to do without all that is indispensable to common Christianity. He approached the subject so disinterestedly, with such an entire disregard of its one presupposition, sin, that many people could never get on common ground with him. He entirely omitted the theology of the cross that had hitherto been the substance of evangelistic addresses. Nobody could say that his gospel was "arterial" or "ensanguined." In the first place, he had, like Emerson, a profound belief in the powers of the human will. That word of Spinoza that has been called a text in the scriptures of humanity might have been his motto: "He who desires to assist other people...in common conversations will avoid referring to the vices of men, and will take care only sparingly to speak of human impotence, while he will talk largely of human virtue or power, and of the way by which it may be made perfect, so that men being moved not by fear or aversion, but by the effect of joy, may endeavor, as much as they can, to live under the rule of reason."[29] With this sentence may be coupled its echo in the *Confessions of a Beautiful Soul* [Goethe]: "It is so much the more our duty, not, like the advocate of the evil spirit, always to keep our eyes fixed upon the nakedness and weakness of our nature, but rather to seek out all those perfections through which we can make good our claims to a likeness to God." But along with this went a passionate devotion to Jesus Christ. Emerson said, "The man has never lived who can feed us ever."[30] Drummond maintained with absolute conviction that Christ could forever and ever meet all the needs of the soul.

In his critique *Ecce Homo*, Mr. Gladstone answered the question of whether the Christian preacher is ever justified in delivering less than a full gospel. He argued that to go back to the very beginning of Christianity might be a method eminently suited to the needs of the present generation. The ship of Christianity was overloaded—perhaps not for fair weather, but when a gale came, the mass strained over to the leeward. Drummond asked his hearers to go straight into the presence of Christ, not as He now presents Himself to us, bearing in His hand the long roll of His conquests, but as He offered Himself to the Jew by the Sea of Galilee, or in the synagogue of Capernaum, or in the temple in Jerusalem.

He declined to take every detail of the Christianity in possession as part of the whole. He denied that the rejection of the nonessential involved parting with the essential, and he strove to go straight to the fountainhead itself. Whatever criticisms may be passed, it will be allowed that few men in the century have done so much to bring their hearers and readers to the feet of Jesus Christ. It has been said of Carlyle that the one living ember of the old Puritanism that still burned vividly in his mind was the belief that honest and true men might find power in God to alter things for the better. Drummond believed with his whole heart that men might find power in Christ to change their lives.

He had seven or eight months of the year at his disposal, and spent very little of them in his beautiful home at Glasgow. He wandered all over the world, and, in genial human intercourse, made his way to the hearts of rich and poor. He was as much at home in addressing a meeting of working men as in speaking at Grosvenor House.[31] He had fastidious tastes, was always faultlessly dressed, and could appreciate the surroundings of civilization. But he could, at a moment's notice, throw them all off and be perfectly happy. As a traveler in Africa, he cheerfully endured much privation.

He excelled in many sports and was a good shot. In some ways, he was like Lavengro, and I will say that some parts of *Lavengro*[32] would be unintelligible to me unless I had known Drummond. Although he refused to quarrel and had a thoroughly loyal and deeply affectionate nature, he was yet independent of others. He never married. He never undertook any work to which he did not feel himself called. Although he had the most tempting offers from editors, nothing would induce him to write unless the subject attracted him, and, even then, he was unwilling. Although he had great facility, he never presumed upon it. He wrote brightly and swiftly, and would have made an excellent journalist. But everything he published was elaborated with the most scrupulous care. I have never seen manuscripts so carefully revised as his. All he did was apparently done with ease, but there was immense labor behind it.

Although he was an ordained minister, he used neither the title nor the dress that goes with them, but preferred to regard himself as a layman. He had a deep sense of the value of the church and its work, but I think he himself was not connected with any church, and never attended public worship unless he thought the preacher had some message for him. He seemed to be invariably in good spirits, and invariably disengaged. He was always ready for any and every office of friendship. It should be said that, although few men were more criticized or misconceived, he himself never wrote an unkind word about anyone, never retaliated, never bore malice, and could do full justice to the abilities and character of his opponents. I have just heard that he exerted himself privately to secure an important appointment for one of his most trenchant critics, and was successful.

For years, he had been quietly working on his last and greatest book, *The Ascent of Man*. The chapters were first delivered as the Lowell Lectures in Boston, where they attracted great crowds. The volume was published in 1894, and though its sale was large, exceeding 20,000 copies, it did not command his old public. This was due very much to the obstinacy with which he persisted in selling it at a net price, a proceeding that offended the booksellers, who had hoped to profit much from its sale. The work is much the most important he has left us. It was an endeavor, as has been said, to engraft an evolutionary sociology and ethic upon a biological basis. The fundamental doctrine of the struggle of life leads to an individualistic system in which the moral side of nature has no place. Professor Drummond contended that the currently accepted theory, being based on an exclusive study of the conditions of nutrition, took account of only half the truth. With nutrition, he associated, as a second factor, the function of reproduction, the struggle for the life of others, and he maintained that this was of coordinate rank as a force in cosmic evolution. Though others had recognized altruism as modifying the operation of egoism, Mr. Drummond did more. He tried to indicate the place of altruism as the outcome of those processes whereby the species is multiplied, and its bearing on the evolution of ethics. In other words, he desired a unification of concept, the filling up of great gulfs that had seemed to be fixed. "If Nature is the Garment of God, it is woven without seam throughout; if a revelation of God, it is the same yesterday, today, and forever; if the expression of His Will, there is in it no variableness nor shadow of turning."[33]

After sketching the stages of the process of evolution, physical and ethical, he develops his central idea in the chapter on the struggle for the life of others, and then deals with the higher stages of the development of altruism as a modifying factor. The book was mercilessly criticized, but I believe that no one has attempted to deny the accuracy and the beauty of his scientific descriptions. Further, not a few eminent scientific men, like Professor Gairdner and Professor Macalister, have seen in it at least the germ out of which much may come.

One of its severest critics, Dr. Dallinger, considers that nature is nonmoral, and that religion begins with Christ. *"No man hath seen God at any time"* (John 1:18)—this is what nature certifies. The only begotten Son of the Father, *"he hath declared him"* (John 1:18)—this is the message of Christianity. But there are many religious minds, and some scientific minds, who are convinced, in spite of all the difficulties, that natural law must be moral, and are very loath to admit a hopeless dualism between the physical and the moral order of the world. They say that the whole force of evolution directs our glance forward....

With the publication of this book, Drummond's career as a public teacher virtually ended. He who had never known an illness, who apparently had been exempted from care and sorrow, was prostrated by a painful and mysterious malady. One of his kind physicians, Dr. Freeland Barbour, informs me that Mr. Drummond suffered from a chronic disease of the bones. It maimed him greatly. He was laid on his back for more than a year, and had both arms crippled, so that reading was not a pleasure and writing almost impossible. For a long time, he suffered acute pain. It was then that some who had greatly misconceived him came to a truer judgment of the man. Those who had often found the road rough had looked askance at Drummond as a spoiled child of fortune, ignorant of life's real meaning. But when he was struck down in his prime, at the very height of his happiness—when there was appointed for him, to use his own words, "a waste of storm and tumult before he reached the shore"[34]—it seemed as if his sufferings liberated and revealed the forces of his soul.

The spectacle of his long struggle with a mortal disease was something more than impressive. Those who saw him in his illness saw that, as the physical life flickered low, the spiritual energy grew. Always gentle and considerate, he became even more careful, more tender, more thoughtful, more unselfish. He never complained in any way. His doctors found it very difficult to get him to talk of his illness. It was strange and painful, but inspiring, to see his keenness, his mental elasticity, his universal interest. Dr. Barbour says, "I have never seen pain or weariness, or the being obliged to do nothing, more entirely overcome; treated, in fact, as if they were not. The end came suddenly from failure of the heart. Those with him received only a few hours' warning of his critical condition."

It was not like death. He lay on his couch in the drawing room and passed away in his sleep, with the sun shining in and the birds singing at the open window. There was no sadness or farewell. It recalled what he himself had said of a friend's death—"putting by the well-worn tools without a sigh, and expecting elsewhere better work to do."

Sir William Robertson Nicoll (1851–1923) was a minister in the Free Church of Scotland, as well as a journalist and an editor.

MEMORIAL PROFILE BY
IAN MACLAREN

He had been in many places around the world and seen strange sights, and taken his share in various works; and, being the man he was, it came to pass of necessity that he had many friends. Some of them were street Arabs, some were foreigners, some were physicians, some were evangelists, some were scientists, some were theologians, some were nobles. Between each one and Drummond, there was some affinity, and each could tell his own story about his friend. It will be interesting to hear what Professor Greenfield or Mr. Moody may have to say. But one man, with profound respect for such eminent persons, would prefer to have a study of Drummond by Moolu, his African retainer. Drummond believed in Moolu, not because he was "pious"—which he was not—but because "he did his duty and never told a lie." From the chief's point of view, Moolu had the final virtue of a clansman—he was loyal and faithful. His chief, for that expedition, had beyond most men the necessary endowment of a leader—a magnetic personality.

It is understood that Drummond's life is to be written at large by a friend in whose capable and wise hands it will receive full justice. But, in the meantime, it may not be unbecoming that one should pay his tribute who has his own qualification for this work of love. It is not that he is able to appreciate to the full the man's wonderful genius, or accurately to estimate his contributions to scientific and religious thought—this will be done by more distinguished friends—but that he knew Drummond constantly and intimately from boyhood to his death. If one has known any friend at school and college, and, in the greater affairs of life, has lived with him, argued with him, prayed with him, had his sympathy in the supreme moments of joy and sorrow, had every experience of friendship except one—it was not possible to quarrel with Drummond, although you might be the hottest-tempered Celt on the face of the earth—then he may not understand the value of his friend's work, but, at any rate, he understands his friend. As one who knew Henry Drummond firsthand, my desire is to tell what manner of man he was in all honesty and without adulation. If anyone be offended, then let him believe that I wrote what I have seen; and, if anyone be incredulous, then I can say only that he did not know Drummond.

His body was laid to rest a few weeks ago, on a wet and windy March day, in the most romantic of Scottish cemeteries; and the funeral, on its way from the home of his boyhood to the Castle Rock of Stirling, passed the King's Park. It was in that park, more than thirty years ago, that I first saw Drummond; and, on our first meeting, he produced the same effect as he did his entire life. The sun was going down behind Ben Lomond in the happy summertime, touching with gold the gray old castle, deepening the green upon the belt of trees that fringed the eastern side of the park, and filling the park itself with soft, mellow light. A cricket match between two schools had been going on all day and was coming to an end, and I had gone out to see the result—being a new arrival in Stirling, and full of curiosity. The two lads at the wickets were in striking contrast—one heavy, stocky, and determined, who slogged powerfully and had scored well for his side; the other nimble, alert, graceful, who had a pretty but uncertain play. The slogger was forcing the running in order to make up a heavy leeway, and he compelled his partner to run once too often. "It's all right, and you fellows are not to cry shame"—this was what he said as he joined his friends—"Buchanan is playing A1, and that hit ought to have been a four; I messed the running." It was good form, of course, and what any decent lad would want to say, but there was an accent of gaiety and a certain air that was very taking. Against that group of clumsy, unformed, awkward Scots lads, this bright, straight, living figure stood in relief. As he moved around the field, my eyes followed him; and, in my boyish and dull mind, I had a sense that he was a type by himself, a visitor of finer breed than those among whom he moved. By and by, he mounted a friend's pony and galloped along the racecourse in the park until one saw only a speck of white in the sunlight; and still I watched in wonder and fascination—only a boy of thirteen or so, and dull—until he came back, in time to cheer the slogger who had pulled off the match—with three runs to spare—and carried his bat.

"Well played, old chap! Finest thing you've ever done," the pure, clear, joyous note rang out on the evening air, while the strong-armed, heavy-faced slogger stood still and looked at him in admiration, and made amends. "I say, Drummond, it was my blame you were run out...." Drummond was his name, and someone else said, "Henry." So I first saw my friend.

I can now identify what impressed me that pleasant evening in the days of long ago. It was the lad's distinction, an inherent quality of appearance and manner of character and soul that marked him and made him solitary. What happened with one strange lad that evening befell all kinds of people who met Drummond in later years. They were at once arrested, interested, fascinated by the very sight of the man, and could not take their eyes off him. Like a picture of the first order among ordinary portraits, he unconsciously put his neighbors at a disadvantage. One did not realize how commonplace and colorless other men were until they stood side by side with Drummond. Upon a platform of evangelists, or sitting among divinity students in a dingy classroom, or cabined in the wooden respectability of an ecclesiastical court, or standing in a crowd of passengers at a railway station, he suggested golden embroidery upon hodden gray. It was as if the prince of one's imagination had dropped in among common folk. He reduced us all to the peasantry.

Drummond was a handsome man—such as you could not match in ten days' journey—with delicately cut features, rich auburn hair, and a certain carriage of nobility; but the distinctive and commanding feature of his face was his eyes. No photograph could do them justice; and, very often, photographs have done them injustice by giving the idea of staring. His eyes were not bold or fierce; they were tender and merciful. But they had a power and hold that were little else than irresistible and almost supernatural. When you talked with Drummond, he did not look at you and out the window, alternately, as is the usual manner. He never moved his eyes; and, gradually, their penetrating gaze seemed to reach and encompass your soul. It was as Plato imagined it would be in the judgment; one soul was in contact with another—nothing between. No man could be duplicitous, or base, or mean, or impure before those eyes. His influence, more than that of any other man I have ever met, was mesmeric—which means that while other men affect their fellows by speech and example, he seized one directly by his living personality....

One sometimes imagines life as a kind of gas of which our bodies are the vessels, and it is evident that a few are much more richly charged than their fellows. Most people simply exist completing their tale of work—not a grain more; doing their measured mile—not an inch beyond; thinking along the beaten track—never tempted to excursions. Here and there in the world, you come across a person in whom life is exuberant and overflowing, a force that cannot be tamed or quenched. Drummond was such a one, the most vital man I ever saw, who never loitered, never wearied, never was conventional, pedantic, formal, who simply reveled in the fullness of life. He was so radiant with life that ordinary people showed pallid beside him, and shrank from him or were attracted and received virtue out of him. Like one coming in from the light and open air into a stuffy room where a company had been sitting with closed windows, Drummond burst into bloodless and unhealthy coteries, bringing with him the very breath of heaven.

He was the evangelist to thoughtful men—over women, he had far less power—and his strength lay in his personality. Without anecdotes or jokes, or sensationalism or doctrine, without eloquence or passion, he moved young men at his will because his message was life, and he was its illustration. His words fell one by one with an indescribable awe and solemnity, in the style of the Gospels, and reached the secret place of the soul. Nothing more unlike the ordinary evangelistic address could be imagined: it was so sane, so persuasive, so mystical, so final. It almost followed, therefore, that he was not the ideal of a popular evangelist, who has to address the multitude and produce his effect on those who do not think. For his work, it is necessary—besides earnestness, which is taken for granted—to have a loud voice, a broad humor, a stout body, a flow of strong anecdotes, an easy negligence of connection, a spice of contempt for culture, and pledges of identification with the street in dress and accent. His hearers feel that such a man is familiar and is one of them; and, amid laughter and tears of simple human emotion, they are moved by his speech to higher things.

This kind of audience might regard Drummond with respectful admiration, but they would consider him too fine a gentleman for their homespun. Place him, as he used to stand and speak, most perfectly dressed both as to body and soul, before five hundred men of good taste and fine sensibilities, or the same number of young men not yet cultured but full of intellectual ambitions and fresh enthusiasm, and no man could state the case for Christ and the soul in a more spiritual and winsome fashion. Without doubt, religion is the better because of the popular evangelist, although there are times when quiet folk think that he needs chastening; in every generation, religion also requires at least one representative of the higher evangelism. And if anyone should ask what manner of man he ought to be, the answer is within his reach—Henry Drummond.

When one admits, without reserve, that his friend was not made by nature to be a successful officer of the Salvation Army, it must not be understood that Drummond was in any sense a superior person, or that he sniffed in his daintiness at ordinary humanity—a spiritual Matthew Arnold. It would strain my conscience to bear witness that working people, for example, however much they loved him, were perfectly at home with him. And it is my conviction, from my observation of life, that this is an inevitable disability of distinction. One may be so well-dressed, so good-looking, so well-mannered, so spiritually refined, that men with soiled clothes and women cleaning the house may realize their low estate, and miss that natural affinity that, by a hundred signs, unites them in five minutes with a plainer man.

While this may have been true, the blame was not his, and no man lived who had more of an unaffected interest and keener joy in human life in the home or on the street. No power could drag him past a Punch and Judy show—the ancient, perennial, ever-delightful theater of the people—in which, each time he attended, he detected new points of interest. In early days, if you please, he would gaze steadfastly into a window in the High Street of Edinburgh, until a little crowd of men, women, children, workmen, loafers, and soldiers had collected, and he would join with much zest in the excited speculations regarding the man—unanimously and suddenly imagined to have been carried in helpless—how he met with his accident, where he was hurt, and whether he would recover, listening eagerly to the explanation of the gathering given by some officious person to the policeman, and joining heartily in the reproaches leveled at some unknown deceiver!

One of his chosen subjects of investigation, which he pursued with the zeal and patience of a naturalist, was that ever-interesting species—"the Boy," whom he studied in his various forms and haunts: at home for the holidays, on the cricket field, playing marbles on the street with a chance acquaintance while two families wait for their food, or living with many resources and high enjoyment in a barrel. There was nothing in a boy he did not know, could not explain, did not sympathize with; and, as long as it lasts, his name will be associated with the Boys' Brigade.

While anyone else would have seen only two revelers in a man and woman singing their meandering way along the street at night, Drummond detected that a wife, who had not been drinking, was luring her husband home by falling in with his mood, and that before it was reached, she might need a friendly hand.

His sense of humor was unerring, swift, and masterful. If he came upon a good thing in his reading, he would walk a mile to share it with a friend, and afterward depart in the strength thereof. And he has been found in his room exhausted with delight, with nothing before him but one of those Parisian plaster caricatures of a vagabond. Lying on his back in the pitiable helplessness and constant pain of those last two years, he was still the same man.

"Don't touch me, please; I can't shake hands, but I've saved up a first-rate story for you"—and his palate was too delicate to pass anything second-rate. This was partly due to his human joyousness, to whom the absurdities of life were ever dear; partly, it was his bravery, who knew that the sight of him brought so low might be too much for a friend. His patience and sweetness continued to the end, and he died as one who had tasted the joy of living and was satisfied.

At the same time, his nature had a curious aloofness and separateness from human life, which one felt but can hardly describe. He could be severe in speaking about a mean act or about someone who had done wickedly; but, in my recollection, he was never angry, and it was impossible to imagine him in a towering passion. He was profoundly interested in several causes, but there was not in him the making of a fanatical or headlong supporter. None could be more loyal in the private offices of friendship, but he would not have flung himself into his friend's public quarrel. In no circumstances would he be carried off his feet by emotion or be consumed by a white heat of enthusiasm. He was ever calm, cool, the self-possessed master of himself, passionless in thought, in speech, in action, in soul. If you were in trouble, he would help you to his last resource, and would conceal his service, if possible; but in his sore straits, he would neither have asked nor wished for aid from you.

He must have received many confidences; he gave none. Many people must have been succored by him; none succored him until his last illness. Toward women, who are the test and revelation of men, he was ever chivalrous, but he left the impression on your mind that neither they nor their company—there may have been exceptions—attracted or satisfied him. He was too courteous a gentleman to give any sign of this, but one guessed that a woman's departure from the room meant to him no loss, and was rather a relief. One was certain that he was loved; one was quite certain that he would never marry. So sexless was he toward women, so neutral toward men, so void of the elemental passions that go to make the color and tragedy of life, yet so noble and true was he, that one regarded him at times with awe, and for a moment thought of him as a being of another race, mingling with our life in all kindliness, yet maintaining and guarding his other-world integrity.

This, at least, is perfectly certain: From his youth, he refused to have his life arranged for him, but jealously and fearlessly directed it by his own instincts—refusing the brown, beaten paths wherein each man, according to his profession, was content to walk, and starting across the moor on his own way. Nothing can be more conventional than the career of the average Presbyterian minister who comes from a respectable religious family, and has the pulpit held up before him as the ambition of a good Scots lad; who is held in the way thereto by various traditional and prudential considerations, and better still—as is the case with most honest lads—by his mother's wishes; who works his laborious, enduring way through the Divinity Hall, and is yearly examined by the local presbytery; who at last emerges into the butterfly life of a probationer, and is freely mentioned, to his mother's anxious delight, in connection with "vacancies"; who is at last chosen by a majority to a pastorate—his mother being amazed at the blindness of the minority—and settles down to the routine of the ministry in some Scotch parish with the hope of Glasgow before him as a land of promise. His only variations in the harmless years might be an outburst on the historical reality of the book of Jonah—Ah me! Did that stout, middle-aged gentleman ever hint that Jonah was a drama?—which would be much talked of in the common room, and, it was whispered, reached the professor's ears. And, afterward, he might propose a revolutionary motion on the distribution of the Sustentation Fund. Add a handbook for Bible classes on the prophecy of Malachi, and you have summed up the adventures of his life.

This was the life before Drummond when he entered the University of Edinburgh in 1866. And it ought to be recorded that he died an ordained minister and Professor of the Kirk, so that he did not disappoint his home nor become an ecclesiastical prodigal—but with what amazing variations did he invest the years between! In what order he took his classes, no one knew, but he found his feet in natural philosophy and made a name in geology. He completed his course at the New College in four years, but with two years' evangelistic touring between his third and fourth year. He once electrified the students by a paper—it seems yesterday, and I know where he stood— that owed much to Holmes and Emerson but revealed his characteristic spiritual genius.

He sometimes spent his vacations in tutorships, which yielded wonderful adventures, or at Tübingen, where his name was long remembered. As soon as Moody came to Edinburgh, Drummond allied himself with the most capable, honest, and unselfish evangelist of our day, and saw strange chapters in religious life through the United Kingdom. This was the infirmary in which he learned spiritual diagnosis. For one summer, he was chaplain at Malta; during another, he explored the Rockies. He lived for five months among the Tanganyika forests, where he sent me a letter dated "Central Africa," and mentioned, among other details, that he had nothing on but a helmet and three mosquitoes. For a time, he was an assistant in an Edinburgh church, and readers of the illustrated papers used to recognize him in the viceregal group at Dublin Castle.

His people at home—one could trace some of his genius and much of his goodness to his father and mother—grew anxious and perplexed. For this was a meteoric course for a Free Kirk minister, and stolid acquaintances— the delicious absurdity of it—remonstrated with him as one who was allowing the chances of life to pass him by, and urged him to settle. His friends had already concluded that he must be left free to fulfill himself, but knew not what to expect, when he suddenly appeared as a lecturer on natural science at the Free Church College of Glasgow, and promptly annexed a working-men's church. Afterward, his lectureship became a chair, and he held it to the end, although threatened with charges of heresy and similar absurdities. You might as well have beaten a spirit with a stick as prosecuted Drummond for heresy. The chair itself was a standing absurdity, being founded in popular idea to beat back evolution and to reconcile religion and science; but it gave Drummond an opportunity of widening the horizon of the future ministry and infusing sweetness into the students' minds. He may have worn a white tie on Sunday duty at his church, but memory fails to recall this spectacle; and he consistently refused to be called "Reverend"—declaring (this was his fun) that he had no recollection of being ordained, and that he would never dare to baptize a child. The last time he preached was about 1882, in my own church, and the outside world did not know that he was a clergyman. From first to last, he was guided by an inner light that never led him astray; and, in the afterglow, his whole life is a simple and perfect harmony.

Were one asked to select Drummond's finest achievement, he might safely mention the cleansing of student life at Edinburgh University. When Drummond was an arts student, life in all the faculties—but especially the medical—was reckless, coarse, and boisterous, and no one was doing anything to raise its tone. In my remembrance, the only visible sign of religion was a prayer meeting attended by a dozen men—one of whom was a canting rascal—and countenance from a professor would have given a shock to the university. Twenty years afterward, six hundred men, largely medicals, met every Sunday evening for worship and conference under Drummond's presidency; and, every evening, the meeting was addressed by tutors and fellows and other dignitaries. There was a new breath in academic life—men were now reverent, earnest, clean living, and clean thinking, and the reformer who worked this change was Drummond. This land, and, for that matter, the United States, has hardly a town where men are not doing good work for God and man today who have owed their lives to the evangel and influence of Henry Drummond.

When one saw the unique and priceless work that he did, it was inexplicable and very provoking that the religious world would have cast this man, of all others, out, and have lifted up its voice against him. Did religion have so many men of beautiful and winning life, so many thinkers of wide range and genuine culture, so many speakers who can move young men by the hundreds toward the kingdom of God, that she could afford or have the heart to withdraw her confidence from Drummond? Was there ever such madness and irony before heaven as good people lifting up their testimony and writing articles against this most gracious disciple of the Master, because they did not agree with him about certain things he said, or some theory he did not teach, while the world lay around them in unbelief and selfishness, and sorrow and pain?

"What can be done," an eminent evangelist once did me the honor to ask, "to heal the breach between the religious world and Drummond?" And I dared to reply that, in my poor judgment, the first step ought to be for the religious world to repent of its sins and to make amends to Drummond for its bitterness. The evangelist indicated that, as far as he knew his world, it was very unlikely to do any such becoming deed, and I myself did not remember any instance of repentance on the part of the Pharisees. Then, growing bold, I ventured to ask why the good man had not summoned Drummond to his side, as he was working in a university town and knew better than any other person that he could not find an assistant as acceptable or skillful anywhere else. He agreed about that, but he immediately declared that if Drummond came, his present staff would leave, and that two men could not do all the work, which seemed reasonable; and, besides, every man knows his own business best, and that evangelist knew his remarkably well. Nothing more remained to be said, and I rose to leave. At the far end of the room, some of the staff were talking together. "I gave them a 'straight talk' at the men's meeting last night, and then we had such a sweet little 'sing,' and thirty souls dropped in." A young man of the better class was speaking, and I looked at the weak, self-satisfied face, but it is not necessary to write down my reflections as I left the place. Never did my friend say one unkind word of the world that condemned him, but it may be allowed to another to say that if anyone wishes to indict the professional religionists of our time for bigotry and stupidity, painful and unanswerable proof lies within his reach in the fact that the finest evangelist of the day was treated as a Samaritan.

One, of course, remembers that Drummond's critics had their reasons, and those reasons cast interesting light on his theological standpoint. For one thing, unlike most evangelists, it was perfectly alien to this man to insist on repentance, simply because he had not the painful and overmastering sense of sin that afflicts most religious minds and gives a strenuous turn to all their thinking. Each thinker conceives religion according to his cast of mind and trend of experience, and Christianity to Drummond was not so much a way of escape from the grip of sin, with its burden of guilt and loathsome contact, as a way of ethical and spiritual attainment. The question he was always answering in his writing and speaking was not how a man can save his soul but how a man can save his life. His idea of salvation was rising to the stature of Christ and sharing His simple, lowly, peaceful life. This was the text of his brochures on religion, which charmed the world, from *The Greatest Thing in the World* to *The City Without a Church*. It is said that even these gave offense to some ultra-theological minds—although one would fain have believed that such persuasive pleas have won all hearts—and I have some faint remembrance, perhaps a nightmare, that people published replies to the eulogy of Love. It was quite beside the mark to find fault with the theology in the little books, because there was none and could be none, since there was none in the author. Just as there are periods in the development of Christianity, there are men in every age corresponding to each of the periods—modern, Reformation, and Medieval minds—and what charmed many in Drummond was that he belonged by nature to the pre-theological age. In his habit and thought, he was a Christian of the Gospels, rather than of the Epistles, and he preferred to walk with Jesus in Galilee rather than argue with Judaisers and Gnostics. It would be a gross injustice to say that he was anti-theological; it would be correct to say that he was nontheological. To him, Jesus was not an official Redeemer discharging certain obligations.

He was his unseen Friend, with whom he walked in life, by whose fellowship he was changed, to whom he prayed. The effort of life should be to do the will of God; the strength of life was peace; the reward of life was to be like Jesus. Perfect Christianity was to be as St. John was with Jesus. It was the idyll of religion.

Perhaps his two famous books, *Natural Law in the Spiritual World* and *The Ascent of Man*, ought to be judged as larger idylls. A writer often fails when he has counted himself strong, and succeeds in that which he himself has belittled. It was at one time Drummond's opinion that he had made a discovery in that fascinating debatable land between nature and religion, and that he was able to prove that the laws that govern the growth of a plant are the same in essence as those that regulate the culture of a soul. It appeared to some of us that the same laws could not and did not run through both provinces, but that, on the frontier of the spiritual world, other laws came into operation; and that *Natural Law* set forth with much grace and ingenuity a number of instructive analogies, and sometimes only suggestive illustrations. Had Drummond believed this was its furthest scope, he never would have published the book; and it was an open secret that, in later years, he lost all interest in *Natural Law*. My own idea is that he had abandoned its main contention and much of its teaching, and would have been quite willing to see it withdrawn from the public.

While that book was an attempt to identify the laws of two worlds that, under one suzerain, are really each autonomous, *The Ascent of Man* was a most successful effort to prove that the spirit of religion, which is altruism, pervades the processes of nature. It is the poem of evolution, and is from beginning to end a fascinating combination of scientific detail and spiritual imagination. Both books, but especially the *Ascent*, were severely criticized from opposite quarters—by theologians because the theology was not sound, by men of science because the science was loose—and Drummond had the misfortune of being a heretic in two provinces. But he had his reward in the gratitude of thousands who are neither dogmatic nor partisan, to whom he has given a new vision of the beauty of life and the graciousness of law.

His books will do good for years, as they have done in the past, and his tract on charity will long be read, but the man was greater than all his writings. While he was competent in science, he was a master in religion; and if, in this sphere, he failed anywhere in his thinking, it was in his treatment of sin. This was the defect of his qualities, for, of him, more than of any man known to me, it could be affirmed that he did not know sin. As Fra Angelico could paint the holy angels because he had seen them, but made poor work of the devils, because, to him, they were strange creatures, so this man could make holiness so lovely that all men wished to be Christians; but his hand lost its cunning at the mention of sin, for he had never played the fool. From his youth up, he had kept the commandments, and was such a man as the Master would have loved. One takes for granted that each man has his besetting sin, and we could name that of our friends, but Drummond was an exception to this rule. After a lifetime's intimacy, I do not remember my friend's failing. Without pride, without envy, without selfishness, and without vanity; moved only by goodwill and spiritual ambitions; always responsive to the touch of God and every noble impulse; faithful, fearless, and magnanimous; Henry Drummond was the most perfect Christian I have known or expect to see this side of the grave.

Ian Maclaren was the pseudonym of John Watson (1850–1907), who was a minister of the Free Church of Scotland, as well as the author of both fiction and nonfiction works.

NOTES

Chapter 1

1. See Charles Darwin, *The Expression of the Emotions in Man and Animals* (New York: D. Appleton, 1872), chapter 3, "General Principles of Expression—Concluded," 79–80, https://www.brocku.ca/MeadProject/Darwin/Darwin_1872_03.html.

2. See Martin Luther, *Table Talk* (originally titled *Divine Discourses*), trans. William Hazlitt (Philadelphia: The Lutheran Publication Society), discourse 319.

Chapter 2

3. Jemima Luke, "I Think, When I Read That Sweet Story of Old," 1841.

4. Author's variation of "O Jesus, Make Thyself to Me," n.d., by Charlotte Elliott.

5. Barbara Miller Macandrew, "Coming," n.d. See B. M. (Barbara Macandrew), *Ezekiel and Other Poems* (London: T. Nelson and Sons, 1871), 30.

Chapter 3

6. Rev. Robert Traill, *"Sixteen Sermons on the Lord's Prayer for His People, in John XVII.24,"* 1705. See The Religious Tract Society of London reprint of this book (1799), 67, www.books.google.com.

7. See William Burgess, ed., *The Religion of Ruskin* (New York: Fleming H. Revell Company, 1907), 242.

Chapter 5

8. The Book of Wisdom of Solomon, chapter 8, verses 10–12. See http://bibles.org/KJVA/Wis/8.

Chapter 6

9. See Thomas Carlyle, *Sartor Resartus* (Boston: Ginn & Company, Publishers, The Athenaeum Press, 1896), 64.

10. John Ruskin, *Modern Painters*, vol. 3 (1856), part 4, chapter 16, "Of Modern Landscape." See http://www.gutenberg.org/files/38923/38923-h/38923-h.htm.

11. Elizabeth Barrett Browning, "Aurora Leigh" (1857), lines 61–62.

Chapter 7

12. John Ruskin, *Modern Painters*, vol. 2 (1846), part 3, chapter 14, "Of Vital Beauty—Thirdly, in Man." See http://www.gutenberg.org/files/29906/29906-h/29906-h.htm.

13. Alfred, Lord Tennyson, "Ulysses" (1833; published 1842), line 18.

14. George Eliot (pseudonym of Mary Ann Evans), "O May I Join the Choir Invisible" (1867), lines 1–3. See http://www.bartleby.com/246/302.html.

15. Author's variation of "Rock of Ages, Cleft for Me," 1776, by Augustus M. Toplady.

Chapter 9

16. George Eliot (pseudonym of Mary Ann Evans), "The Legend of Jubal" (1870).

17. See James Martineau, *Hours of Thought on Sacred Things* (Boston: Roberts Brothers, 1882), 215.

18. Alfred, Lord Tennyson, "In Memoriam" (1849).

19. William Shakespeare, *The Tempest*, 4.1.147–148.

Chapter 11

20. Latin for "the highest good."

21. Bartolomé Esteban Murillo (1617–1682), Spanish Baroque painter.

22. Apparent variation by the author of a poem entitled "He Knows." See http://quote-investigator.com/2013/05/10/walk-with-friend/.

23. Benjamin Schmolck, "My Jesus, as Thou Wilt," n.d., translated by Jane Borthwick, 1854. See Jane Borthwick, *Hymns from the Land of Luther* (New York: Anson D. F. Randolph, 1857), 48.

Chapter 12

24. Variation by the author of the following quote by Johann Wolfgang von Goethe: "Talents are best nurtured in solitude; character is best formed in the stormy billows of the world," http://www.bartleby.com/348/authors/210.html.

Chapter 13

25. The Westminster Shorter Catechism was written in 1647 for the purpose of Christian instruction and consists of a series of 107 questions.

Chapter 15

26. Anna Laetitia Waring, "Father, I Know That All My Life," 1850.

Memorial Profile by W. Robertson Nicoll

27. A split in the Church of Scotland called the "Disruption of 1843."
28. Latin for "All life is from life."
29. See Joseph Ratner and Shawn Conner, eds., *The Philosophy of Spinoza* (El Paso: Norte Press, 2010), 222.
30. See Ralph Waldo Emerson, *Nature; Addresses and Lectures* (1849), "The American Scholar" ("an Oration delivered before the Phi Beta Kappa Society, at Cambridge, August 31, 1837"), http://www.emersoncentral.com/amscholar.htm.
31. The London home of the Duke of Westminster.
32. *Lavengro* (1851) is a work by English author George Henry Barlow.
33. From *The Ascent of Man* (1894).
34. Nicoll was quoting from a book that Henry Drummond edited, in which Drummond wrote of the subject of the work, "Sometimes, in such trouble as his, the land recedes with painful slowness, amid farewells and regrets, *and a waste of storm and tumult lies between the traveller and the further shore. But it was not so here. The symptoms ripened with a rush...*" (emphasis added). See Henry Drummond, ed./comp., *The Unsearchable Riches of Christ and Other Sermons* by John F. Ewing, M.A., 2nd ed. (London: Hodder and Stoughton, 1891), xxvi–xxvii.

ABOUT THE AUTHOR

Henry Drummond (1851–1897) was born in Stirling, Scotland, and was educated at Edinburgh University. In 1877, he became a lecturer on natural science at the Free Church College of Glasgow. Drummond was a geologist and an explorer, and he spent a portion of time away from the classroom on scientific expeditions. As a Christian, he combined his knowledge of science with his understanding of God the Creator and His diverse creations. Beyond his work as a scientist, Drummond desired to see men and women come to Christ. He accompanied Dwight L. Moody on many of his revival missions in England and Ireland, and he presented an address on biblical love during this time that deeply affected Moody. Drummond wrote several works on science, but his most famous and enduring book, based on that address on love, is *The Greatest Thing in the World.*

Welcome to Our House!

We Have a Special Gift for You ...

It is our privilege and pleasure to share in your love of Christian classics by publishing books that enrich your life and encourage your faith.

To show our appreciation, we invite you to sign up to receive a specially selected **Reader Appreciation Gift**, with our compliments. Just go to the Web address at the bottom of this page.

God bless you as you seek a deeper walk with Him!

WE HAVE A GIFT FOR YOU

whpub.me/classicthx

WHITAKER
HOUSE